3-31-12

D1545370

Best Always
J.D. Crowe

CROWE ON THE BANJO

MUSIC IN AMERICAN LIFE

*A list of books in the series
appears at the end of this book.*

CROWE ON THE BANJO

THE MUSIC LIFE OF J. D. CROWE

MARTY GODBEY

University of Illinois Press

URBANA, CHICAGO,

AND SPRINGFIELD

© 2011 by the Board of Trustees
of the University of Illinois
All rights reserved.
Manufactured in the United States of America
P 5 4 3 2 1
∞ This book is printed on acid-free paper.

Library of Congress Cataloging-in-Publication Data
Godbey, Marty.
Crowe on the banjo : the music life of J.D. Crowe /
Marty Godbey.
    p. cm. — (Music in American life)
Includes bibliographical references, index,
and discography.
ISBN 978-0-252-07825-5 (pbk.)
1. Crowe, J. D. 2. Banjoists—Biography.
I. Title.
ML418.C76G63   2011
787.8'81642092—dc22   2011006827
[B]

Dedicated to
the memory of
Orval Dee Crowe
1916–1989

CONTENTS

Illustrations follow page 112

PREFACE

In the mid-1960s, my husband and I were deeply immersed in the bluegrass music scene in and around Columbus, Ohio. At least once a week, usually more often, we ventured into some dark, sleazy, possibly dangerous "hillbilly" bar to listen to the excellent local musicians. Occasionally, some of the "name bands" such as Bill Monroe, the Osborne Brothers, Reno and Smiley, and the Stanley Brothers appeared in the larger ones, and we followed them religiously.

We traveled to outlying towns for "package" shows in school and civic auditoriums—if there was a bluegrass band in the lineup and we could find out about it, we were there. We heard Bill Monroe and His Blue Grass Boys at the High School in Delaware, Jimmy Martin and the Sunny Mountain Boys in Zanesville, Reno and Smiley and the Tennessee Cut-Ups in Springfield, Wilma Lee and Stoney Cooper in Ashland, and Flatt and Scruggs and the Foggy Mountain Boys, booked with the Stanley Brothers, at the Dennison Square Theatre in Cleveland. From information gleaned from their 5:45 a.m. radio broadcast, we stalked Flatt and Scruggs in a 150-mile radius, managing to see them twelve times in one calendar year.

When the weather was warm, we attended Sunday afternoon shows at outdoor country music parks: Frontier Ranch, near Columbus; Hillbilly Park, in Newark; Ponderosa Park, in Warren; and lovely, historic Chautauqua Park, near Dayton. In this picnic atmosphere, we met musicians and fans from other areas and shared information; until *Bluegrass Unlimited* began publication in 1966, there was no clearinghouse for bluegrass news, although a few newsletters did provide sources for recordings and some listings of upcoming performances.

It was from the "Now Appearing" section of *Bluegrass Unlimited* that we learned that legendary 5-string banjo player J.D. Crowe, who had recorded extensively with Jimmy Martin and the Sunny Mountain Boys, was playing in Lexington, Kentucky, with his own band, the Kentucky Mountain Boys. This would be, for us, the first in a lifetime of overnight—and longer—forays to hear bluegrass music.

On Easter weekend of 1968, we arrived in Lexington just before dark on Friday night, only to discover that we had left the *Bluegrass Unlimited* issue, with its all-important address, in Columbus. All we could remember was that the place was on Limestone Street, so we drove slowly north, trusting our ears and instincts to give us the location.

Sure enough, music sounded from a corner bar, the Limehouse, at Third Street, near downtown, and we went in to sample it. The place was high-ceilinged, dimly lit, practically empty, and a little seedy, and there was a bluegrass band on a low stage in the corner, but the music lacked something, and the banjo player neither looked nor sounded like the J.D. Crowe whose work we had absorbed from those great Jimmy Martin records of the 1950s and early '60s.

After only a few tunes, the band took a break, and the guitar player ambled over to tell us, "I think you're looking for J.D. Crowe. He's at Martin's Place, at Seventh and Lime, just a few blocks north." Muttering something about his band being good, too, we scuttled out and found what we were looking for: a small, yellow-brick building with bluegrass music and college students spilling out the screen door onto the broad sidewalk.

It was in, we learned later, a questionable part of town, but, nestled among small, cozy houses, each with a porch and a front yard, and with its crowd of students and young professionals, Martin's Place was more welcoming than the wall-to-wall honky-tonks of North High Street in Columbus. We felt perfectly comfortable there, and the music more than justified our drive—it was electrifying.

J.D. Crowe was exactly what we expected, a skinny young man with abundant red hair gleaming in the lights, hunched over his banjo. The crisp, clear notes of his playing, often with a bluesy flavor, featured the perfect timing and rich tone he had shown on Martin's recordings and was loud enough to drown out the noisy chatter and clink of beer bottles in the tavern.

With him behind the collection of mike stands in the corner were a couple of guitar players, a mandolin player, and a bass player, with a left-handed fiddle player on J.D.'s right. They leaned into the single microphone in turn, performing vocal standards and instrumentals from the bluegrass repertoire. The audience, though noisy, was extremely appreciative, particularly of Crowe's "breaks" on the banjo, but his backup playing behind the singers and the other instruments was extraordinary, contributing a texture and fullness to the total sound.

Crowe was impressive in 1968 with a part-time band (which included experienced professionals Bobby Slone, fiddle, and a young, already proficient Doyle Lawson on mandolin); he has been no less so in the hundreds of times we have seen him since. Obviously, there have been personnel changes during the forty-eight years he has managed his own band, but there has always been a long list of musicians eager to work with him, and he has consistently chosen the best people available for any vacant slot.

The sound of the Kentucky Mountain Boys, later renamed the New South, has reflected these changes and the tastes of the times, but the music has always been of the highest quality. As each new member brought with him new songs and different experiences, so he assimilated something of J.D.'s professionalism, solid rhythm, attention to detail, and insistence on perfection in harmony singing. Through Crowe's band have passed many musicians who became luminaries of bluegrass and country music; they have spread his methods to those with whom they worked after Crowe, and thus to more and more musicians in ever-increasing numbers. In addition to being a superb performer, J.D. Crowe has been—and is—a teacher.

The innovations made by J.D.'s bands of the 1970s and 1980s have forever changed the concept of what bluegrass music is; bands after that period were as different from those before as those who followed Lester Flatt and Earl Scruggs were from the ones who preceded them. The timing, the way of approaching nontraditional material, the ensemble work, and the attitude have been copied thousands of times, and while Crowe's subtleties and deep knowledge of earlier music may be missing, the effect is unmistakable.

J.D. Crowe's influence on other banjo players and aspiring "pickers" cannot be overstated. He would be the first to acknowledge his debt to Earl Scruggs, who first inspired him to play the banjo and, literally, at whose feet he absorbed his early insight into Scruggs's three-finger style. Hard work and practice developed this awareness into Crowe's own distinctive sound, and now three generations of optimistic banjo players have crouched in front rows to watch J.D.'s famous right-hand "claw" in hopes of acquiring something of *his* skill.

Those who have been most successful have taken their gleanings back into their own spheres, creating their own ways of playing and their own followers and, almost as Crowe's former band members have done, have caused ripples that extend, possibly, to people who don't even know the origins of the "licks" and inflections they try to reproduce. That is, however, most unlikely—J.D.'s total understanding of the 5-string banjo and his knowledge of how to get the best, most consistent sound from it have made his name and his prowess world renowned.

Because of his enormous popularity among bluegrass fans and banjo enthusiasts, it was inevitable that fallacies would become a part of his mystique, many of which have been perpetuated in conversation and print. The most popular of these is that the "1975 band" that included Tony Rice, Ricky Skaggs, Jerry Douglas, and Bobby Slone played for a long time at Lexington's Holiday Inn. They did not; in their entirety, they never played there at all. To correct some of these errors, I have tried to present Crowe's music life in the words of those who have known him best. They were there.

Remarkably stable and "normal" among musicians, whose lives are too often blighted by alcohol, substance abuse, poor living habits, and mental problems, J.D. Crowe has grown from a painfully shy, intense young man into an affable, accessible, patient elder statesman, seemingly unaware of his iconic status. His patience and generosity with his time have been of invaluable help to his band members, fans, fellow musicians, and at least one grateful interviewer.

As a musician, he is as proficient in his seventies as he was at twenty, his fingers as quick and agile as ever, and his enthusiasm for his music as great. He accepts only the engagements he wants to, these days, and he enjoys what he does. J.D. Crowe is a master of his craft and one of only a handful of banjo players whose touch is immediately recognizable.

ACKNOWLEDGMENTS

This book would not have been possible without the cooperation and memories of J.D. Crowe, who talked with me on numerous occasions, sometimes for hours, occasionally to answer a quick question on the telephone. He was always helpful and generous with his time, and said, at one point, "If we're going to do this thing, we need to do it *right*."

Those I interviewed about their experiences with J.D. Crowe were enthusiastic and eager to share their stories. That they did so was due to their respect and admiration for a consummate musician and exceptional human being. Their names and words are in the text—I thank them all.

I would also like to express my deep appreciation to Frank Godbey, my live-in techie, the other half of my memory, and my best friend.

Marty Godbey

On December 23, 2010, Marty Godbey, my wife and dear companion, died unexpectedly. The manuscript for *Crowe on the Banjo: The Music Life of J.D. Crowe* was then "in production" at the University of Illinois Press, and it became my job to see it through all the processes that lead to publication. I hope that I have been true to her vision, and that she would approve of the final product. Marty had many friends in the world of bluegrass music, and I know that they miss her as much as I do, and that they will treasure this book in her memory.

With undying love,
Frank Godbey

CROWE ON THE BANJO

CHAPTER I
I NEVER HEARD
A SOUND LIKE THAT

Centered in the Commonwealth of Kentucky and the Bluegrass Region, Lexington, seat of Fayette County, was the prosperous market center of an agrarian economy at the end of the Great Depression. Here were the famous horse farms, with their bluegrass pastures surrounded by white fences; tobacco was the "money crop" for farmers.

Lexington, with a population of nearly fifty thousand, had little industry. There were stores that sold feed, seed, farm implements, and horse supplies, and auction barns for horses and tobacco. Two racetracks, the new Keeneland Race Course for thoroughbreds and the Red Mile trotting track, attracted thousands to their meets.

The Depression had not devastated the area as it had industrialized cities, but recovery was slow, hampered by a severe drought, until 1937, when a devastating flood of the Ohio River destroyed many river towns. The Bluegrass was unaffected, except that the saturated soil helped to produce a record tobacco crop that signaled a return to normality.

It was into this optimistic atmosphere that James Dee Crowe was born on Friday, August 27, 1937, at St. Joseph's Hospital in Lexington, then at Second and Jefferson streets. The first child of Orval Dee and Bessie Lee Nichols

Crowe, the little red-haired baby was special; most of his family had dark hair, and although there was red hair on both sides of his family, it was uncommon.[1] "My dad's dad's brother had red hair, and my grandmother, my mom's mom, didn't have really red hair, but it had a kind of reddish tint. My mom's brother's first son and my dad's brother's first son were redheaded; then I was redheaded. None of the other children in either family were," J.D. said.[2]

Orval and Bessie had grown up in large farming families; Orval was born in Montgomery County, some thirty-five miles east of Lexington. His immediate family was living north of Lexington, on the Scott–Fayette County line, when he and Bessie met, and music was already an important part of his life.[3] "His family lived right across from my family on the Newtown Pike." said James "J." Wood. "[Live] music was more important then; there was no television, and hardly any radio. There was no electricity out here on Newtown Pike until the mid-1930s, and if you wanted to hear music, somebody had to play it. People would have parties, especially the young people, and if you could play, you were always welcome."

"My dad," J.D. said, "was the oldest of thirteen children; he quit school to help on the farm, and then after a while, he was the only one working, so he left and got a job so he could make some money."[4]

Bessie's family lived in Jessamine County, just south of Fayette. She and Orval met in 1934, and Orval immediately asked for a date. "He came to my house in Jessamine County," she said, "and we went together for two years. We were married in 1936, at Keene, in Jessamine County, and went to his mother's before we went to housekeeping."[5] Shortly after J.D. was born, they moved to Lincoln Avenue, in a subdivision just east of downtown Lexington. Orval drove a truck for the Donaldson Bakery Company.[6]

According to his mother, little J.D. (he was never called anything else) had a sunny disposition and showed his musical talent at an early age. "When J.D. was two years old, he started singing—the music came from my mother's side—and the first song he learned was 'The Books of the Bible.' He sang it in church, and they gave him a little Bible for doing that."[7]

To the young family, with their extended families nearby, Lexington must have seemed the ideal place to live. J.D. remembers his childhood impressions:

Lexington was a fun town, because it *was* downtown. It was all downtown, and you had your ten-cent stores—Woolworth's and Kresge's—and there were a lot of restaurants around, and a lot of movie theaters we used to go to. In fact, there's only a couple still left I used to attend when I was a kid: the Opera House (but they no longer show movies there, they just have concerts and plays) and the Kentucky Theatre (that's where the Woodsongs Old Time Radio Theatre is). There were a lot of other theaters, probably three or four more, but they're all gone; they're now parking lots. Urban renewal; it's changed a lot.[8]

In the early 1940s, Orval became manager of a 443-acre farm about six miles south of Lexington, in Jessamine County, where the family would live for twelve years.[9] "It was located on the east side of the Harrodsburg Road, where the Crosswoods shopping center is now," J.D. said, "and my dad raised everything on the halves."[10] The Crowes lived on a 5-acre tract across the road in a white frame house on a hill. "My dad tried to buy that tract after [the owner] died," J.D. said, "but his son wouldn't sell."[11] The house where they lived is no longer standing, but the office of present-day Bluegrass Memorial Gardens cemetery is on the same spot.[12] "The cemetery was my mom's brother Milton Nichols' farm," J.D. said.[13]

The Harrodsburg Road curved through wooded acres and large and small farms that raised essential food, with some tobacco, during World War II, and the farm where the Crowes lived was somewhat isolated. Today, the rolling terrain is still there, but hardly recognizable from that time; the road has been widened, and subdivisions have replaced the farms.

J.D.'s teenage thin frame was no indication of the family's eating habits—his mother, an excellent southern cook, always kept a garden, and the family had three hearty meals every day. "My family's always been good eaters," she said.[14]

"My mom's rare, I'll tell you," J.D. said. "She's ninety-four years old, or will be the first of March. I can remember her working on the farm, doing whatever needed to be done. She was always there and supportive. Of course, she didn't spare the rod, either, which I deserved. I got into all kinds of meanness when I was growing up. She's always been there, and still is; she was a great cook, and still is. One of the things I really remember is all the good food we had, that she'd fix from scratch, off the top of her head."[15]

"When we moved out to Jessamine County," Bessie said, "we were there twelve years. That's where J.D. started to school, the Providence School, in Jessamine County, and he graduated from the eighth grade in Nicholasville [the county seat]."[16]

During J.D.'s childhood, music was prominent in the family's life. "As far back as I can remember," J.D. said, "I know my mom and dad always enjoyed music. They'd always listen to the *Grand Ole Opry* on Saturday night, and if there were any music shows around, they'd usually try to go. I remember as a kid, probably four, five years old, I always had a ukulele, a little guitar or something around to play on, and I enjoyed that. They said I used to go around singing all kinds of little songs, saying I was somebody or another in the business."[17]

One of his favorite performers to imitate was Ernest Tubb, one of the stars of the *Opry*. Tubb's distinctive deep voice was not what attracted his interest, but the sound of the electric guitar in his band did. Crowe had heard Tubb on radio but had never seen him. "I thought Ernest Tubb played the [electric] guitar. My big thing, after all, was to play guitar. I thought Ernest Tubb's was the best band, and it featured that guitar. That was the sound I wanted to play like."[18]

Blues and other forms of country music also interested J.D., who loved the guitar, in any format. "I started out playing country music, not bluegrass," he said. "I started playing guitar, and if it was not for one man, I'd probably be as proficient on electric guitar as I am on banjo. I would probably be playing guitar behind somebody on the *Grand Ole Opry*."[19]

J.D. didn't have a great deal of time to play the guitar after he got older—he had to fit it in between his duties on the farm and the normal activities of any growing boy. "There were chores, plenty of chores," he said. "There were stoves and fireplaces, and there was wood to be brought in. I had to feed the dogs—Dad had coon dogs—lots of other things. I had two cousins next door, and we rode bicycles. And I played my little 'Gene Autry' guitar. At least, I knew the chords," he joked. "We visited kin, or they came to see us; we had a lot of company."[20]

During their time there, the Crowes were saddened by the short life of their second child, Lee Roy, who was born on January 18, 1942. He lived only three days and died of a lung ailment.[21] On June 8, 1945, J.D.'s baby sister, Rosa

Marie, was born. She would become his strongest supporter and biggest fan. The whole family is close, but Rosa's attitude toward her brother is one of hero worship—there is no jealousy or sibling rivalry, as you might expect in a family where one child has achieved public recognition.

"From the time I was four years old," Rosa said, "I was proud of J.D. Then, to me, he was a star. He was my big brother and he played music, and he was very good at what he did. He used to play constantly, and I was his audience; I clapped for him. We would sit for hours, and he'd play songs and say, 'Can you name this?'"[22]

"Even though we were that far apart in age," she said, "he would take the time to play with me. You know, when you live on a farm, you don't have anyone to play with unless you have a lot of brothers and sisters. He made me a playhouse and made me a go-cart to pull behind his bicycle. We'd go down that steep driveway, and he'd turn me over. Then I'd scream and then get back in the wagon to do the same thing over again."[23]

On the farm, Orval's hours were long. "He worked from daylight 'til dark," J.D. said, "seven days a week, but he always found time to take us to music shows. Every Saturday night the *Barn Dance* was there; we'd go to that, whoever was there. It didn't matter. He enjoyed it as well as I did—he liked that."[24]

"Dad wasn't a musician," Rosa said. "He didn't pick anything, didn't dance, had no timing of any kind, but I don't remember a time when there wasn't music in our home. From the old Victrolas—the ones that played 78s—and radios, and when the newer equipment came along. It was like we went to bed to it, and we got up to it."[25]

Among the shows J.D. attended with his parents was a Bill Monroe tent show. "That was before Lester [Flatt] and Earl [Scruggs] were in his band," he said. "He had Clyde Moody, Stringbean, 'Cousin' Wilbur [Bill Westbrooks] on bass, and Tommy Magnus playing fiddle.[26] That was in the 1940s, but that music didn't get to me, although I enjoyed it. Maybe if I'd seen Bill with Flatt and Scruggs [in his band] it would have had the same effect [that Flatt and Scruggs's own band had on him later], but Flatt and Scruggs was the first band I saw doing that type of music.

"For years, when we'd go to country music shows," J.D. said, "the music was all a lot alike—the same kind of singing, speed, and so forth. I liked it, and everything, but I always liked the instrumentals as something different.

When I heard Cliff and Bill Carlisle, the Dobro stood out, and I started noticing that 'Hawaiian sound,' I called it, in country music. Then I saw Uncle
Josh [Burkett Graves] with [singer and guitar player] Esco Hankins, who came
here from Knoxville. Josh was flashy, stood out, was quicker and did more
than others I'd heard."[27]

The Dobro sparkled, and the electric guitar was exciting and dominating—
"Back then, every country music group had an electric guitar," J.D. said. "That
was just hillbilly music."[28] The banjo, however, didn't particularly impress him;
its use as a rhythm instrument meant the banjo didn't have the presence or the
status of the fiddle, the steel guitar, and the electric guitar. Among the featured
banjo players he had seen or heard were Louis Marshall "Grandpa" Jones,
David "Stringbean" Akeman, and "Uncle" Dave Macon, whose performances
owed as much to Vaudeville traditions as to country music. Consummate
entertainers all, they used their instruments as props in their comedy acts.
"Everything with a banjo was comedy—good entertainment to watch, but
just not good listening music," J.D. explained.[29] He could enjoy whatever he
saw, but it didn't shake his determination to play electric guitar.

There were many opportunities to see and learn from guitarists of all
styles; some performances were held in schools, and some in movie theaters.
"The Ada Meade Theatre on Short Street was where all the western shows
were, and some at the Opera House," J.D. said.[30]

In 1949, an association of businessmen purchased and demolished the Gentry Stock Yards on West High Street (also called "the Versailles Road") at An-
gliana (also called "Anglin") Avenue, and rebuilt it to include radio broadcast
facilities, a seating capacity of 800, and its own attached restaurant. Renamed
the "Clay Gentry Stockyards," it could be converted to an air-conditioned,
soundproofed theater and became the home of the Saturday-night *Kentucky
Mountain Barn Dance*.[31]

As with many similar ventures, patterned on the *Grand Ole Opry*, the *Barn
Dance* relied on a core of country performers of many styles, with visiting acts
from time to time. A sponsor, the Eureka Flour Company of Beaver Dam,
Kentucky, ensured broadcasts of the show to the surrounding states of Indiana, Ohio, West Virginia, and Tennessee, and as far away as the Carolinas.[32]

Advertised to open September 10, 1949, the arena was evidently still under
construction, so the first performance of the *Barn Dance* was held at Wood-

land Auditorium, located in a park at the intersection of East High Street and Woodland Avenue.[33] The auditorium was the venue for many kinds of music performers, including many internationally known luminaries. Fritz Kreisler, Sergei Rachmaninoff, Jascha Heifetz, the New York Philharmonic, and Vladimir Horowitz were among those who appeared there.[34]

Rarely mentioned in the local press, except in advertisements, were occasional country music performances and regular Thursday-night wrestling there, as well as Sunday-afternoon country music shows at Joyland Park, an amusement park on the north side of town. Lexington's public face was turned toward "high culture," and despite numerous popular country music radio programs and large crowds at performances, as far as the newspapers were concerned, country music might as well not have existed.

A large boxed ad on the entertainment page proclaimed the first *Kentucky Mountain Barn Dance*. The headliner was Molly O'Day, with her Cumberland Valley Folks, and a "large cast of stars of radio and stage," including, presumably, Casey Clark and his Lazy Ranch Boys, who are pictured but not mentioned. (Casey Clark and his band were frequent performers on the *Kentucky Mountain Barn Dance* and at Joyland Park. In the mid-1950s, he was in Detroit, with a barn dance and radio show at which Crowe would perform with Jimmy Martin.) The *Barn Dance* was to be broadcast over "Mutual Station WVLK."[35]

By September 17, 1949, the Clay Gentry Stockyards was ready for the *Barn Dance,* and the show was held in the new arena; that night, one of several featured acts was the Stanley Brothers.[36] That was the night that changed young J.D. Crowe's life: Lester Flatt and Earl Scruggs and the Foggy Mountain Boys were surprise guests and, according to J.D., were possibly auditioning. "Ed Mills [one of the emcees], announced, 'If you like them, we just might hire them.'"[37]

"I asked Lester about it, years later, and he vaguely remembered," J.D. said.

He said they really were passing through and heard they were having a *Barn Dance.* And, of course, they were trying to get started at that time. They had just released their first record, on Mercury, and they stopped in to try to get a job on the radio show. At that time, they [the *Barn Dance*] were broadcasting an hour from Clay Gentry, and when Flatt and Scruggs stopped in to ask about the radio job, I guess whoever was head of the *Barn*

Dance at that time asked if they would like to do a guest shot on the *Barn Dance,* and they did. And nobody knew they were going to be there, because it wasn't advertised. And I happened to be there, when they did that.[38]

J.D. has often talked about that night; it has been sixty years since he first saw Flatt and Scruggs, but he still shows the excitement and enthusiasm of the kid he was then. For him, it's still happening. "I was sitting there one night," he said, "and they introduced this new group which I'd never heard of at the time. Five guys came out and just tore the house down and me with it. I couldn't get over it! All I'd ever heard of the banjo was frailing, clawhammer, which I really didn't like—of course, I can appreciate it now, more than I did then. But I never heard a sound like that!"[39] J.D. continued, "Their music was so different, so powerful, and they didn't have any electric instruments or anything [as other country bands did]. It was like it was going to explode. The speed, and even the slow things, had such a timing factor. It was just so different from anything you heard.[40] That's what inspired me to play the banjo," J.D. said.

It was the drive, the rhythm. You could just feel it. It seemed like, to me, that everybody in the whole place came alive when they [Flatt and Scruggs] hit the stage. That was the fastest half hour I ever spent in my life; it seemed like five minutes.[41] When I first saw Flatt and Scruggs, [in their band] there was [John Ray] "Curly" Sechler, Cedric [Rainwater, whose real name was Howard Watts], and Benny Sims.[42] That was my first exposure to what we now know as "Bluegrass." Then, it was still "Hillbilly Music," and I'd never seen or heard anything like that.[43] To me, the banjo was the one instrument that stood out. It was the hardest sounding, the most lively—the most *different.* The sound of Earl's banjo was so different, not at all like the clawhammer sound I'd heard before.[44]

When J.D. first saw them, Flatt and Scruggs knew they had created something so different that even a young boy could recognize it. They had left Bill Monroe's Blue Grass Boys in February 1948 and soon teamed up to play music that had their own stamp on it. They were young and enthusiastic, ready to share their music and to try to make a living doing so, and they were having a wonderful time in the process.

What sold me also on that music was the way they worked the mike—of course, an electric guitar player didn't have to work the mike, and they [country bands] didn't have the trio sound—they did duets, mostly. The way [Flatt and Scruggs] worked was like they'd been choreographed. I'd never seen that many of them moving in and out, because they all sang; they all did something. You heard everything that was going on, just like they had electric instruments, but they had to get tone and volume by themselves, and it combined to make up their sound.[45] Most of the time, when you saw other entertainers, they featured one vocalist and they stood in one spot, and all the other guys and everybody stood in one spot. They didn't need to come around the mike, like Flatt and Scruggs did. So that just amazed me, when I first saw them, I couldn't get over that, and the way they played. That was my first introduction to the banjo, as far as being played like that. I decided, well, I had to try to do that.[46] Anybody that didn't get to see that really missed something, especially when they [Flatt and Scruggs] were in their prime. It was a new music, that's all—and it's all right up here. [He pointed to his head.] That band was as different to country music then as rock and roll was to country music later.[47]

The most obvious thing that made Flatt and Scruggs sound "different" was Earl Scruggs's playing on the 5-string banjo, in a three-finger style he had developed from the two- and three-finger picking he heard as a boy in North Carolina. Propelled by smooth rolls, punctuated with syncopation and subtle dynamics, it elevated the banjo to a starring role that was equally at home with both his rapid-fire instrumentals and the slower songs that featured Lester Flatt's "honey-coated" voice.

Like a jazz band in their interaction, the band members worked together to produce a unified music, coalesced by the solid underpinning of bass and Lester's guitar. He used a thumb pick on the bass strings and strumming fingers on the higher ones, and his sound was once described as "the glue that held it all together." Flatt and Scruggs's timing had a rolling pulse, a surge, that floated around the beat with a forward energy that was much more sophisticated and complex than the straightforward beat of traditional string bands and electric country bands.

Extremely versatile vocally, the Foggy Mountain Boys provided solos, duets, trios, and gospel quartets with equal ease, moving in and out around the microphone with terpsichorean artistry. Scruggs's three-finger guitar picking on gospel songs contributed to a rich, full-bodied sound. It was, indeed, a new kind of music.

Flatt and Scruggs's audition was more than successful, and the following week, the *Barn Dance* ad features "The Original Foggy Mountain Boys,
formerly with Bill Monroe and his Blue Grass Band [*sic*] WSM, Nashville,
Tennessee," to be broadcast over WVLK.[48]

When they came to Lexington, they had recorded two sessions, eight
sides, for Mercury Records, the first at Knoxville, and the second at Cincinnati. "Mercury was a very small company," Earl Scruggs said. "I think we
were about their third artist. They would make the arrangements for a studio
someplace, and we'd record at some radio station."[49]

In December 1949, shortly after joining the *Kentucky Mountain Barn Dance*,
Flatt and Scruggs returned to Cincinnati to record their third session for
Mercury, an additional eight sides. Their material, all written by Flatt and
Scruggs and present or former band members, showed the heady buoyancy
of a new collaboration and included what would become some of their
most enduring songs. This body of work, with a few of the songs they had
performed with Monroe and some traditional instrumentals, was what J.D.
listened to and learned from.

In addition to the Saturday-night *Barn Dance,* Flatt and Scruggs had a radio
show on WVLK in Versailles, Kentucky, about twelve miles west of Lexington and played schools, shows, and theaters as well. This was a period when
people enjoyed eating and watching movies in their automobiles, so drive-in
theaters offered additional venues. Most drive-in concession stands had flat
roofs, and bands performed on them while it was still daylight. "The Foggy
Mountain Boys played about every drive-in in central Kentucky, southern
Ohio, and the western section of West Virginia."[50]

By the time J.D. saw Flatt and Scruggs, he was fairly competent on the
guitar, but it was clear that he had been completely seduced by the sound
of Earl Scruggs's banjo. "To me," he said, "it [playing the banjo] looked so
easy—course everybody has that in their mind: 'I can do that; that looks
easy.'"[51]

"I remember telling my Dad, 'I want a banjo,'" he said, "and I remember
he said, 'Why, you couldn't play like that,' and I said, 'Well, I'd like to try it.'
It was a while before I got one; you know how that is, and back then, you
couldn't afford a lot of things."[52]

When he asked for a banjo for Christmas, "I said, 'J.D., honey, you'd better get a guitar,'" Mrs. Crowe said. "'I don't think you can play a banjo.'"[53]

"Probably, as most parents do," J.D. said, "they thought it [wanting to play music] was all just fun. I don't think they really realized that I would ever take it seriously. It was just something that I wanted to do, and they were good enough to get me instruments and see how far I wanted to go with it. I'm sure they didn't, either one of them—and I didn't either, at the time—expect me to be in the position I'm in now."[54]

J.D.'s interest in the banjo, once he had seen Earl Scruggs, never flagged. He watched Flatt and Scruggs with rapt attention whenever they appeared; there are photographs of the stage of the *Barn Dance* that show part of the crowd, and J.D. is sitting on the aisle steps, chin on hand, concentrating on what Scruggs is doing.[55]

"Before he got a banjo," his sister, Rosa, recounted, "he would sit around and drum on things."[56] She said, "He was always working his fingers on his side, on the table, a broom, anything."[57]

"I was thirteen when I got my first banjo," J.D. said. "It was a Kay, like most beginners get. I probably kept that a year, a year and a half. Course, I wanted one like Earl's, you know. If his had been a Kay, that would have been all right, too."[58] There is a charming snapshot from that Christmas Day, of J.D., clutching his brand-new banjo and grinning like a jack-o'-lantern, and Rosa, next to him, grinning, too.

"When I got my first banjo," Crowe said, "I had visions of being able to pick it up and play some of the things I'd heard Earl play, which was *wrong*. I'll tell you, it was hard, because I had nothing to go by but just records. Watching him also helped me a lot; to be around them as much as I was, it did help. You just had to try to remember it, and I would visualize, when I saw him, certain positions where his hand was on the neck; as I said, it wasn't easy."[59] But he persisted. "Anyhow, I stuck with it. I think in the process of learning how to play the banjo, after about a year I laid it down and played the mandolin a little bit, learned a little on that. Then I went back to the banjo, and I've played it ever since."[60]

"The first time I ever really heard him play the banjo was the Christmas he got that first banjo," Rosa said. "He woke us all up at three in the morning, playing 'Cripple Creek,' and nobody had showed him anything. We were all amazed. Daddy was just overwhelmed, he was so proud!"[61]

That was only the first of many nights that J.D. disturbed. He played his banjo every available minute, and when he was thinking about it so hard he could not sleep, he would get up and try to work things out, but even a quietly played banjo is hardly conducive to sleep. Always patient and encouraging, even Orval could stand just so much, and would finally call out, "J.D., you know I have to get up at four in the morning."[62] Mrs. Crowe said, "Orval never told him to put the banjo away. He was just so tickled that he could play it."[63]

"Dad really didn't know much about music," Rosa said, "except when Brother made a mistake, and he did know that. Then he would tell him that. I can remember one of the main things that he said when he was playing was, 'Earl Scruggs doesn't just stay on that fifth string.' J.D. kind of frowned sometimes, and then he found out Daddy was right."[64] Of his dad, J.D. said, "He always could tell if you muffled a note or if you didn't hit one right. He would tell you quick, but he never played anything."[65]

"We went to see Flatt and Scruggs every night they were in town," Rosa said. "He [Orval] would say, 'J.D., now watch Earl's hands, watch his thumb.' Then, later, he'd say, 'J.D., you're riding that fifth string. Watch Earl next week and see what he does.' Daddy had a real ear for music; he knew when J.D. was making a mistake."[66]

J.G. "Lightning" Bartlett knew J.D. in high school and played with the Kentucky Mountain Boys, J.D.'s first local band, in the 1960s. "Orval," he said, "told me he asked J.D. what he wanted [for Christmas] and he said a 5-string banjo, so he bought it, and thirty days later, J.D. was playing understandable music on it."

In learning, J.D. placed his right hand in the position that seemed most natural to him, although it might have looked awkward to others. This made his picks strike the strings at a 90-degree angle, resulting in his clean, clear sound and a later nickname for his hand: "The Claw."

"J.D. rode the bus to school every morning," Mrs. Crowe said. "He had to wait on the bus, and he'd say, 'Mama, give me my banjo,' so I gave it to him—he was sitting by the window. Well, he picked that banjo until he saw the bus, then he said, 'Mama, take it, here comes the bus.'"[67]

Rosa said, "And as soon as he'd come home, it was the same thing again.[68] One time," she added, "the school called, because J.D. was staring out the window all the time. The principal called, and Mama and Daddy had to go to the school over it. The teacher said he [J.D.] was always looking out the window and picking on his desk, and they didn't know how to handle him. He was not a bad kid; he was just daydreaming all the time."[69]

"He cranked up that old Victrola," Mrs. Crowe said, "that's what we had, then, and turned Lester and Earl on, and when he [worked out] something, the next morning at breakfast he'd say, 'Mama, I caught something last night.'"[70]

"Crowe told me," Richard Bennett said, "that when he was young and just learning, he'd be listening to Earl on record and playing along, and Rosa would be there to lift the needle off the record and put it back, so he could go back to the beginning of the section." Bennett was guitar player and lead singer with Crowe from 1989 until 1995.

As Flatt and Scruggs were based in Lexington, there were frequent opportunities to see them, and the Crowes did not miss many. J.D. attempted whatever he heard them play as soon as he could get back to his banjo. "The first thing I tried to play was 'Cripple Creek,'" J.D. said, "because it seemed easier to work with. Then I wanted to learn 'Down the Road,' and 'Cumberland Gap,' just whatever Earl did. I was more interested in trying to learn the breaks to songs and backup than instrumentals, but I tried 'Foggy Mountain Breakdown' and 'Pike County Breakdown.'"[71]

"When we'd go to see [Flatt and Scruggs]," Rosa said, "J.D. would get right up there next to the stage, and his eyes would be glued to Earl's hands. He watched him constantly. And when we'd go home, he would practice, and we would hear it, and Daddy would holler, 'J.D., you've got to go to sleep, Buddy, you've got to go to school.' J.D.'d have to get that lick in there; he couldn't stand it, and he'd have to make sure he didn't miss it."[72]

Flatt and Scruggs's time in Lexington may have been the most important event in J.D.'s life, but for them, it was just another stop in the arduous travel schedule that was necessary for survival for country entertainers in the radio age. Bands would locate in an area with a popular radio program that featured several acts, establish a place in the lineup, acquire their own daily radio program, and book performances in the station's listening area. By selling songbooks, records, and pictures at their appearances, they not only supplemented their income but also advertised themselves and upcoming shows. When they decided the area was saturated, or when a better offer came from a different locale, they relocated.

Each band, moreover, was a complete show within itself, including a comedy act, frequently a "girl singer," and part of the program devoted to gospel songs. The emcees often joked with the audience, and perhaps awarded small prizes or coupons for products of their sponsor, if they had one. Their object was not only to play music but to entertain as well.

Before coming to Lexington, Flatt and Scruggs had been at WCYB, in Bristol, Virginia, and at WROL, in Knoxville. With a brief hiatus in Tampa, they were based in central Kentucky from the autumn of 1949 until July 1951, then returned briefly in November 1951. By this time, the *Barn Dance* was established at Woodland Auditorium.[73]

"They had a radio show in Versailles that came on at 11:45 every Saturday morning," J.D. said, "and Dad would take me—I think at the time it [the radio station] was in the library in Versailles, in the basement. They [Flatt and Scruggs] would come in at probably nine thirty or ten o'clock, and they would rehearse the show they were going to do, so we would get over there about ten, ten thirty, and watch them rehearse. That was a big help, there, because I was close. I wish I would have had a video camera then, or even a tape recorder, but there were no such things back then."[74] At first, J.D. said, "I was just in awe of them, all of them. They were like movie stars, to me, just as big. I finally got to meet them. Dad introduced me to them, and they shook my hand, and all that."[75]

"J.D. was just a waist-high boy when I met him in Lexington, Kentucky," Earl Scruggs said, "about 1949 or 1950. We were living in Bristol and would drive to Lexington. At one point, we moved there. It was a wonderful experience, and we met some wonderful people, especially J.D. and his family. J.D. and his dad would come by to see us, but J.D. never had anything to say, and I didn't know he was so interested in the banjo. I don't remember J.D. ever asking me one single question."[76]

"My dad was a big talker, and they were real friendly and nice," J.D. said. "We got to know them pretty well, and they always let us in."[77] He remembered Benny Sims: "He was just a fine dude, he was a great guy, and he said, 'Hoss, are you picking banjo, too? Get that banjo there, boy, and pick one with me.' Of course, I wasn't about to do that. No. But all those guys, they always treated me like 'one of the guys.' A lot of people now, you get this feeling when you come up that they don't want to be bothered. They never did that. Most of those guys, the ones I did meet, were very cordial and nice."[78] Of course, "then I was probably the only one around here learning to play the banjo. That was unheard of."[79]

> I remember my dad asking Earl if he would be able to show me anything, or give me lessons, or whatever, and I remember Earl saying, "No, I don't have the time," he said, "and I don't really know what I'm doing—I do what I do, what I hear." He said, "He's welcome to watch me all he wants to, but I can't show him anything 'cause I don't know what I'm doing." Which I learned later, that's a fact. He was doing what he needed to do, but he didn't realize what he was doing.[80]

Unknown to either J.D. or Earl, there were other aspiring banjo players who wanted to learn Scruggs's technique, some of them from the time they heard him on the *Opry* with Bill Monroe, but without J.D.'s day-to-day exposure to Scruggs, they had to learn in a more indirect manner. One of them, fellow Kentuckian Sonny Osborne, was only two months younger than J.D., but acquired an interest in the banjo earlier, possibly because his older brother, Bobby, was a musician. Living in Ohio in 1948, eleven-year-old Sonny had never seen Earl Scruggs at all, but he had seen Larry Richardson (who was working with Bobby) play the banjo. Sonny managed to work some things out by himself quickly and pretty easily. "It was just something that I saw, in my head," he said. "I mean, I never had to work at it really hard. My fingers would always do everything I told them to do. As far as playing the banjo, it was never, never, ever a problem. That's just what I did."

> There was one thing that Bobby showed me one time, the only thing I remember anybody showing me, ever. Bobby had been to West Virginia and had played on a show with Lester and Earl, and he saw how Earl did the one thing—it's the roll on "Roll in My Sweet Baby's Arms"—and Bobby showed me how to do that, and that's the only thing I couldn't figure out. What I was doing, the timing wasn't working, and no matter how I played, the timing wouldn't work. Bobby showed me that backward thing in there, and it just opened everything up. The reason for that backward roll is quite simple: it makes the timing work. Without that, the timing won't work.

Or your notes on the left hand won't match the notes for the song. To play exactly the song, you have to do the backward roll.

After that, all it took was a lot of practice and listening to Scruggs's recordings. By the age of fourteen, Sonny Osborne was appearing and recording with Bill Monroe.

Throughout his long and illustrious career, Osborne worked primarily with his brother; the Osborne Brothers later brought bluegrass to a wider audience with the addition of electric instrumentation and more mainstream country music–oriented material. Sonny built on Scruggs's work with licks he heard on electric guitar, steel guitar, and piano to create a style that is individual and immediately identifiable, although his affection for and quotes from Scruggs's music are always apparent in his playing. At the age of sixteen, before he developed his own musical identity, he told Jimmy Martin, who had criticized him for playing like Scruggs, "If I could learn how to play that way, I would do so, and I would play that way from now on. He's that good."

Virginian Eddie Adcock, just ten months younger than Crowe, had to learn banjo in a hurry. He was almost sixteen in 1954 when his favorite band advertised for a 5-string banjo player. Not only did he not know how to play one, he didn't even own a banjo.

> I'd liked the banjo all along, but I played mandolin and guitar and a little bit of tenor banjo. Smokey Graves had been a fiddle player for Clyde Moody, and started the Blue Star Boys. When he said he needed a 5-string banjo player, I sold my calf and bought a banjo. We wrote back and forth, and I said I could be there in probably two or three weeks. In that time, I had to learn to play the 5-string banjo. I had no idea they used a three-finger roll! So I just taught myself. I got over there for the job, and Smoky Graves said, "You're a musician, but you're not a 5-string banjo player." I slowly developed a roll, but it [learning to play] wasn't easy for anybody back then.

While working with Graves, Adcock began to develop his own innovative style, which, although it incorporates the usual right-hand-roll techniques, also features a single-string melodic approach with colorings based on guitar-influenced chord structures and rhythmic patterns drawn from guitarists Merle Travis and Chet Atkins. It lent itself well to the ballads of Mac Wiseman, with whom he worked in 1956, yet fitted with Bill Monroe's harder edges when he was a Blue Grass Boy in 1958. Most important, it was of overwhelming significance in establishing the breakaway sound of the Country Gentlemen, which he joined in 1959, and his own bands that followed. "Eddie invented a lot of banjo styles," J.D. said. "He was a good innovator, with great timing."[81]

About learning to play, Adcock said, "The best thing that ever happened to Sonny, J.D., and me was not having a teacher."

J.D., paying attention to everything Scruggs did, was also thinking about what he heard. "You can't just listen to the notes," he said. "You've got to listen to *all* of it, the timing, the pop, the authoritative sound. You have to get inside that banjo and learn it. Fiddle, mandolin, guitar—I've studied all of it and how it went together."[82]

He reflected, "When I first started doing this, I didn't think about doing it for a living; I didn't have a goal. I was just doing it 'cause I loved it. I really never thought about it, probably. I knew I liked it and often thought it'd be fun to do that [perform onstage]. I saw the guys—not banjo players—I'd idolized for years, and wondered how it would be to be in their position."[83]

For J.D., concentrated effort was the key. "I wish I had a dollar for every hour I practiced," he said. "Course, I still found time to do other things, but when I practiced, I was serious about it. I aggravated my mom and dad with it! Mom and Dad would be sleeping in the next room, and you know how a banjo carries! Back then, I couldn't play without picks."[84]

Scruggs's style was the standard, and J.D.'s goal was to get it *right*. "When I started out I consciously tried to imitate Earl. Definitely. I just stuck with what Earl played—it hit my ear, the timing factor and the fullness, the drive. The combination was unbelievable."[85] To that end, "[I practiced] day and night. It was really just all the time. I would go to bed and think of something, and I'd get up and try it, and sometimes it would work, and sometimes it wouldn't. In all, it was probably a year [after getting a banjo] before I started with Esco Hankins."[86]

Hankins was "top dog in Lexington," J.D. said, "as far as country music was concerned. He was a hell of an emcee—he brought on all the acts and did commercials. I learned a lot from him. He had an amateur contest, like a lot of them did, and I won several. Then I played with the band—some of the guys in the band liked bluegrass, and they enjoyed it and so did I."[87]

"I played for him quite a bit," he said. In fact, "It was my first paying job."[88]

CHAPTER 2
I JUST WANTED TO PICK

"How I got with Esco Hankins, for the very first time," J.D. said, "they used to put on amateur contests. As an aspiring picker, everybody goes through that phase—at least back then they did—and so I entered the contest, and I happened to win. The prize—the big prize—was you got to appear on his radio show, which he had every Saturday night from six to seven, and it was live, and the studio [WLAP], only held about thirty-five or forty people, so it was usually full."[1] For J.D. it was a good experience. "It wasn't very many people, but enough to make you nervous. I thought it was kind of neat."[2]

Tennessee singer and guitar player William Esco Hankins, known for the similarity of his singing style to that of Roy Acuff, had been active in the Knoxville country music scene from the late 1930s and had recorded for King Records after World War II.[3] In his band the Crazy Tennesseans when he moved to Lexington in 1949 was Dobro player Burkett "Buck" Graves, called "Uncle Josh," in a comedy routine with bass player English P. "Junior" Tullock Jr., known as "Cousin Jake."[4] After joining Flatt and Scruggs in the mid-1950s, they resumed their comedy act as well as playing and singing as part of the Foggy Mountain Boys.

Hankins soon became a regular member of the *Kentucky Mountain Barn Dance*. The *Crazy* was dropped from the band's name in 1950, resulting in "the Tennesseans."[5] As a band leader, disc jockey, and record shop owner, Esco Hankins would remain a radio presence in Lexington until his death in 1990.[6]

"Old Esco," J.D. said, "boy, he was a good old fellow!" The period that I worked with him [about 1951–52] was a real good learning period. You know, I was very fortunate; I never really had to work with amateur musicians. I never had to do that. I think that helped me a lot, because I was working with professional people. You can learn a lot more from people that know more than you do. Esco had been in business for a long time; [Andrew Tipton] 'Tip' Sharp was in the band, and a fellow named Dean Faulkner—they called him 'Spike'—who played mandolin, and sang, and [Harold] 'Red' Stanley played fiddle."[8]

J.D.'s sister, Rosa, said, "I embarrassed [J.D.] one time at WLAP. I think I was about six, and they were doing a live thing, and J.D. was looking up to watch the guy signal for them to start, and I hollered out 'Pick it, Crowe!' just as he was about to kick it off. I was proud because he was my brother, and I was just a kid. Oh, he got kind of got aggravated with me, and I think Mom and Dad said something to me too, if I recollect right. It embarrassed him, but he got over it, I guess."[9]

"Esco was a fine fellow," Mrs. Crowe said. "He would come to my house maybe once or twice a week, and J.D. played over WLAP with him as long as Esco was there. I guess J.D. was thirteen or so when Esco wanted him to go play show dates."[10]

"After I had won the amateur contest that Esco put on," J.D. said, "he asked my mom and dad if he could take me on some shows. Well, that started it, right there, as long as I could get back in time to go to school. We'd probably go in a hundred-mile radius, which back then was quite a bit. I know a lot of times we'd get back at two or three o'clock in the morning, and I'd have to get up and go to school—which I did."[11] They played anyplace that could accommodate an audience. "We played schools, theaters, and courthouses on weeknights—probably more schoolhouses than anything. Back then, the courthouse had the biggest auditorium in some small towns, and they weren't really all that big."[12]

It was fortunate that J.D. was broken in with small hometown audiences who welcomed the opportunity to see live music. They were kind and generous with the young banjo player, and so were the musicians with whom he came in contact. "When I was playing with Esco," he said, "that's when I met Red Allen. He was playing with the Stanley Brothers. We jammed a little, and then he took me over to meet Carter and Ralph at the hotel where they were staying."[13] Harley "Red" Allen's distinctive country-flavored tenor voice and his authoritative rhythm guitar led to a long career, mostly with his own band, the Kentuckians, but also with the Osborne Brothers and a tour with the Foggy Mountain Boys during Lester Flatt's illness. He would become one of J.D.'s Kentucky Mountain Boys in 1968.

"Working with Esco really helped me," J.D. said, "as far as learning the different styles of music, because he was a country artist. Now, Tip Sharp and Dean Faulkner did a comedy act; they would dress up and play this comedy act. They were called 'Ike and Spike,' and, I mean, they were funny. Tip was singing a lot of bluegrass, and that helped me also. [Later on,] he was a DJ [disc jockey] in Winchester, Kentucky [at WEKY] for quite a few years, the *East Kentucky Jamboree,* he called it."[14]

In April 1950, there was some question of where the *Barn Dance* shows were to be held and which radio station had the rights to broadcast them. With the scanty editorial coverage of country music that Lexington papers provided, it is difficult to ascertain the exact circumstances, but essentially, the Stockyards changed from WVLK to WKLX for their broadcasts, and WVLK retaliated by advertising their own barn dance called *WVLK's Original Kentucky Mountain Barn Dance Show,* to be held at Woodland Auditorium.

The Stockyards then sought an injunction to prevent the Foggy Mountain Boys from performing anywhere except the Clay-Gentry *Kentucky Mountain Barn Dance* on Saturday nights, according to their contract.[15] A court order on April 12 declared the Stockyards company the originator and owner of the *Barn Dance* and that WVLK could not produce a similar show under the same name. Flatt and Scruggs, if they were to perform at all on Saturday nights, must do so for Clay-Gentry.[16] On that same date, the usual display ad for the *Barn Dance* was accompanied by a smaller boxed ad stating the *Barn Dance* would be broadcast over WKLX.

It is clear that the Stockyards instituted the *Barn Dance* and the radio broadcasts to enhance their reputation and that Flatt and Scruggs accepted the job because the radio broadcasts would advertise them and help them book performances on the nights they were not on the *Barn Dance*. Without the broadcast, their *Barn Dance* appearances would be just a low-paying job without any other benefits.

The disagreement provided free publicity for both, and the Foggy Mountain Boys continued to perform at Clay-Gentry Arena. The *Kentucky Mountain Barn Dance* did eventually move to Woodland Auditorium, but not until December 16, 1950.[17]

"I can't remember how long the Clay-Gentry Arena went," J.D. said, "before they moved to Woodland Auditorium. I do remember some of the people who came to Woodland Auditorium were Pee Wee King and the Golden West Cowboys, the Maddox Brothers and Rose, Roy Acuff, Ernest Tubb, and Lefty Frizzell. Then you had some local stars like Homer Harris and his trick horse, Stardust. I remember seeing Sunset Carson there, onstage, and Lash Larue," J.D. said. "They had all kinds of different acts that would appear there. I remember seeing Jimmie Skinner there, for the first time."[18] Skinner had a special guest, "and it was Tip Sharp. He got up there, wearing a little derby hat, like the one Lester Flatt used to wear, and a buckskin jacket with fringes, and he came out and sang 'Muleskinner Blues.' He just tore it up! The crowd really loved it. He sang it in the key of A."[19]

Ruby Whitaker, a bluegrass fan and singer, grew up in the little community of Austerlitz, Kentucky, in Bourbon County, about fifteen miles east of Lexington. She knew Tip Sharp when she was a girl. "He was a neighbor of ours," she said. "Tip lived with his aunt and her husband, who worked on the railroad. [Tip] was a very shy young man in his twenties, and he started singing and playing the guitar one day [when she was visiting]. Beautiful songs—I remember one was '[When the] Bluegrass Is Covered with Snow'— and I asked him where he got the songs. His aunt said, 'He wrote them!'"

Ruby remembers her family making the trip to Lexington to see Flatt and Scruggs at Woodland Auditorium whenever they were there. "The first time I ever saw J.D.," she said, "was when he and Orval went to Woodland. He was just a little old skinny thing in a pair of yellow shorts; his little arms weren't any bigger that that," she said, making a circle with her thumb and middle finger, "and he had red hair cut short and lots of freckles. [J.D.] and Orval sat right there on the front row, and he watched everything that went on. When Flatt and Scruggs took a break, they'd go backstage, and J.D.'d watch Earl back there. Orval was so proud of J.D., and kept pushing him; I don't know if J.D. would have been where he is today without Orval and that pushing."

J.D. listened to whoever played. "At that time, I don't remember hearing anybody [who featured a banjo] other than Flatt and Scruggs for quite a while. Then, later on, I heard the Stanley Brothers, and Don Reno and Red Smiley. And of course I had heard Bill [Monroe] on the *Opry*, some. But I never really heard—I can truthfully say I don't remember ever hearing Bill with Flatt and Scruggs on the *Opry*, whether we missed them, or whether they weren't on that particular Saturday night, 'cause a lot of the time they'd be out [of town] playing shows. Of course, on Saturday night, if there was a show in town, we went to the show."[20]

Mrs. Crowe said, "Every night they [Flatt and Scruggs] were there, J.D. was there. That's when he was playing with Esco Hankins."[21]

J.D. was interested in and listened to many different kinds of music, but his involvement was limited to country music, and he played with Esco, went to school, practiced every chance he had, and watched Earl Scruggs when he had the opportunity. He had never played with other musicians his own age until he got together with the Joslin brothers, Charlie and Bobby.

"I had known the Joslins growing up," J.D. said. "We didn't live too far apart. I know when I was just learning to play the banjo, they found out where I lived and came to my house. Course, I was just really young, and so were they. Charlie was old enough to drive, and that's how I met Bob and Charlie, and we were friends ever since."[22]

"I'm a year and a month older than J.D.," Charlie Joslin said. "Esco Hankins was a DJ here [in Lexington], and J.D. picked with him when he was about fourteen years old, on WLAP on Saturday nights. The studio was on Short Street, and I think that's where I first saw him [J.D.] pick."

More opportunities to play soon appeared:

It was right after I won that contest with Esco. I remember this old car coming up that steep drive, and these two boys got out of it, one with a guitar and the other with a fiddle, and they wanted to start a band. They wanted me to go with them over to Danville [about thirty miles southwest of Lexington], where there was this other boy, Carlos Toadvine. We went way out in the country—I mean out in the boonies; I couldn't find it now—and drove up to an old house in Hogue Holler. Carlos played left-handed guitar upside down and over the top. That's just the way he learned. He was older, then Charlie, and Bobby was about my age.

Anyway, Carlos came back to Lexington with us, and the Joslins got us a job at Mrs. Martin's [a bar on North Limestone Street where they would play again a decade later] and a fifteen-minute radio show on WLEX, down on Short Street. Carlos and I slept upstairs over the bar—Mrs. Martin lived across the street in a big old house—and we ate with my grandmother Nichols. We didn't have any money, and I sure wasn't going to ask my dad for any. It didn't last long, just until the new wore off.[23]

It was summertime, "and I was out of school. We walked almost everywhere, and from Seventh Street [Martin's Place was at Seventh and Limestone] to Carlisle Avenue, where my grandmother lived, is a pretty good haul. Sometimes we'd catch a bus, if we had a dime. I didn't care; I was wanting to play—we all were wanting to play."[24]

A few years later, Carlos Toadvine became an early Elvis Presley imitator, took the name "Little Enis," and worked as a single.

Bill McGinnis, a longtime Lexington jazz musician, was playing in a dance band at the Zebra Bar, a popular nightspot on Short Street. "The first time I met Little Enis," he said, "he was working at the Lafayette Hotel [a few blocks away], and they got him to come in [to the Zebra] and sing like Elvis once an hour. The stage was behind the bar, and he got to stomping so hard he jarred over trays of glasses."

J.D. agreed. "Enis was a showman," he said. "He loved to get onstage and show out. He'd do anything for you, if he liked you—give you the shirt off his back, lend you money, anything. Little Enis and the Fabulous Tabletoppers played at the Palms, a cocktail lounge, and just packed 'em in."[25]

"The Palms was on the New Circle Road [Lexington's early beltway], on the outer side, between the railroad crossing and Liberty Road," Bill McGinnis remembered. "I played there a few times."

"When it first went in, the Palms was one of the more elite places around,"

J.D. said. "Later, it got kind of rough. Everybody and his brother played there, country, rock, and jazz. We [the Kentucky Mountain Boys, in the 1960s] even played there a weekend or two."[26]

Enis was more than a carbon copy of Elvis; he had a ready wit and a strong country voice, and he incorporated many country songs in his primarily rockabilly act. He toured for a time as an opening act for Jerry Lee Lewis but returned to work in Lexington for the rest of his short life.[27] In the early 1950s, however, he was just another kid, like J.D., who wanted to play music, and they enjoyed jamming together from time to time.

"About 1950 or '51," J.D. said, "I got my first Gibson banjo. Back then, you couldn't get a [new] banjo unless you ordered it from the factory. Joe Rosenberg's [a respected instrument dealer and pawn shop in Lexington] was a Gibson dealer, and I think Cecil Jones [who worked there] talked Dad into getting me a Gibson. Probably Dad had in mind getting a secondhand banjo. Cecil said, 'You don't need to get an expensive one,' so I got an RB-100 Gibson."[28]

Gibson's banjo line is defined by the uses to which the banjos are to be put: the TB is a "tenor" banjo, with a nineteen-fret neck and four strings; the PB is a "plectrum" banjo, with four strings and a twenty-two-fret neck. The RB, or "regular" banjo, also has twenty-two frets, but has a fifth string at the fifth fret. Gibson's postwar models, whether TB, PB, or RB, are designated by numbers; the 100 model originally sold for $100 and had dots in the fingerboard and a brass hoop between the drum head and the wooden rim; the 150 model originally sold for $150 and was the same construction but had a "bow tie" pearl inlay in the fingerboard and decorative inlaid rings on the back of the resonator. It was discontinued in 1958. Gibson would not reintroduce their "Mastertone" banjos until 1954.

The RB-100 was a wise choice for a boy who might not keep on with what was perceived as a hobby. "It cost about a hundred bucks," J.D. said, "maybe a hundred and fifty. I remembered Cecil Jones when I first heard about his studio [Lemco] and asked him about it. It was in his studio [in 1968] that we made the two records with the Kentucky Mountain Boys."[29]

That was J.D.'s introduction to Gibson banjos and the world of mystique, superstition, opinions, and passion that surrounds them. Put any two serious banjo players in the same room, on the telephone, or on the Internet, and you'll start a discussion that includes numbers, dates, wood types, interchangeable parts, makers of new banjos and tone rings, and dozens of esoteric terms known only to banjo lovers. A banjo, like any good musical instrument, is more than the medium with which a musician communicates; it is a love object.

There are people who mistakenly equate the banjo with the accordion, the bagpipe, and the soprano saxophone as the earth's most obnoxious musical instruments. This is probably due to the volume of the banjo, which, in the hands of the wrong person, can sound like a pickup truck full of empty garbage cans. To the uneducated listener, even a well-played banjo can be noisy. To the individual willing to look beyond the surface, however, the banjo may be enjoyed on many levels—as a work of art, a hobby, an artist's medium, an obsession, or all these things at once.

With both wood and metal components, banjos are so intricate, their shades of tone and richness so exquisitely differentiated, the adjustment of their parts so variable, and the personality of each instrument so individual that years of application and study are required just to *hear* them properly. Until Earl Scruggs came along, no one had paid much attention to the 5-string banjo for years.

Considering that Flatt and Scruggs had no national radio presence after they left Monroe in 1948, their impact—especially Earl's—was astounding. In the decade from 1948 to 1957, hundreds of people, mostly boys and young men, wanted to learn to play the 5-string banjo. "Earl was the one that caused that resurrection of the banjo," J.D. said. "He got national exposure [while with Monroe], and everyone wanted a banjo like Earl was playing."[30]

Dan Foy, on his Web site Banjophiles.com, has a database of Gibson banjo shipments from 1948 to 1979, compiled with the aid of Walter Carter, former historian for Gibson, USA.[31] Although Gibson was not the only manufacturer of banjos during this period, it was the most prominent, and their instruments were easiest to obtain. Besides, Earl Scruggs played a Gibson banjo.

"If Earl had not played a Gibson," J.D. said, "if he'd been playing a Vega, a Paramount, or a Washburn, that's what everybody would have wanted to play. He knew in his mind, heard something in those flathead Gibsons, the volume, the tone. Others did not have that tone."[32]

Shipments to dealers of Gibson 5-string banjos went from 2 in 1948 to 236 in 1949, after Earl Scruggs's appearances on the *Opry* with Bill Monroe. Another jump came in 1953 when Flatt and Scruggs began broadcasting on Nashville's

50,000-watt, clear-channel radio station, WSM, and another in 1954 when the RB-250 (with a real tone ring) was introduced. Numbers remained high through the emergence of Elvis Presley and rockabilly, probably influenced by Flatt and Scruggs's becoming members of the *Opry* in January 1955, and with only a slight decline in the late 1950s and early '60s surged upward again in 1962, when the *Beverly Hillbillies* television program debuted, using Flatt and Scruggs's music as its theme.[33]

These figures do not take into account the sales of used banjos, other brands, or hopeful players getting Grandpa's old banjo out of the attic, but they are a partial indication of the level of interest at the time; dealers would not order banjos unless they expected to sell them. Clearly, they can be tied to what Earl Scruggs was doing, but Gibson never sought an endorsement at that time and never capitalized on what might have made a substantial difference in their sales.

Earl "didn't go with Gibson until the 1970s," J.D. said. "By then he had popularized the banjo. Gibson never approached him. Vega [an instrument company] did, but their banjos never came up to his old Gibson."[34]

Many of the banjo players of this first generation of Scruggs enthusiasts became professionals and worked in bands that had the same sort of makeup as those of Flatt and Scruggs and Bill Monroe. Traditional string bands that had used a banjo as a rhythm instrument began to incorporate the new style of banjo playing as a way to associate themselves with its popularity, and even a few country bands had a banjo as a specialty act, as J.D. was with Esco Hankins.

Don Reno, who replaced Scruggs in Monroe's band in 1948, originated a three-finger style on the 5-string banjo, which, like Scruggs's, was loosely based on the Carolina players around whom he had grown up. Initially a guitar player, he was attracted to the sound of the Delmore Brothers and other hot flat pickers of the period and incorporated into his banjo playing not only guitar licks but notes he picked up from other instruments and other types of music as well. With the addition of single-string work and many jazz chords, he created a sound as identifiable as that of Scruggs and also increased the popularity of the 5-string banjo.

With his longtime partner, Red Smiley, Reno, a prolific songwriter, would create another "new sound" band that emphasized a dance beat and Smiley's country-flavored lead vocals, blended with Reno's tenor in their signature duets. Theirs was a sound that was equally acceptable to what would soon be called "bluegrass" audiences and to those who followed electric country music.

Reno was succeeded in Monroe's band by Virginian Rudy Lyle, another of the earliest three-finger pickers. Malcolm "Mac" Wiseman was the guitar player when Lyle joined, until Jimmy Martin, introduced to Monroe by Lyle, came for his first hitch with Monroe in December 1949 and Wiseman left to do a single act. Wiseman had been with Flatt and Scruggs the previous year as a tenor singer.[35] It is easy to see by this one example the cross-pollination that would characterize bluegrass music forever, whether it was caused by economic conditions, family complications, or the restlessness of many musicians.

Flatt and Scruggs, during their time(s) in Lexington, had little personnel change. When they made their brief, unsuccessful, foray to Tampa in the fall of 1950, bass player Howard "Cedric Rainwater" Watts left to work with country superstar Hank Williams. He was replaced by Charles "Chuck" Johnson, who used the name "Jody Rainwater."

While in Tampa, Flatt and Scruggs recorded their fourth and final session for Mercury, twelve sides drawn from material they performed at shows. These, too, would become classics, and such favorites as Jimmie Skinner's "Doin' My Time," "Pike County Breakdown," Charlie Monroe's "Roll in My Sweet Baby's Arms," and the Morris Brothers's "Salty Dog Blues" are still played by amateur "parking-lot pickers" at bluegrass festivals everywhere.

Earl Scruggs used a different tuning on two of the tunes, an open-D tuning on "Cora Is Gone" and a C tuning on the jazz classic "Farewell Blues," which he had known in his childhood. "Dad bought a 'Graphophone,' we called it," he said, "a wind-up machine with a half-dozen or so records. That's the only place I could figure I ever heard 'Farewell Blues,' played by one of those old-time orchestras."[36]

The music to which Scruggs was exposed, from whatever source, affected what he wanted to produce on the banjo; another person with the same influences would filter what they heard through a different personality to produce different sounds. Scruggs's music is filled with his humor, charm, and intelligence, which, combined with his ear for tone, make it irresistible.

It is no wonder that J.D. and hundreds of others tried to duplicate what they heard, and some years would pass before J.D. realized that the music he himself listened to disposed him to play in a way that reflected his own personality. As a teenager, he was determined to play just like Earl, and he worked toward that goal in every spare minute.

After the death of the owner of the farm where Orval worked, the Crowe family moved to Newport, Kentucky, just across the Ohio River from Cincinnati. "J.D. was graduated from the eighth grade in Nicholasville," Mrs. Crowe said, "and Rosa finished the first grade there. J.D. started high school in Newport in 1953."[37]

"Dad's brother, Arthur, lived in Newport for years," J.D. said. "He'd moved there after he got out of service, and talked Dad into going up there. He worked at Rex Engineering; they made stuff for the government, and when Dad started to work there, too, we moved. We lived there about a year, a year and a half. When I was a freshman, I played second-string basketball."[38]

When J.D. lived in Newport, "Jimmie Skinner had a record shop [in Cincinnati] where we bought all our records. He was not going full force with his recording career, and he broadcast live every Saturday from his record shop."[39]

At that time, J.D. said, "Tip Sharp was living in Covington." (Newport and Covington are adjacent.) "He would come over to the house. There was me, Tip Sharp, Benny Williams—he played mandolin, fiddle, and guitar; he could do it all—and the fiddle player was Red Stanley, who had worked with Esco. We had a little band.[40] We went to the Wurlitzer building [in Cincinnati] and made a recording right to the disc; it was 78 rpm.[41] Tip was writing songs, and when we recorded [two that he wrote,] 'Bluegrass Covered with Snow' and 'Moonlight Waltz,' Benny played the mandolin in a weird D tuning. It reminded me of the 'Get Up John' tuning [a D tuning with mismatched pairs of strings on the mandolin: F#A DD AA DE] or 'Black Mountain Rag' tuning [A E A C# on the fiddle]."[42]

Venturing from their home turf one weekend, "We went to Knoxville . . . and played the Mid-day Merry Go Round. I think Benny had some connection there. We got to see Red and Fred, Jamup and Honey, and the McCormick Brothers while we were there."[43]

Benny Williams went on to play with Mac Wiseman, then both fiddle (three tours of duty) and guitar with Bill Monroe; Red Stanley would also play fiddle with Monroe, and Tip Sharp became a popular disc jockey. The four stayed friends for years after their time together. "But they're all gone now," J.D. said.[44]

The family eventually moved from Newport. "The company Dad worked for went out of business," J.D. said. "We moved to Cynthiana [a small town about thirty-five miles northeast of Lexington], and I hated it. Dad was farming, and we stayed there about a year. He [Orval] didn't really like it either. Mom's sister lived there—still does—and her husband's people are there."[45]

Despite his dissatisfaction with the town, several things happened while they were living in Cynthiana that would have a profound effect on J.D.'s career. On a visit to Lexington, J.D. and Orval went to Versailles to see Esco Hankins's radio show, and J.D. was invited onstage to "pick one." The broadcast had astonishing and far-reaching results.

"I heard him playing 'Roll in My Sweet Baby's Arms' with Esco Hankins," Jimmy Martin said. "Heard it on my car radio on the way to Middletown, Ohio, to play with Enos Johnson."

"Jimmy Martin," J.D. said, "had left Bill Monroe for the second time [1954] and was driving through Lexington on his way to Middletown, Ohio. He heard me on the radio, and he stopped and called the station and asked who that was playing the banjo, 'cause he was looking for banjo players, mandolin players, fiddle players. They called my dad to the phone, so they talked, and Dad told him where we lived, and Jimmy came out to the house. That was my first meeting with Jimmy, and I was on cloud nine. Man, this guy had played with Bill Monroe, and he was a pro."[46] Jimmy continued on his way to Middletown, but he didn't forget J.D.

J.D.'s next venture into professional music came when he went to work with Ray "Curly" Parker and Darrel "Pee Wee" Lambert during the early summer of 1954.[47] Lambert, who played mandolin and sang in the style of Bill Monroe, had worked with the Stanley Brothers from 1946 until they disbanded in 1951, when Carter Stanley went to play guitar with Bill Monroe. The Rich-R-Tone and Columbia recordings made by the Stanley Brothers during this time showcase Lambert's mandolin playing and fine tenor voice. It was he who created the high baritone part on trios that produced the Stanley Brothers' distinctive sound at that time and influenced countless trios later.

"Curly Parker had played fiddle with Monroe," J.D. said, "but played guitar with Pee Wee. He used a thumb pick. They had day jobs, and we didn't do that much. I think it was Russell, Kentucky, where they were living, near Ashland. Scott Hatfield had been their banjo player, and he quit; that's when I got the job, but I don't remember how I met Curly and Pee Wee.[48] That's when Flatt and Scruggs were doing their TV show in Huntington [West Virginia], and I got to see some of them."[49]

Parker and Lambert worked as the Pine Ridge Boys when they first teamed up, changing their name to the Bluegrass Partners about the time they hired J.D. At some point while J.D. was with them, they made some recordings in Lexington. "Bill Hunley and Ann Hunley had a record shop where we all bought our country records," J.D. said, "and later on set up a small recording studio in the basement of their house. Pee Wee and Curly hoped to put out a 45-rpm record, and we recorded some demo tapes. I can't remember if the whole band recorded or just Pee Wee and Curly and me. I'd like to know what happened to those tapes; they were never released." The band included, at that time, "Pee Wee, Curly, and myself, and a guy named Bill Moats, who was the fiddle player. He was a Benny Martin fiddle player—I mean, if Benny didn't play it, *he* didn't play it! The bass player was Bob Tincher. He was a hell of a bass player."[50]

During his time with them, the group went to Springfield, Ohio, prompted by Parker's work as a surveyor, and the band members worked on his project during the day. "We were building runways at an airport," J.D. remembers. "It didn't last that long."[51] They played nights and weekends and had a show on radio station WJEL. When the job was completed, Parker and Lambert went back to Russell, Kentucky, and J.D. returned to Cynthiana.[52]

It was not long before Jimmy Martin came to get him. "I went with him to Middletown [Ohio]," J.D. said. "I was out of school at the time for summer vacation. I stayed a couple of months; that was my first deal with Jimmy, and we played up there with Smokey Ward, who did a live program [on radio station WPFB] around lunchtime every day. [Luther "Smokey" Ward had appeared occasionally on the *Kentucky Mountain Barn Dance* with his then wife, "Little Eller," while they were regulars at the *Renfro Valley Barn Dance*.] I believe the mandolin player was Bill Price, and there was another fellow with him named Bobby Simpson, who played bass. That was my first encounter with Jimmy."[53]

After his first tour with Monroe, Jimmy had worked in Middletown in 1951–52, with Smokey Ward and a young Sonny Osborne; he had worked with Sonny's brother, Bobby, in the Lonesome Pine Fiddlers, and the two had recorded for the King label in 1951. They later started a band called the Sunny Mountain Boys in Bristol, Tennessee, before Bobby went into the U.S. Marines. When Jimmy returned to Monroe in the summer of 1952, he took Sonny with him to play banjo. After another year in school, Sonny returned to Monroe for the summer of 1953.

The reason for all the swapping and changing among adult musicians was primarily economic, combined with a little "grass is greener" syndrome. Monroe worked regularly during this period, and some of his recordings with Jimmy Martin were among the best he ever made, but he was a notoriously bad money manager, and while his band members loved the music they made with him, they found it difficult to make ends meet while working for him. Radio stations with popular shows attracted musicians from across the Southeast, but when local bookings did not live up to expectations, or when an area was deemed to have been "played out," it was time to move on, either individually or in groups.

"When I left Bill," Jimmy Martin said, "I went to Middletown, Ohio, with J.D. and Bill Price. We never got to record. J.D. came with me when he was fourteen. [Jimmy was mistaken; J.D. would have been sixteen in the early summer of 1954.] J.D. was willing to learn, and I've always liked to help other people if I can. If I didn't like him and hadn't wanted him to be a good baritone singer and banjo player; if I hadn't worked as hard on J.D. as I did, I don't believe he would ever have gotten his name put on a Gibson banjo."

"Jimmy was young and excited," J.D. observed. "He'd just left Bill. He was with Bill from 1949 to 1954, and this was 1954. Because he'd played with Monroe, I thought he was a big deal—which he was—he'd played the *Opry,* and that's the ultimate. I was wanting experience, and I was wanting to play. We did Tommy Collins songs, George Jones songs, Ferlin Husky songs—different things, things nobody else was doing at that time. When I was with Jimmy, I wasn't obsessed with making any money as long as I got to eat—I just wanted to pick."[54]

Jimmy Martin was a cocky, energetic little man with supreme confidence in his considerable talents. His voice was actually in the tenor range, and he sang both lead and tenor with Monroe. Their duets had been sky-high, leading to the term *high lonesome* that came to characterize Monroe's work. Jimmy knew how to use his voice, too, grabbing every molecule of emotional and musical tension from each syllable. His solid, powerful guitar playing was as steady as a metronome, punctuated with the "runs" with which he propelled his music forward. And it was *his* music, once he left Monroe. He had a clear idea of what he wanted to do, how he wanted his music to sound, and what he wanted the musicians who played with him to do to help him get that sound.

"Jimmy told me," J.D. said, "'Everybody is trying to sound like Earl. You can't sound like Earl because you don't have Lester [Flatt] and Cedric Rainwater. You need five people to make that sound.'"[55]

"When J.D. was playing with Jimmy," J.D.'s sister, Rosa, said, "Jimmy would say, 'I know you love Earl Scruggs, and he's good, but, if I'd wanted Earl Scruggs, I'd have hired Earl Scruggs. You need to get your own stuff.'"[56]

Although he was somewhat resistant to change at first, J.D. attended to what Jimmy said and at that point began slowly to develop his own style, still heavily based on Scruggs's, but incorporating things that seemed to fit better with what Jimmy was playing. He also began learning to sing baritone.

"You couldn't learn [J.D.] baritone," Jimmy Martin said, "because he'd never sung; his voice was very weak, and his baritone was very weak."

"[Jimmy] was like a movie star, to me," J.D. remarked. "I didn't really realize how good he was at teaching the music, and I didn't know at the time that he was, I guess, grooming me to play what he wanted to hear in his music. That turned out to be a good thing, in later years. But he did, he showed me a lot, and I knew I had to go back to school, so I was trying to make the best of it and learn all I could at that time."[57]

In addition to what he learned from Jimmy, he had a number of first-class musicians around him to observe and question. Like a baseball rookie up for a few weeks with a Major League team, he became a sponge, soaking up the music and the atmosphere around him, and there was a great deal of both in Middletown.

Dayton and Middletown, in southwestern Ohio, share an Appalachian heritage and a community of fine country musicians. People from the mountains of Kentucky and West Virginia were drawn to work in factories there during World War II and the prosperous period that followed.

The money and steady work were often offset by a feeling of displacement. Family units might have lived there for generations, and transplanted individuals might be surrounded by friends and families, but they still had ties to their places of origin. Listening to "hillbilly" music strengthened those associations, evoking memories of pastoral contentment and the heartbreak of separation and homesickness. Successful radio stations there have catered to—and profited from—that emotional connection, with their station personalities keeping up a folksy, friendly conversation with their listeners.

Radio station WPFB began in 1947, when businessman Paul F. Braden deliberately set about to capture that audience. For a time, the station sponsored a popular jamboree, and many of bluegrass music's top names got their start playing music there, but what held the whole thing together was the relationship between the listeners and the announcers.[58]

"Smokey Ward," J.D. said, "could sell an igloo or a refrigerator to the Eskimos. He had the craziest sayings; that's where Paul [Mullins, a later, equally popular, disc jockey at WPFB and other stations] got a lot of that. You never heard stuff like it—he'd talk about sponsors, and when you'd go by there, you couldn't get in the parking lot. Every sponsor he had did great business. There were tire stores, restaurants, service stations, furniture stores, everything, and he had a nickname for everybody. He advertised a restaurant, a good old country restaurant called the B and B, and he called it the Buckshot Biscuit Stop."[59]

"Smokey Ward," said Sonny Osborne, "had a nickname that he called J.D., and it was 'Birdseed.' He called him 'Birdseed Crowe,' and I always wanted to see what 'Birdseed' looked like. When I saw him, he probably weighed maybe a hundred pounds. Maybe. A real skinny guy, thin. Boy, he could play, though. He could always play. The tone of the banjo that he played, you'd think it was solid gold. He always had a good tone, played with good tone."

The atmosphere was lively. "There were people playing around the Dayton area like Carlos Brock, Dorsey 'Little David' Harvey, and Frank Wakefield," J.D. said. "[Wakefield] was real young, playing with Red Allen."[60]

Carlos Brock and Enos Johnson had recorded with Sonny Osborne in the winter of 1952–53, and both would later play guitar with Bill Monroe. Enos Johnson had worked with the Osborne Brothers in Knoxville for about a year. Both Brock and Johnson would remain prominent musicians in the Dayton-Middletown area for decades. Dorsey Harvey was a semireclusive but outstanding mandolin player whose nickname was derived from the gospel song line "Little David, play on your harp." He was the father of David Harvey, also a mandolin player, head of the mandolin division at Gibson, and founder of the band "Wild and Blue" with his wife, Jan, and her sister, Jill Snyder.

Frank Wakefield was a mandolin prodigy from Tennessee about three years older than J.D., who had been discovered by singer-guitar player Red Allen. "I didn't have a mandolin player at the time," Red Allen said. "Tommy Sutton had a jamboree on WING [a Dayton radio station]. I saw Frank Wakefield sitting on a porch on the corner of Montgomery and Fifth, playing a cheap mandolin. I told him I'd pay him ten dollars, and he'd never been paid for playing. We played 'Blue Moon of Kentucky' in C, and he took a whole mandolin break in B. You couldn't hear for the clapping. He was fifteen years old."

Red Allen and Frank Wakefield had a love-hate relationship that took them through twenty years of intermittent partnership and recording. Wakefield was one of the first to straddle the line between country music and folk music, appearing in the folk-bluegrass Greenbrier Boys in the 1960s. His mandolin playing ranges from traditional—Monroe is alleged to have named him his successor at one time—to wildly innovative, as in his "classical" style, but continues to be interesting and exciting.

Bobby Osborne's mandolin playing was, in its way, as distinctive as Wakefield's. Based on his early work as a guitarist, it incorporates electric guitar licks and is highly melodic, characterized by crisp, clear notes over a pulsing rhythm. Like his brother's banjo playing, it was influenced by Earl Scruggs, who has described his music as "playing the words of the song," and also by his own fiddle playing. His style is like no other, and has been greatly influential.

"I never saw Bob and Sonny [Osborne] play until we were at WPFB," J.D. said. "Enos Johnson was with them at that time. Bob and Jimmy [Martin] and Larry Richardson had worked together before Sonny was playing banjo."[61]

When Bobby Osborne got out of the U.S. Marines in 1953, Sonny left Bill Monroe (his second tour), and the two formed a band with Enos Johnson and fiddle player L.E. White (who had been in Monroe's band with Sonny) to work in Knoxville. The brothers returned to Dayton while J.D. was in Middletown with Jimmy Martin, who had worked with them separately but not together. Martin and the Osbornes decided to form a group, despite obvious personality and temperamental differences. Perhaps it was these issues, and the resulting tension, that produced such remarkable music in the year that they were together; they recorded six sides for RCA Victor that have remained classics for more than fifty years.

At the end of the summer, Jimmy and the Osborne Brothers departed for Detroit (another "Appalachian sink" of uprooted southern mountain people, drawn to the automobile industry) and Casey Clark's *Lazy Ranch Barn Dance* on WJR, and J.D. returned to school in Cynthiana.

"I remember [Jimmy] told me," J.D. said, "if there ever came a time when he could use me again, he'd call. Well, of course, you know how that is, but it did work out that way, because in 1956, he did."[62]

CHAPTER 3
THE ROAD TO DETROIT:
WE REHEARSED

"I went back up to Middletown after school was out," J.D. said. "Enos Johnson was still there, and Bill Price, who sang tenor and played mandolin with Jimmy—he was from North Carolina—and Bobby Simpson was there also. Smokey Ward called me, and I went back up there and worked with them. Smokey tried to play the fiddle, Bill sang, and me—I was trying to learn some baritone. Enos would sing, too. There were always guests. I'll tell you what, he [Smokey Ward] had so many commercials we didn't have to play much. He could talk ten minutes and never play a song. He was a pro, now."[1]

"The first contact I had with J.D.," Kentucky-born banjo player Noah Crase said, "was before I went with Bill Monroe, when I was in Middletown. I had sold my brother an RB-150 banjo. [Kentuckian] Jimmy Skidmore had been playing banjo there in Middletown with Smokey Ward, and J.D. came to Middletown to take his place. When they got J.D., I guess he didn't have a banjo with him, or something, but he borrowed the banjo I'd sold my brother."

Crase had played with Jimmy Martin, recorded with Red Allen and Frank Wakefield, and played with Monroe two different times in the 1950s. Known for highly accurate, intricate playing that combines Scruggs licks with unconventional progressive inventions of his own, his work has been drawn upon by others as stepping-stones in the development of Keith-style playing. He has worked with many Ohio-based bands and traveled extensively with the Boys from Indiana in the 1970s.

"I didn't see J.D. around for years," Crase said, "but we remembered each other. When I was with the Boys from Indiana at Renfro [Valley Bluegrass Festival], I got off the bus and J.D. was standing there; he came over, and we stood around and talked for a long time. He said, 'Old banjo players never die, they just fade away.'"

One accidental experience in Ohio would have a strong effect on J.D. "The first time I heard Elvis was in Middletown, in a restaurant," he said. "They used to have those nickel juke boxes, and we'd look through and see what they had. I saw 'Blue Moon of Kentucky' and played it, and I thought, 'That was the *worst!*' I was a bluegrass diehard and thought if it didn't have a banjo it wasn't worth listening to, but the more I listened, the more I liked it. He [Elvis] was totally different than anybody else—different beats, different everything. Then he started singing ballads, and I thought, 'Hey, he can sing!'"[2]

J.D., like most banjo players, always had his eye out for another, better, instrument. Serious banjo players are rarely satisfied, until they locate—and obtain—*the* banjo (or banjos) they feel to be their destiny. Banjos are complicated, difficult, and temperamental, sometimes seeming deliberately uncooperative. They are all individuals, not only in appearance and voice but also in the way they respond to one player and not to another.

Gibson introduced its TB-250 and RB-250 in 1954, having finally become aware of the increasing interest in the banjo; in 1953, the shipments of RBs were exactly twice those of TBs—230 to 115—while the PBs lagged far behind, with only 16 shipped.[3] The new banjos, which had the same decorative trim as the 150s, were the first postwar banjos to have bell-brass tone rings mounted on the wood rim for greater volume and a more metallic tone. They were given the "Mastertone" designation that had been used on Gibson's more expensive banjos before World War II, but instead of reproducing the prewar "flathead" ring, Gibson brought back the less favored—at least by most Scruggs-style players—"raised-head" tone ring.

The difference in profile of the two tone rings can be seen through the drumhead of the banjo, but it also makes itself known in other ways. The new banjos were certainly louder than the RB-100s and RB-150s that preceded them, but the raised-head tone ring produces a keener, more metallic sound, rather than the mellow, woody tone of Earl Scruggs's flathead. Once again, Gibson had failed to study the market.

They shipped 62 of the RB-250s in 1954, however, and 152 in 1955.[4] One of the early owners was young J.D. Crowe. "It was probably '55," J.D. said. "Dad paid $350. That was the ultimate—they had started making the Mastertone. It was a bow-tie style, the 'fancy' one, top of the line.[5] I got a new Mastertone," he said, "but I got a dang raised head! That's what I had when I went with Mac [Wiseman]."[6]

In 1955, Mac Wiseman was in his prime as a bluegrass singer and recording star. Known for his sonorous, expressive tenor voice and his vast repertoire of heartfelt ballads, he had a contract with Dot Records and many popular hits and was a member of the *Old Dominion Barn Dance* in Richmond, Virginia. Before establishing his own band, he had performed with Molly O'Day, Flatt and Scruggs, and Bill Monroe. When he needed a banjo player for a summer tour, J.D. was recommended.

"How I got that job was," J.D. said, "a friend of mine, Benny Williams, was working with Mac, playing fiddle and mandolin at that time. I think Donny Bryant had just left Mac, and I was out of school, so Benny called and asked if I'd be interested in going to work with Mac for a while. I said, 'Well, I'm going to school, so I'd have to be back,' and he said that would be all right. I said 'Well, sure, I'd love that!' So I hopped a bus, and went to Richmond, Virginia, and I worked with Mac about two and a half months."[7]

Williams picked J.D. up at the bus station, and the two roomed together. "Don Reno and Red Smiley stayed right below where we were then, and we'd go down to the trailer park and pick."[8] Mac's band consisted of "just the four of us, Mac, Benny Williams, and the fiddle player was Curtis Lee. Mac didn't carry a bass player at the time."[9]

"I only carried three besides myself," Mac Wiseman said. "I didn't carry a bass, because I could handle that with the guitar. We had a [record] release schedule with singles every six weeks, and were fortunate enough that we'd have two or three playing at a time, and just built up a tremendous catalog. I did mostly solo performances, with some duets, and worked as hard as I could to make it sound like the records. I don't know who was singing lead with me at that time, and I don't recall J.D. singing at all."

"We played the *Old Dominion Barn Dance* every Saturday night that we were in," J.D. said. "We worked a lot of concert dates; I know we worked some in Canada, and that was the first time I was ever in Canada. Mac did a lot of package shows, with *Opry* acts, back then. He had just bought a new vehicle, and I remember I asked him how many miles it had on it. He said, 'Well, I just bought it, but we'll put a few miles on it this summer,' and we did. I think we put thirty thousand miles on it in the time I was with him, and that's a lot of miles. So we stayed pretty busy, but I had a good time. I learned a lot during that time period with Mac."[10]

By the summer of 1955,

"The Ballad of Davy Crockett" had been out two or three months, and we played "Love Letters in the Sand," "I'll Still Write Your Name in the Sand," "Wildfire," and "By the Side of the Road" (a gospel song), "I'd Rather Die Young," "'Tis Sweet to Be Remembered," "Shackles and Chains," and "I Wonder How the Old Folks Are at Home"—that was the biggie. We really rehearsed that stuff; Mac was hard to play with, and you had to listen to his singing to get your timing. Benny switched to mandolin, and when [a song] needed twin fiddles, switched to fiddle.[11]

By then, I'd gotten into more than Flatt and Scruggs. I liked Mac's music, and Reno and Smiley's. Country music was always what I listened to—Ernest Tubb in the '40s and '50s; Roy Acuff was a great entertainer. My favorite singer was Lefty Frizzell, and I liked Carl Smith and Hank Williams. He really started that trend, and just set the world on fire. I always liked western swing, especially Bob Wills and Hank Thompson. Floyd Tillman wrote some great songs, and was a good stylist in his own right. Big bands—I liked Spade Cooley. The Sons of the Pioneers—I didn't like their songs so much, but liked the harmony. Skeets MacDonald had that California sound, like [Merle] Haggard and Buck Owens had later. George Jones was one of my all-time favorites. You could recognize all of them when you heard them; you can't do that, now.[12]

With the new ideas he had come up with while playing with Martin and this exposure to other banjo players and other styles of music, J.D. was aware of the changes in his own music. Like most teenagers, he listened to rockabilly; it was 1955, the big hit was "Rock Around the Clock," and things were changing fast in the music world.

At that time, of course, I was pretty young and still learning, and I was just fascinated with the whole deal. Don Reno and Red Smiley were there, and that was a big thrill for me, because I'd never seen those guys before. I'd heard them on record, but I'd never seen them, so I got to meet all of them. Carleton Haney was their manager, and he was there. There was a brother act, Hack and Clyde Johnson, and playing the banjo with them was Allen Shelton, so I got to meet those guys.[13]

Reno and Smiley had one fine show. They were so funny, and probably some of the nicest guys I ever met. They made you feel like you were just like they were. Ronnie Reno, Don's son [who played mandolin], was just a little kid, and they put him on a box so he could sing. They didn't want to raise and lower the microphone because they were broadcasting.[14]

"They were so entertaining," J.D. continued, "not only their music, but the comedy, with 'Chicken Hot Rod' and 'Pansy' [their comedy alter egos]. A lot of times we'd follow them [on the show] and I'd worry, but old Mac would go out there and have them eating out of his hand. He was a great emcee, a lot like Lester [Flatt] in some ways.[15]

"I was listening to Reno, and I took some of Reno's instrumentals and converted them to Scruggs style with a Reno left hand," J.D. explained. "Mac really liked that. Mac featured a lot of fiddles, and had a totally different style from Jimmy or Lester and Earl."[16]

"J.D. was around sixteen [actually seventeen] years old," Mac said, "and we were touring extra heavily then. As I recall, he was quite shy. I don't think he'd done any traveling with a top group. Each time I hired a man in, I tried to impress on him: you've got to apply yourself and give me everything you've got. Apparently, he [J.D.] had listened to my records; he knew all my material. He did an excellent job and never caused me a minute's trouble or worry. We were traveling in a car at that time, and if you're spending that much time in a car, you have to get along, or it doesn't work."

When J.D. returned from the summer with Mac, his family had moved to a horse farm on Greenwich Pike, north of Lexington, where Orval had accepted a job. In September 1955, J.D. enrolled as a junior at Lafayette High School. "Back then, you started to school after Labor Day," he said.

I played hooky half the time; I wanted to pick. I had got it in my blood, and that's all I wanted to do. They had my schedule screwed up [at school] and told me I wasn't supposed to be there, so I went down to the pool hall.

I ran into "Lightning" [J.G. Bartlett], and he had a part-time job at Good Samaritan [Hospital], taking food on big carts up on the elevators. I got a job, too, and, of course, they had to do a physical. They found a spot on my lung and really scared all of us. I wasn't sick. I'd never had a sick day except when I had the measles. They sent me to a specialist, who said, "You've got to get that taken care of!" I had just turned eighteen.[17]

What J.D. and the following year his sister, Rosa, had was bronchiectasis, a condition of the lungs that causes destruction and widening of the large airways. It is sometimes congenital but may occur as a result of infection or other diseases.[18] "It may be hereditary," Rosa said. "It's more heard of in London than here, due to the fog."[19] It is rarely seen today, due to the use of antibiotics in the early treatment of respiratory infections, but even in the 1950s, if the bronchiectasis was isolated, surgery could leave the patient with no further problems.[20]

J.D. had the lower lobe of his left lung removed. "I went into the hospital around Thanksgiving time," he said, "and after that, I didn't go back to school. The surgery technology wasn't what it is now; I was probably on the operating table about seven hours, and now they'd do it in a lot less—maybe even outpatient! I remember staying ten days in the hospital, and then staying home, recuperating."[21]

"J.D.'s lung grew back," Rosa said. "He was stronger [than she], and it didn't affect him as much. He has not had pneumonia; I've had it nearly every year. My scarred lungs made me more susceptible. My surgery was in 1956, and they removed the lower third of my lung."[22]

J.D. didn't want to return to school. He wanted to pick, but there was nowhere in Lexington to play.

When rockabilly music emerged in the 1950s, its immense popularity forced recognition, often coupled with disapproval, by mainstream listeners; there was a raw, unbridled aspect that was frightening to some. Although its growth, according to jazz musician Bill McGinnis, did not affect the work of dance bands and combos that played traditional popular music around Lexington, it completely overshadowed country music and eventually almost caused its demise.

Opry stars still played "package shows" in large auditoriums, but the shows were less frequent, and smaller acts found their usual venues were now occupied by rock-and-roll bands, and their audiences—particularly the younger ones—had deserted them. Many of the younger country music performers converted to playing more up-tempo, Elvis-influenced music; the country roots of rockabilly were obvious, and the switch was not difficult. Radio stations, always eager to pander to the most income-producing sounds—and possibly influenced by what would become known as "payola," a system whereby disc jockeys, and sometimes radio station executives, were paid under the table to play certain records frequently, or to add performers to their playlists—refused to play anything that sounded "too country" or too far out of the mainstream.

Corporate Nashville panicked, and record companies cut many of their traditional country recording stars (although Jimmy Martin and Bill Monroe continued to record for Decca, and Columbia held on to Flatt and Scruggs) and attempted to broaden the appeal of country music by replacing fiddles with string sections and generally softening and citifying both the content and the sound of the performers they retained.

J.D., like others of his generation, loved rockabilly, yet he was ambivalent about its effects. "I hated it," he said, "in a way, because it took away from what we were doing. Country music hung in there, though, and still had big artists and big country [radio] stations. Elvis opened a lot of doors and put a lot of bands to work that wouldn't otherwise have gotten to work if Elvis hadn't popularized the music. Then there were artists who would have made a hit whether he'd been there or not—you don't know. I guess the good side outweighed the bad."[23]

With the absence of venues for bluegrass, J.D. relied on playing with friends from other musical backgrounds just to keep "loose," in pickers' parlance. "When Elvis came in," Rosa said, "he loved that stuff too. [They played] Fats Domino, all that, lots of blues stuff. Mama and Daddy really went through it."[24] She added, "They all came to our house, and it was fun. Esco, Jimmy Lee Ballard and his brother, Johnny, who was blind; Carlos Toadvine—everybody called him 'Little Enis,' later—and they'd get in there and they didn't just do bluegrass. J.D.'d get on the guitar, and he could burn the guitar up, and do the Elvis stuff, too. Enis would sing, and J.D. would do the Scotty Moore part on the guitar."[25]

Although it was fun, it didn't satisfy J.D.'s restlessness, or his desire to play serious bluegrass music. He had kept in touch with Jimmy Martin after that summer in Middletown; many years later, Jimmy still had at least one letter from J.D. written during that period.

Jimmy Martin and the Osborne brothers parted company in August 1955; Jimmy stayed in Detroit and recruited Earl Taylor, mandolin, and Samuel "Porky" Hutchins, banjo, from Baltimore, to work with him. They played in the "clubs" (a euphemism for taverns) and on *Casey Clark's Jamboree,* and recorded four well-received sides for Decca. "Before the Sun Goes Down," "Skip, Hop, and Wobble," "You'll Be a Lost Ball," and "Hit Parade of Love" had just been released when J.D. joined Martin in 1956. These included studio musicians Tommy Vaden on fiddle and Howard "Cedric Rainwater" Watts on bass.

"Sam Hutchins had gone back to Baltimore," J.D. said. "They had two 78s out at the time. Jimmy thought about me, and called the house. It was warm weather, in June or July of 1956. Jimmy'd been to Sneedville [Tennessee, his hometown] to see his mom and stepdad, and stopped by the house. I just got in the car with him and went."[26]

Mrs. Crowe was reluctant to let him go. "At first," J.D. admitted, "I don't think she wanted me to leave school. Of course, I don't think any parent would want a kid to leave school. I know she kind of contested that a little bit. I think Dad wanted me to play; he didn't really want me to leave school, either, but I think he realized you had to leave home to play. It's like driving a truck you know, if you're on the road, that's where you've got to go. But once I got into it, I think she was very supportive of it. I think, overall, they were glad I did, 'cause I wasn't that far from home, really, and I got back to visit quite often."[27]

"Jimmy," Mrs. Crowe said, "would bring J.D. to my house on Greenwich Pike every summer and stay about a week. He took care of him dearly and allowed no smoking and no drinking. He was a good guy, and J.D. thought a lot of him."[28]

"I was excited about leaving Lexington and moving to Detroit," J.D. said.

I'd never been there before, and I really looked forward to it; I stayed for five years. Earl Taylor played mandolin. We played a barn dance with Casey

Clark and the Lazy Ranch Boys [who played] western swing. They played some good music.[29] A barn dance, in, of all places, Detroit, Michigan, which was kindly odd, I thought. Casey Clark was the man that ran that show, and he also had a TV show across the river in Windsor, Ontario, for a while. Jimmy and the Osbornes did the TV show; I think I did that only one time, because they stopped having it for some reason.[30]

Casey [Clark] had been in Lexington when I was a boy; he played fiddle.[31] I asked him if he remembered being in Lexington, and he said he did.[32] After the *Barn Dance* on Saturday nights, we'd go to the club and play from 10 p.m. until 2 a.m.[33]

"When J.D. first come with me," Jimmy Martin said, "now, he could take the lead [on the banjo], but when he stepped away from the microphone, you couldn't hear him. His bad problem was saying, 'You can't' when [I told him to play] so you don't sound like Earl Scruggs. Where Earl would play a lick one way, I told J.D., 'Just play it backwards.' J.D. would play every note just like Earl, if he could, 'cause he loved Earl and his music so good, but I told him, 'If you want to get anywhere, you've got to get your own style.'"

"It didn't dawn on me until later," J.D. said. "What Jimmy was trying to teach me, but later I thought, 'Oh, that's what he was talking about!'"[34]

Of course, when I went with him I was green, just like everybody is when you first start out. He was a good man to learn from. He wanted his timing down right, and he knew his timing. It was different from Scruggs's in that some of the notes were a little quicker. Some of Scruggs's runs will not fit Jimmy's material because he comes back in with his singing a little quicker than Lester would do; things like that. And therefore it will not work; it will not sound right. So you have to work on something that fits what he is doing. That's what he taught me to do, and I worked it out.[35]

"I enjoyed going to Detroit. We played clubs and rehearsed; never a day went by that we didn't rehearse. I liked Earl [Taylor]. He was one of those guys you couldn't keep from liking."[36] Remembering Detroit, J.D. laughed:

Some of the clubs that we played in Detroit are probably gone by now, and it would be a good thing. They were rough, a lot of 'em were. Some of 'em were nice, some of 'em were mediocre, but there was a lot of rough clubs at that time. We never had any trouble, but I saw a lot of it. That's just the way it was, in those days. One good thing about it: the musicians, I guess because we'd befriended so many people, and they liked us, they weren't going to let anything happen to us. So that was good. But, now, among theirselves, that was a different story. There was fights, a lot of fights, a lot of arguments. You know, anytime you mix booze and a crowd together, that's what you get."[37]

J.D. still had his mind on banjos. "Sam Gastin was an old fellow who lived down below Danville, [Kentucky]," he said, "in Junction City."[38] J.D. thought "the world of him, and tried to pick up stuff from him, but he played an older three-finger style, using his fingernails."[39]

Mr. Gastin "could play waltzes—with a roll—as pretty as anything you ever heard; he had an odd timing, but he was good.[40] I wish I had learned to play like that, but I wanted to play like Earl."[41] Gastin's banjo "was an old plectrum, and all he had done was put a fifth string on the neck. It was a ball-bearing [banjo], not that loud, but it had a pretty tone."[42] In fact, "I ended up getting that banjo."[43]

A Gibson ball-bearing banjo is a type of raised-head banjo; the tone ring rests on ball bearings that ride on springs inserted into holes drilled into the wood rim. It was designed to keep constant tension on hide heads, which contracted and expanded with changes in humidity.

J.D. traded his RB-250 to Mr. Gastin for the ball bearing, "right after I went with Jimmy. I liked the sound of it better," he said.[44] Later, "I swapped that to a raised-head Granada."[45] Gibson's "Granada" was a curly maple Mastertone with gold-plated, engraved hardware. From J.D.'s viewpoint, however, his Granada was still a raised-head banjo and not the flathead he really wanted.

In December 1956, J.D., Jimmy, and Earl Taylor went to Bradley's studio in Nashville to record Hylo Brown's "Grand Ole Opry Song," "I'm the Boss of This Here House," "I'll Drink No More Wine," and "Dog Bite Your Hide," written by Smokey Ward. Session musicians included Gordon Terry on fiddle and bass vocals, and Howard "Cedric Rainwater" Watts on bass.

"A lot of people don't know," J.D. said, "but my main banjo at that time was [that] raised-head Granada; in fact, I recorded those four cuts with that banjo.[46]

"Bradley's Barn," he said, "was my first time in a big studio. After recording in little rinky-dink places like someone's family garage, to go into a place like that! I was excited, to say the least."[47]

"When we recorded with Owen Bradley," Jimmy Martin said, "J.D. had found him a Mastertone. They said, 'Can you hold the banjo down a little bit? It's coming through every microphone.' I said, 'Pour it on, J.D., play it louder!' God almighty, when you'd get through singing, he'd come in so strong with that banjo, you couldn't hardly stand it."

Earl Taylor left not long after the recording session to return to Baltimore and team up again with Sam Hutchins, Charlie Waller, and Vernon "Boatwhistle" McIntyre in a new version of the Stoney Mountain Boys.[48]

In early 1957, Jimmy put together another band. "Billy Gill played bass," J.D. said. "He was a good tenor singer, kind of like Ira Louvin. Like Bob Osborne, he sung 'Ruby' in D. Frank Wakefield played mandolin. Billy couldn't play the mandolin, and Frank couldn't sing tenor. Frank was pretty normal back then—he was just a big cutup."[49] Wakefield "sang solos; on the trios, Billy Gill sang tenor, and I sang lead."[50]

J.D. stayed with Jimmy Martin in an apartment in Detroit. "Frank Wakefield lived right above us. He was playing with different groups around Detroit at the time. When we weren't working, I'd go up to his apartment, and he'd be playing the mandolin and drinking coffee. He played *all* the time."[51]

> I liked Detroit, I really did. At that time it was a little tamer than it is now, and you didn't have to worry about anything. I think there was a few gangs around, but, you know, every city had that happening. It was just a lot of fun for me, back then; there I was in the big Motor City.
>
> In our off times, when we weren't playing clubs and places, I did a lot of sleeping. I, of course, stayed up late—we were all night people—and we'd go to pool halls and play pool—Jimmy was a good pool player. We'd go to movies, just hang out and do normal things. We'd visit—I'd made a lot of friends up there, and I'd spend time with them.
>
> We'd go out to a lot of different clubs on our nights off and listen to country music. Back at that time, they had a lot of good musicians up there in Detroit, and a lot of those clubs would go all night. I know one club up there would play twenty-four hours of continuous music, and they had four or five bands. When they'd work four hours, another band would come in. We used to go over there quite often.[52]

J.D. was still underage, but got into the clubs without difficulty. "Most of them knew me," he said, "and at the time, I didn't drink, so I didn't have much problem getting in."[53]

One of the best things that happened to J.D. in Detroit was the discovery of what would be a lifelong friend, companion, and workaday tool—a banjo:

I found the first old flathead Mastertone—that I still have, by the way—in Monroe, Michigan. How that came about, I'd bought a guitar that somebody had crushed the top of. It was a Martin Herringbone, a newer one. I was wanting to get it fixed, and found out this guy who repaired guitars was in Monroe, Michigan, had a little music store down there, and a repair shop. Jimmy and I went down and took it, and when we did, Jimmy spotted it [the banjo] before I did. It was laying in a chair, had no neck in it, did not have a head on the banjo, and all the parts were laying in the resonator, covered with about an inch of dust, like it had been there for a period of time.

I had another banjo I kept for a spare, and I had it with me in the car. Jimmy asked the fellow whose banjo that was, because he thought maybe somebody had left it for repair. The guy said that it was his, that he had taken it in when somebody owed him for repairs. He said, "I'd like to have one that had a neck in it, because I don't want to fool with putting it together." That's how I got that banjo. I immediately went to the car and got this banjo I had, and brought it in, and we swapped. Of course, I had to get a neck, and I got that done, but that's how I came to get that banjo.[54]

The banjo he found that day is a solid flathead (or "no-hole") Gibson-style three; with volume, richness, and warmth in its sound, it is one of the most desirable banjos—to a 5-string picker—ever made. This particular banjo is familiarly known to banjo fans as "the Banger."

"The spare banjo," J.D. said, "was a Gibson RB-100 that a friend of mine had made a tone ring and put in it."[55] Setting aside the provenance of the banjos having belonged to Crowe, today the RB-3 would be worth at least forty times what the RB-100 would sell for, so the trade, for J.D., was as successful economically as it was artistically.

The friend who improved the RB-100 was Lee Vance, who lived in Willoughby, Ohio, outside Cleveland:

I met him when we played the Circle Theatre in Cleveland. We went to his house. He played banjo some, and I let him have my raised-head Granada once I got my no-hole. He, in turn, gave me a neck for that no-hole. He had made me a tone ring for that RB-100, and it helped it a lot, so I swapped [even]. You don't get that kind of deal too often!

The neck had blocks [pearl inlays in the fingerboard] and a "boat-paddle" headstock, cut down to be a fiddle headstock. I played that neck as long as I was with Jimmy, and cut *Good 'n Country* with that neck. It was a 150 or 250 neck like the one Earl had. I had homemade tuners—crude, but they worked—that Lee made, also.[56]

The banjo had a thicker rim than the neck was designed for, and they did not fit together properly, resulting in string action so high that J.D. could slide his little finger under the strings at the rim end of the fingerboard. He played it that way until the early 1960s.[57]

In the 1950s and '60s, 5-string banjo players, aware that the banjos in current production did not measure up to the prewar ones, were frustrated in their searches for old 5-string banjos, which were always in short supply—tenor and plectrum banjos were more plentiful, having been used in dance bands from the 1920s through the 1940s. A cottage industry developed in which woodworkers made reproduction 5-string necks for the "pots" of tenor and plectrum banjos.

They also did pearl-inlay and other decorative and repair work as needed. Pickers were wary of sending instruments back to the Gibson factory for repairs, because workers there often put on just any style neck or fingerboard without consideration for appropriateness. There were horror stories about that sort of treatment: Earl Scruggs had sent his banjo to the factory to have work done on his fingerboard (constant playing wears depressions into fingerboards and can abrade frets so that they do not "note" correctly), and when it was returned, Gibson had completely replaced his familiar, authentic fingerboard with a new one that had the current style of inlay.

Old-time banjo player Wade Mainer, when his original 5-string Granada came back from Kalamazoo, found his original gold-plated hardware—all of it—had been replaced with new, for no reason other than that it was "dirty." And when Rudy Lyle, who played with Monroe in the late 1940s and early 1950s, sent his richly toned wreath-pattern RB-3 to the factory for repair, it was returned completely refinished and reworked, with its beautiful voice gone forever.

It was not until a brief period in the late 1980s and early '90s that Gibson, under new management, tried to replicate prewar banjos. When this did not last, existing workshops and new small factories began to build more banjos to early specifications. Careful craftsmanship and advertising in the trade papers made them known, and often successful, but their banjos never achieved the prestige of an old Gibson 5-string, "like the one Earl plays."

While J.D. was with Jimmy, the Sunny Mountain Boys worked regularly; Jimmy had several popular records that brought in crowds, and his showmanship and perfectionism made them real audience pleasers wherever they went, but the shadow of rock and roll was always on them, and country music everywhere suffered. It was with mixed feelings that J.D. assessed Elvis's influence:

> Around 1956 or '57, Elvis came in and killed every damn thing. The *Barn Dance* fizzled out. We played clubs and survived, but he took everybody in all kinds of music, and they followed him like the Pied Piper. He opened up a whole new way of looking at things.
>
> I have to admit I liked him, though. He had talent, looks, movement, and one hell of a manager. I saw Elvis perform twice—you wouldn't believe it. Jimmy Martin and I went down to one of those big halls in Detroit, an arena where they had basketball, hockey, and wrestling matches. Jimmy knew somebody—I believe he had met Scotty [Moore] or Bill [Black] years before. They knew who he [Jimmy] was, so we got to talk to Scotty and Bill, but there was no way you could get back to see Elvis.
>
> All the flashbulbs! It was just a continuous pop, pop, pop all the time. There were girls and grown women passing out, and paramedics coming in. It was unreal, like a slaughter. I've never witnessed anything like that in the music business.[58]

As the musical landscape around him changed, J.D.'s tastes broadened. "I listened to rhythm and blues, and rock and roll, then turned around and put those licks on the banjo. I watched Dick Clark on *American Bandstand,* faithfully, and Jimmy would say, 'Why don't you get a job playing rock-and-roll guitar?' It used to aggravate him so much."[59] One night, Jimmy said, "'Why don't you just play rock and roll?' so I said, 'Hell, I might as well,' and played and sang 'Slippin' and Slidin'' [a Little Richard song]. The crowd loved it, and I did that several times, but that was the only song I ever did fool with."[60]

Paul Williams was just out of the service when he went to work with Martin in November 1957. "I caught the bus and went to Detroit," he said, "and that's when I met J.D. Crowe. I was twenty-two years old, and he was a little younger. J.D. was a very slim, red-haired young man, and I was about 220 pounds. I envied him, going to the store and getting kids' pants; I'd have to go to the large men's section. I hadn't played mandolin in eight years, and J.D. was a great help to me."

Young Paul McCoy Humphrey came from southwestern Virginia and teamed up musically with a distant cousin, Jimmy Williams. The two had a radio program when Paul was twelve or thirteen years old and already possessed of a remarkable high, clear voice. Paul recalled:

> We auditioned with Ezra [Cline] and the Lonesome Pine Fiddlers at Blue-field, West Virginia. He was without a band at that time; Bobby Osborne and Larry Richardson had left to play with Jimmy Martin. Ezra, on his morning broadcast, was asking for anyone who wanted to audition on mandolin and guitar or two guitars—he was trying to get a duet. We rode the Greyhound across Big Walker Mountain.
>
> Ezra had Curly Ray Cline on fiddle and Charlie Cline on banjo at that time, and we went to work with him in, roughly, 1951. At that time, I was playing guitar, and that was my first professional job; I was fourteen years old.
>
> At the point when Ezra hired us, he asked, "What name do you go by?" and Jimmy spoke up and said, "The Williams Brothers." He thought, with the Stanleys and others, brother groups sounded better. Williams or Humphrey, I pay tax on both of them.
>
> We were [with Ezra] less than two years. Jimmy [Williams] went with Mac Wiseman on WPAQ in Mount Airy [North Carolina]. That left Paul Williams of Jim and Paul, the Williams Brothers. "My Brown-Eyed Darling" was the first song I ever wrote; "Paul Williams" was on the record, so that further cemented the name.

The Lonesome Pine Fiddlers at that time included Paul, Ezra, "Curly" Ray Cline, and Rex Parker; Charlie Cline had left to play fiddle with Bill Monroe. "Ezra hired Ray Goins on banjo, and he and I did all the singing," Paul said. "Ray had a different voice, deeper, and we were limited to what we could sing together because of the range. My voice has always been high-pitched; my range has been that way all my life." Between May 1952 and August 1953, Paul recorded fourteen sides with the Lonesome Pine Fiddlers.

Paul left the Fiddlers in late 1953 to join the U.S. Air Force. "I knew they would draft me. I had a brother in the infantry, and knew if I waited to get drafted, I would be in the infantry, too." This was during the Korean "conflict," the almost-forgotten war between World War II and the Vietnam War, in which many early bluegrass musicians served and about which several bluegrass songs were written, notably Curly Sechler's song "A Purple Heart" and Louise Osborne's tribute to Bobby Osborne, "A Brother in Korea."

"I was in the Far East, in troop carriers," Paul said. "We flew in troops and their equipment to South Korea; coming back, if we had no cargo, we would fly out coffins. I was over there eighteen months and was released from active duty in October of 1957."

It was in 1951 that Paul first met Jimmy Martin, "but [I] was only familiar to a point with Jimmy's music, what he'd recorded for Decca, and so forth. J.D. was great at showing me what the other mandolin players had done. He showed me what to do to get the sound on Jimmy's records. His patience and tolerance were phenomenal."

"Jimmy and Paul and I," J.D. said, "we rehearsed. We wanted to get it right—or at least what we thought was right—and we loved it. Jimmy said, 'If you don't feel a song, don't sing it,' and you could tell he was feeling everything he did. He had a lot of sense about music, how to get that timing together, how to get that same feeling. 'If you've got two in a band,' he would say, 'or if you've got five in a band, everybody has to think the same.' It's hard to do that, but it was easy with him and me and Paul Williams. We worked at it; that was the key. We didn't even have to look at each other. That's why Flatt and Scruggs were so good. That's what makes good bands; that's what makes it click."[61]

To get it right was grueling, Paul found:

I needed to pick. I had to work hard. The music was new to me, and [Jimmy's] style was new to me. And all the time that had passed since I'd played made it difficult. At first, the job looked like a big booger to me; I didn't know whether I'd get it or not. Too, Jimmy wanted me to sing tenor, and I hadn't done that in a while, so I had a lot to learn.

Jimmy worked with me on phrasing and [vocal] tone—we worked hard on that. Jimmy and J.D. both worked with me on timing. I'd been playing country [music, while in the air force], and bluegrass is a whole different ball game. I've always tried to play the melody. I never was interested in just the notes; I love the melody.

J.D. was sort of backward. We had to learn him baritone, and there I am, trying to learn to sing the tenor part. He [J.D.] would get so aggravated, and then he'd come back and try again. Baritone is a harder part than tenor. I can sing baritone, but it's harder because it's a lower tone and has more ups and downs than there is in the tenor part. The range of a song has a lot to do with the baritone, 'cause there are more variations in highs and lows than in lead and tenor.

Jimmy agreed. "There's lots of ways to sing baritone," he said. "It takes a different baritone to sing with Jimmy Martin than with Carter Stanley."

"[Rehearsing] was every day, just every day," Paul said. "I can't remember a day, unless it would be Sunday, when we weren't working on things. We had to work in phrasing, saying words alike, and singing in the same tone. It's the same with instruments: if J.D. was playing the introduction, I had to play rhythm on the mandolin. Jimmy on guitar always played rhythm. One thing about acoustic music, whether it's three, four, five, even sometimes six [musicians], each member is supportive of the others."

"Paul was somewhat of a natural," J.D. said, with admiration. "He came by it, well, I think, anyway, a lot easier than a lot of people would have. He was quick to catch on to things Jimmy wanted to do. You know, we were all reading off of the same page; we were all trying to create this music together. Musically, Paul and Jimmy blended together, to me, in as good a duet as there ever was, 'cause their phrasing was just uncanny, it was so close. It was just a natural feel for them."[62]

"We'd pick and rehearse for three hours," Jimmy said. "I'd leave and go somewhere and come back, and J.D.'d still be practicing. That's what it takes. That's a pro."

"We would both be practicing," J.D. said, "me and Paul. We worked hard, because we wanted to get it the way he wanted it, and Jimmy liked that."[63]

"The vocal part," Paul said, "is tone and phrasing, but one real important ingredient you've got to have is *feeling*. If you don't do it with feeling, it may sound good, but they won't remember. Knowing how to express 'Lost Ball in the High Weeds,' and doing it with feeling. J.D. plays with such feeling; he's always done that, and that's what I've tried to do. Here's a strange comparison: it takes all the ingredients to make good music. If any of those are missing," he warned, "it'll be mediocre. If you're baking a cake and leave out the eggs, it'll be a mediocre cake that nobody would eat. It takes working it out."

"Paul was playing the best mandolin rhythm to fit with my guitar playing," Jimmy Martin said. "He was the best I ever heard. Paul never owned a mandolin all the time he worked for me. We were looking for an F-5 [Gibson mandolin] and saw an F-4 in a pawnshop in Nashville. They were asking forty-five dollars. I said, 'It looks pretty old, would you take thirty?' I've still got it and have been offered ten thousand dollars for it."

Gibson F-style mandolins with "f-holes," similar to those on a fiddle, produce a louder, harsher sound that competes well with a banjo. Bill Monroe played one, and it became the standard in bluegrass music. The F-4 is a "round-hole" mandolin, with an oval opening under the strings, resembling that on a flat-top guitar, and has a sweeter, more rounded tone. Paul Williams's choice was unusual, but not unique—Curly Sechler also played an F-4 but used it primarily for rhythm and turnarounds, rather than taking breaks, as Paul did.

"That F-4 really helped set the tone of the trio we had," Paul said. "It was more of a bassy, woodsy sound. Old F-4s got a different tone than the F-5s did."

"Fans say," Jimmy said, "J.D. and Paul Williams got the best sound with me of anyone in bluegrass, and we did it all in one mike, so you know the soundman didn't have nothing to do with it. I'll never have a band as good as J.D. and Paul, and I'll never have one as good as me and the Osborne Brothers. I pay 'em a lot more money, now, but they aren't as good."

As J.D. recalled, "Jimmy liked a three-chord song. Actually, he didn't know but that many [chords]. He couldn't get it because he didn't want to. He wanted his music to sound like Jimmy, and that's why his music sounded different than anybody else. He knew he couldn't play like somebody else and try to beat a man at his own game."[64]

"We didn't know at the time that what we were doing would turn out to be classic stuff," Paul said. "We were just trying to make good music, good records."

"We didn't look at it as new," J.D. said. "We just looked at it as *different*."[65]

CHAPTER 4
LOUISIANA TO WHEELING AND HOME AGAIN

The music Jimmy, Paul, and J.D. made was "different" in many ways. "Jimmy's rhythm patterns are definitely a little different," J.D. said. "I'm sure Alan Munde and Kenny Ingram [both played banjo with Jimmy; Ingram also played with Lester Flatt] will tell you it's a lot different playing with Jimmy than it is with Lester. And I'm doing different timing now than I did when I was with Jimmy. When you play with Jimmy, you play what suits what he is doing. That's what makes for a good musician. A lot of pickers don't know that."[1]

Always prominent in Jimmy's music is his emotional involvement. "When I sing 'Shake Hands with Mother Again,'" he said, "every time, I think about my mother laying there in the casket, and how good she was to me when she was alive. I'm not thinking about the audience. Your baritone's got to put that same feeling in it."

Doyle Lawson, who played both banjo and mandolin with Jimmy, said, "I recorded that with him in 1970. I remember he had tears streaming down his face—it was not long after his mother had died."[2]

Other things that set their music apart were the beat set by Jimmy's strong right arm and the tight trios. Most bluegrass bands of the period had good harmony, but constant rehearsal with J.D. and Paul created one of the tight-est trios ever heard. Novelty songs showcased Jimmy's vocal tricks, his way of accenting a note by pausing just before it and singing it a bit louder, or perhaps higher. Possibly most outstanding was the energy, the electricity, that reached out into the audience from the moment Jimmy hit the stage. According to J.D.:

> I think sometimes Jimmy maybe had a multiple personality I remember, I looked at him one time and said, "Jimmy," I said, "you know, you're two different people. I've just figured this out. When you're off the stage, and we're just sitting around, you're a lot of fun, but when you put that hat on, you totally change." And I always thought that. He became like a different person, but, I guess, in a way that was good, because he became strictly musical, a performer, totally. He shut out everything else. It was serious and down to business, and very professional. When we got through play-ing and he took that hat off, he was totally different.
>
> Jimmy, mostly, was into the music; that was his life. I'd say 75 percent of his life was music—maybe more. Jimmy was a sincere person; he might not have come across that way to a lot of people, but he had a big heart. He said, "When you're on that stage, give a hundred and ten percent," and he did. Jimmy was really a lot smarter than people give him credit for; even with all his shenanigans and the way he did things, Jimmy was pretty wise.[3]

In February 1958, they went to Nashville for a recording session. All the rehearsing and effort paid off; the six sides recorded included some of the strongest and most popular songs Jimmy ever recorded. "Ocean of Dia-monds," Alton Delmore's "Sophronie," "I'll Never Take No for an Answer" (which Jimmy had written with Billy Gill), "Rock Hearts," and two gospel songs, "I Like to Hear 'Em Preach It," written by Jimmy and Paul, and "Voice of My Savior," were cut in four hours at Bradley's Barn. Nashville session men were "Lightnin'" Chance, bass; Gordon Terry, fiddle and bass vocals; and Buddy Harmon, drums. This was the first time Jimmy used drums on a recording.

"Times were getting a little harder in Detroit," J.D. observed, "and I guess Jimmy had talked to someone about our coming to the *Louisiana Hayride*. Jimmy's records were doing pretty good; he was recording for Decca at the time. We went to Shreveport, Louisiana, and joined the *Hayride*."[4]

The *Louisiana Hayride*, established along the lines of the *Grand Ole Opry*, began in 1948, and became known as "The Cradle of the Stars," due to its early presentation of country music performers who became well known. Broadcast over Shreveport's KWKH, its first big success was Hank Williams, and many other big names in country music started there as well. Johnny Cash, George Jones, Johnnie and Jack with Kitty Wells, Jim Reeves, the Browns, Johnny Horton, and the Wilburn Brothers were only a few; bluegrass music's great singer and guitar player Charlie Waller began there, and Elvis Presley did too, in 1954.

"The *Hayride*," Paul said, "was aimed northwest and west; it was a 50,000-watt clear-channel station like WSM. One Saturday out of the month, half an hour was live over the CBS Network, to the whole country."

It was an exciting opportunity for Jimmy, J.D., and Paul. In addition to performances on the *Hayride* itself, there were package shows and concerts booked through the *Hayride*; although the *Hayride*, like many other country music institutions, was not what it had been, it was still the *big time*:

We left Detroit and were in Shreveport in '58. That was me and Paul Williams and Jimmy, and Jimmy would hire people to play bass when he could. When we went to the Louisiana *Hayride*, appearing on the *Hayride* at that time were Johnny Horton, Carl Belew, James O'Gwynn, and "Country" Johnny Mathis of the Johnny and Jimmy duo. There was Margie Singleton—her husband, Shelby, is head of Mercury Records—and Jerry Kennedy, now a big guy at Mercury Records, who produced Jerry Lee Lewis, Tom T. Hall, and a lot of good music.

That's when Johnny Cash was just getting hot—real hot. Once a month or so, the *Hayride* would have big artists come there, all those people I held in such high esteem. Getting to see them and meet them—I'll never forget that.

They had people like Cash, George Jones, all my favorites. The Louvin Brothers, Ferlin Husky, the Browns. Cash and the Browns had crossover hits played on both country and rock radio stations. Bob Luman was one of the best performers I ever saw on stage. "Think about Living, Think about Loving" was one of his big hits. He did the best imitation of Walter Brennan I ever heard, with his walk and everything.

That's when I met James Burton. He was playing with Bob Luman, and went on to play guitar with Rick Nelson, and later on with Elvis. Even while we were there, the *Hayride* was a real hot commodity. It still had excitement and pizzazz. Maybe it was because Elvis had been there, and it carried over; after he left, he came back and did a show there.

The *Hayride,* for me, as a picker, was probably the greatest time. It was the type of show that you could not wait until Saturday night to get down there and perform. I've never had that feeling since; never enjoyed it as much as I did there. I think everyone there felt that way then; it was like a big family. The *Hayride* was very professionally produced, and everything was just like the *Opry.* Everything clicked.

I was twenty-one years old and caught up in all that, and I was part of that; it was just an excitement.[5]

"We had good success on the *Hayride,*" Paul agreed. "I think when people started accepting Jimmy's music and our point of view—there had never been bluegrass on the *Hayride* before—my personal opinion is that there was a certain element of jealousy in the mix. When we'd go on the *Hayride* and encore, and Johnny Horton didn't, that didn't go over too well. For what we were doing, we were a hit."

"Jimmy could work those crowds!" J.D. said.

We would go onstage after Johnny Horton, when he had a number-one record, and we'd encore and he wouldn't. Jimmy would tell people that and they'd think he was bragging, but it's true. The trouble was, Johnny Horton could sell those records, and Jimmy couldn't; the country music stations wouldn't play his records. Jimmy never could understand that. All he was interested in was getting out there and working those crowds.[6]

Probably one of my favorite places to live was in Shreveport, Louisiana. We were there two, two and a half years. Of course, we all lived in the same house, Jimmy and Paul and myself, and we had a lot of really good friends, there, some really nice people. Seems like, some of those people, when you met them, you felt like you'd known them all your life, and we met quite a few like that. We did the same things we had done in Detroit—we had a good time.[7]

In November 1958, the three of them drove to Nashville to record six more sides for Decca: "Night," "It's Not Like Home," "She's Left Me Again," "Hold Whatcha' Got," "Bear Tracks," and "Cripple Creek," given a new treatment. All of the original songs have Martin's name on them, but "She's Left Me

Again" was written by Billy Gill, and the others were actually written by Paul Williams, possibly with some input by Jimmy. It may not be the right way to publish songs, but for years, it was common practice in many kinds of music.

"I think we recorded sixty-eight songs [during the time Paul was with Jimmy]," Paul said, "and I wrote thirty-eight of them. Out of that thirty-eight, I think twenty-five of them are classic bluegrass songs. Even the songs that have Jimmy's name and my name on them, I wrote. It was a deal: 'If you put my name on it and publish it with my Sunny Mountain Publishing Company, I'll record it.' Jimmy was a good friend."

"Bear Tracks," an unconventional instrumental requiring the use of tuners to bend the strings, is credited to Martin and Crowe, but it actually originated with Sam Hutchins. "The first time I heard it," J.D. said, "I hadn't been with Jimmy that long, and he had this tape. He said, 'Listen, this is Sam playing.' I'm not sure if it was named 'Bear Tracks' then, or if we named it later. There was about half of it—the first part of it. Jimmy said if I would put another part on it, him and I would split it. Being a youngster, I thought that was pretty good. So I put the second part on it, and we recorded it in 1958." J.D. saw Sam later and told him, "Had I known about it [being his composition], I'd have put his name on it. I did get to apologize to Sam, and he said, 'Don't worry about it.'"[8]

"When we played something like "Hold Whatcha' Got," Jimmy said, "I told him [J.D.] 'Play it so you don't sound like Earl Scruggs.'"

J.D. adapted a Buck Owens electric guitar lick for the banjo, and that was the start of his utilization of passages from other instruments—notably steel guitar—to make his banjo sound right for Jimmy's music.

"J.D.'s famous words with me and Paul was 'I can't do that!'" Jimmy said.

I would say back to J.D., "J.D., don't ever say, 'I can't.' Say, 'I can, I will, I do believe.'" Paul then said to J.D., "Get me a pencil and a piece of paper. We will write a song about that." So me and Paul, after the rehearsal, went down to a little restaurant in Shreveport called the Jayhawks, where they had hamburgers, french fries, and hog tongue sandwiches. Me and Paul would drink us some cold beer and write the song on napkins, "I Can, I Will, I Do Believe I'll Fall in Love with You."

The song was recorded in July 1961, but J.D. was not on the session; it was played by Paul Craft, who followed J.D. as Jimmy's banjo player.

Once J.D. got a neck for his flathead three, he played it constantly, but it was not trouble-free. "I used skin [banjo] heads," he said. "In 1956 or '57, plastic heads came in, and people said I ought to use them, but I didn't want to. In Shreveport in 1958, it was so hot and humid I was using [too many heads] and in 1959, I finally used a plastic head. The tone was different, and I hated it, but I had to get used to it. I don't think Earl used a plastic head until 1961. The first album I recorded with Jimmy, *Good 'n Country*, I used a hide head. That was the best-sounding banjo I ever had."[9]

Hide (or skin) heads of water-soaked leather were stretched over a metal ring by the banjo player, then held taut on the banjo with a stretcher band (or "tension hoop"). Installing one was time-consuming and tedious, and highly inconvenient on the road. Later versions came already stretched and were simpler to use but were still affected by changes in weather. Most musicians carried an extra banjo in case the head split, sagged, or was otherwise unfit for performance. There was controversy when plastic heads were introduced, but convenience won out, and hide heads are rarely used by 5-string pickers today.

The *Good 'n Country* album included the six sides from the November 1958 session; "Before the Sun Goes Down," recorded when Sam Hutchins was in the band; "I Like to Hear 'Em Preach It" from the February 1958 session; and four sides from a session in January 1960: "Who'll Sing for Me?" Jimmie Skinner's "You Don't Know My Mind," "All the Good Times Are Past and Gone," and "Homesick." When the album was released, the Sunny Mountain Boys were at WWVA in Wheeling, West Virginia. "The fourth person in the cover photograph," J.D. said, "was Floyd Busby, who was not even in the band. They just thought they needed a fourth man for the picture."[10] The D-18 Martin guitar that Jimmy is holding was borrowed for the photograph from Donna Darlene, a "girl singer" who frequently performed with the band.

"Every vacation," Rosa said, "we'd go wherever J.D. was to see him, and we got to go to a lot of neat places. We went to Detroit and Shreveport, and Richmond, when he was with Mac. At Shreveport, when Jimmy, Paul, and

J.D. went out onstage, the three guys sounded like six. The place was packed every time they played—not compared to Elvis, of course. They had fun; they enjoyed it and the people knew it and enjoyed it, too."[11]

"While we were in Shreveport, Paul left twice," J.D. said, "once to work with James O'Gwynn, and the second time with Stonewall Jackson."[12] J.D. talked Jimmy into bringing back Billy Gill, with whom they had worked in Detroit. "We had to go get him in Detroit," he said. "Jimmy drove until the first time we had to stop for gas, then I drove. We picked Billy Gill up and turned around, and I drove all the way back. It was quite a turnaround—there were no interstates."[13] Gill had a "really good voice, strong, with a wide range; he wasn't much of a mandolin player, but he could sing."[14]

Paul's decisions to leave were likely influenced by economics; their outside bookings had fallen off, due to the general lack of interest in country music as rockabilly continued to surge. "I liked Shreveport and the people and all," J.D. said, "but we didn't play that much, even though Jimmy was the highest-paid act on the *Hayride*. You can't live on what you get playing once a week. If I'd had to depend on music I couldn't have made it; I worked in a service station the whole time we were there."[15]

J.D. was fortunate in his traveling; when he worked with Esco, the musicians were home every night, no matter how late. With Pee Wee and Curly, they had day jobs and did not travel far, and with Mac, there were only four people in a brand-new car, with no upright bass to share the space. His experiences were far from typical, until he started with Jimmy. "There were five people in a band, usually," he said, "riding in a car. When I was with Jimmy, we'd put the bass in the car, and two men in back, one on either side of it. Usually the shortest guy rode in the middle of the front, with the bass [neck] over his shoulder."[16]

"People don't realize," Eddie Adcock said, "on Highway 40, going across the country, if two cars or a car and a truck met, both had to put their wheels in the ditch. You'd be sleeping sitting up in the car—the bass held your head up so you could sleep."

That was when musicians were "hungry to pick," and would travel any distance in crowded, un-air-conditioned cars on narrow, two-lane roads, often driving all night to get to the next show, just to have the opportunity to perform. Food was frequently a loaf of white bread and sliced bologna shared among the band, or something that could be picked up at a gas station and eaten in the car. Sometimes the hunger was real, when there was not enough time to stop, or enough money. Perhaps the money had run out, or they had been "stiffed" by a promoter. Gasoline had to come first, because there was always the next show, the next radio station, or the next prospect of work, and hope sustained them as they kept on traveling.

"There were no motels, and no money," Adcock said. "When I played with Monroe, I nearly starved. Monroe, then Carter and Ralph [Stanley], those guys had the idea, 'Keep 'em poor so they can't afford to leave us and start a band.'"

"When I first went with Monroe in 1954," Noah Crase said, "it was an experience. I'd never been used to sleeping in a car all night with your head leaning up against the window. You learned to do that, or you didn't sleep." They traveled in a 1953 Cadillac limousine. "Not a stretch limo, but there was a seat in the middle," he said, "kind of small, and not as luxurious as the one in the back. Bill sat in back with Bessie [Lee Mauldin] and her two dogs—Pekingese, they were." Others in the car were Carlos Brock, Bobby Hicks, and Charlie Cline. "We'd travel six days a week, come back Saturday for the *Opry,* then go out again. Times were slim, and bluegrass wasn't the most popular kind of music. We didn't always have good crowds; it was not all a bed of roses. I didn't get paid when I should get paid; I've had Bill owe me for two or three weeks, but I always had money to eat on. Bill would take us to a restaurant and see that we got something to eat."

"There were no truck stops," J.D. said. "You stopped at filling stations to get cleaned up and dressed for a show. What gripes me now is some of these young ones, who get off an air-conditioned bus and stretch and say, 'Oh, I'm so tired.' They don't know what it's all about."[17]

While the road might be tiring or stressful sometimes, Jimmy's band never had the problems some other bands had. "To be on the road with Jimmy," J.D. said, "was really a lot of fun. Jimmy had his moments, like we all did, but I can really, truthfully say that I had a lot of fun working with Jimmy."[18]

Traveling gave J.D. opportunities to indulge some of his other interests. "I was always into that western stuff, cowboys. I'd make Jimmy stop at every tourist attraction that had anything to do with heroes or outlaws that were made into heroes."[19] When they were playing package shows and went to San Antonio, "we stopped and went through the Alamo. I probably never would have gotten to do that. It was a very enjoyable time, in every way."[20] He continued:

> When Jimmy first mentioned to Paul and myself about leaving the *Hay-ride*—of course, I don't think we really wanted to go—but I think there was a situation where the money was a lot better in Wheeling, probably, and I think that had to be a big factor. Also, I think the concerts were a lot better; you had a better chance of playing a lot more concerts, because the *Wheeling Jamboree* covered a lot of territory. It went to Canada, and just really reached out; [WWVA] was a clear channel station at the time, so I think that's probably why Jimmy left Shreveport.
>
> I think we were there two, two and a half years. We left in the early part of 1960. It was a drastic change from Shreveport to Wheeling, West Virginia. I never really liked [Wheeling], and I still don't, to this day.[21]

"Gene Johnson was the manager of WWVA," Jimmy said. "He was my booker and manager, and had twenty-seven show dates booked before we got there. We weren't in Wheeling no time before we could outdraw anybody," he added with pride.

"Herb Hooven joined us in Wheeling," J.D. recalled. "He was actually living in Boston, Massachusetts. He had played Wheeling before with Toby Stroud. He played both fiddle and bass, but played fiddle with Jimmy. He moved to Wheeling while he was playing with us."[22]

In January 1960, they went to Nashville for two recording sessions; the first included "In Foggy Old London," "The Joke's on You," "Wooden Shoes," and "Home Run Man," written by Texan Buck White, later founder of the Whites. The second was devoted to the four songs for the upcoming album, plus "God Is Always the Same." Nashville musicians who helped record were "Country" Johnny Mathis, bass vocal; Benny Martin, fiddle; "Junior" Huskey, bass; and Buddy Harmon, drums.

There were two sessions in August 1960, during which they recorded Paul's "Old-Fashioned Christmas"; "Hi-De-Diddle" and "Undo What's Been Done," by Paul's brother, Sam; "Don't Cry to Me"; "My Walking Shoes"; and "Hold to God's Unchanging Hand." "Deep River" and "What Was I Supposed to Do," written by Paul with his brother, were issued as a single under Paul's name, with "Hank" Garland on electric guitar. Herb Hooven was on the sessions, with "Junior" Huskey, bass, and Willie Ackerman, drums.

Decca released two or three of Martin's singles every year, and in November 1960, "Hold to God's Unchanging Hand" and "Old-Fashioned Christmas" came out.

"Jimmy," Rosa said, "had promised he would always bring J.D. home for Christmas and in the summertime, and he did, but in 1960, there was snow up to the windowsill and he couldn't get home. Mom and I would play 'Old-Fashioned Christmas' and cry and cry."[23]

"I left Jimmy in 1961," J.D. said.

I'd been thinking about it for a while. We were in Wheeling, at *The World's Original [WWVA] Jamboree.* I probably left because I'd gotten tired. We did a lot of traveling, and the money was not as good as I thought it should have been. We stayed pretty busy, but it was still rough times back then, and I don't think Jimmy was getting the money that he should have gotten, and, of course, he could just pay a certain amount, and that's all he could do, but it really wasn't enough. That's probably the two reasons why I left, and I didn't like the place, anyway. I was just tired of the whole deal, and I knew I could do other things.

Jimmy didn't like that too much. He tried every way in the world to talk me out of it, but to no avail. Like I told him, nothing lasts forever; things change. Paul didn't want me to go, either, 'cause, since being musicians, we were also great friends. I hated to leave in a way, also, but I knew it was probably for the best. We left on pretty good terms. A while after I left, [Jimmy] was doing a recording session, and he called me to come down and help him because the banjo player at that time had just started and didn't know the material real good, and I did, so he called me to help him finish the instrumental album *Big Country.*[24]

Jimmy, never extravagant in his praise, told one interviewer, "I always liked the way J.D. picked, and I always called him the number one Jimmy Martin banjo player, because he stayed with me and got the style down that I liked. It suited my voice."[25]

Doyle Lawson's experience amplified Jimmy's assessment:

The role model [Martin] used for his banjo in his music was J.D. Crowe. He would talk about when J.D. was young, and how he developed, how many hours J.D. would sit and pick, and how they would ride in cars and J.D. would play his banjo, so what you had to do was try to get as close to that level as you could, and I honestly don't think, in Jimmy's eyes, that anybody ever got to that level, because there was only one J.D. Crowe. Everybody's an individual, but that was the plateau that you had to shoot for. J.D. was a *big* part of Jimmy Martin and the Sunny Mountain Boys. Jimmy, and J.D. Crowe, and Paul Williams: I think that was the premier Jimmy Martin sound.[26]

Doyle was only one of the banjo players Jimmy had after J.D.; another was Chris Warner, from Pennsylvania, who played two years in the late 1960s (with two recording sessions) and four in the late 1980s. He had been playing only three years the first time.

> I knew the notes to the breaks, but obviously not all the things J.D. or Bill Emerson had played. Jimmy said, "You're not playing the right timing." To me, that meant speeding up or slowing down.
>
> Vassar [Clements] said, "What I think he means is not only meter, but dynamics, rhythm, and punch." All that was "timing" to Jimmy. I was about to give up. Then I had a "lightbulb minute," and I was better able to decipher what he was trying to say. He would stay on you—not just banjo players. He would never let anything slip by, but he wouldn't tell you when you got it right, either. Being young like that, Jimmy was getting to me.
>
> Tough as it was for me, looking back, I wouldn't give it up. It was like a two-year college education in bluegrass.
>
> When I came back in 1986, I'd had twenty years to think it over and realize he was right, and I knew better what to play. He hardly ever had to say anything to me then.

An excellent banjo player today, Chris, like all the others, owes something to the "Jimmy Martin School of Bluegrass."

Returning home brought new challenges to J.D., but he was in his hometown, and his family was there. There had never been any heavy industry in Lexington, but in the 1950s, several light industries were built on the north side. IBM's electric typewriter factory began production in 1956; Orval went to work there in 1960 and retired in 1978. The Crowes lived nearby while their house was under construction, and in 1961, they bought the house in which Mrs. Crowe still lives. Coming home meant some adjustments for J.D.:

> When I left Jimmy and came back to Lexington in 1961, and, as they say, got into the reality of life—an eight-to-five job—there wasn't really anybody around Lexington playing the kind of music I liked. Somebody said, "Hey,

Bob and Charlie [Joslin] are playing [country music], and they said for you to come over." So I did, I went over and sat in with them. That's actually the first time we'd played together [since they were boys]. We had a lot of fun, enjoyed it, and the people enjoyed it, so we decided to get together and get us a place to play, which we did, but we went into it with the attitude that, look, we're going to play what we want to play. And we did, primarily, that's what we did.

I remember we discussed running an ad in the paper, to let people know where we were going to be playing, and we had to come up with some kind of a name. I guess the thought was, we're from Kentucky, and, of course, back then everybody was the "mountain boys," that was the deal, so we came up with the Kentucky Mountain Boys.[27]

Musicians who played what had come to be called "bluegrass" were limited in their choice of places to play in the 1960s. A few professional musicians, such as Flatt and Scruggs and Reno and Smiley, maintained their traditional rural southern audience through television shows. Jimmy Martin, Bill Monroe, and many country music acts still followed the basic pattern: they connected with a barn dance, a jamboree, or other established organization and "played out" from this base, booking concerts and package shows from their headquarters. This was great, until country music lost its postwar popularity and the bookings began to dry up, at which point the "sidemen" (including J.D. in Shreveport) were forced to take a part-time job to make ends meet—most sidemen, then and now, are paid only for those days they actually work.

Part time musicians, such as the Kentucky Mountain Boys, had a regular job, like anyone else, and played music for fun—and perhaps a little extra income—on the weekends at some nearby tavern. They had the benefit of a middle-class life, with a regular paycheck and time for their families, but the price they paid was playing in those taverns, where the smell of smoke and stale beer pervaded even the inside of instruments, and the noise of thirsty customers often drowned out the music. They did it for love of the music, to stay in practice, and to be a little special, a little different from the next guy on the line, so they could think of themselves as *musicians*.

The taverns were usually just beer joints where factory workers relaxed at the end of a hard week; some were rough, and a few were downright dangerous, with wire fences between the band and the audience to protect the instruments from flying bottles. Tensions can run high in any barroom. Perhaps someone hates his job, or his neighbor, or his two-timing wife; perhaps he has been chewed out by his boss, or called an opprobrious name by someone of a different heritage. Perhaps he is homesick, or feels futile and looked down upon. Perhaps it is all of these, and he has had a few drinks he cannot afford—and now he is a lighted stick of dynamite, ready to explode. In a crowded bar, there might be several like him, looking for trouble.

Women in bars have their frustrations, too: wandering husbands or boyfriends, problems at work, too many children and not enough money, or, again, all of these, and more. Women, however, are more adept at causing fights than participating in them, and, even though their disagreements are more likely to be screeching matches than exchanges of blows, their unhappiness can make itself known to all those present when it boils over.

But not at Mrs. Martin's.

Martin's Place was, perhaps, the best of all possible taverns. First, there was Mrs. Martin's personality, which permitted no misbehavior, and she had a family of policemen to smooth any little disturbances. Second, Lexington was a peaceful town, with few displaced, angry people. And third, the folk music boom had alerted the average person to bluegrass, which was now "cool," and those who came to listen to music were not looking for trouble.

Following Earl Scruggs's solo appearance at the Newport Folk Festival in 1959, city dwellers who had never heard country music fell in a big way for bluegrass, which many believed was an "authentic" folk form rather than the commercial country music it actually was. Spurred on by Alan Lomax's "Folk Music in Overdrive" article in the October 1959 issue of *Esquire* and, in the ensuing decade, the use of Flatt and Scruggs's recording of "Foggy Mountain Breakdown" in the movie *Bonnie and Clyde,* their appearances on the popular *Beverly Hillbillies* television show, and those of the Country Boys and the Dillards on *The Andy Griffith Show,* bluegrass bands—and particularly bluegrass banjo players—became the darlings of the country's wildly enthusiastic love affair with "folk" music.

Bluegrass bands that fell in with the folk idea and were "hip" enough to carry it off found themselves playing in hitherto unlikely locations: coffeehouses, concerts on college campuses, and at events such as weddings and corporate receptions. Prestigious auditoriums that would never have held country music package shows hosted bluegrass to enthusiastic folk music fans. Earl Taylor and the Stoney Mountain Boys performed at Carnegie Hall in New York City in 1959, and in 1962, Flatt and Scruggs and the Foggy Mountain Boys did also, recording a live album that was overwhelmingly popular with the folk audience, as was their recording made at a concert at Vanderbilt University the following year.

People who rarely, if ever, frequented taverns found themselves eager to go wherever bluegrass music could be found; in Lexington, that was wherever J.D. Crowe might be playing, whether it was at Comer's Restaurant, the Limehouse, or Martin's Place. Dan Brock recalled the ambience:

> Martin's had a mixed environment. There were college kids and people from the neighborhood. You went up a step or two into a big room; on the immediate left was the bar, and Mrs. Martin. She was an older woman who worked behind the bar, and was right congenial.
>
> There may have been some tables on the right, then the room opened up, and the bandstand was in the left rear corner. There was a series of tables—I don't know how many people it held, but it usually felt quite cozy. The bathroom was on the right; there was a room next to it, and you could park in back and come in through that room.

Brock was a law student and part-time folk musician then, but would later be involved in the Kentucky Mountain Boys' first recordings.

Martin's was a small, two-story building with a yellow-brick façade and a large window on either side of a central door. There was a broad paved area outside, up a few steps from street level, and clapboard houses with front porches crowded close on both sides.

It drew bluegrass fans, young professionals, and students from nearby Transylvania University and the University of Kentucky to create a lighthearted crowd with an adventurous, holiday spirit. Everyone was aware that there was something special going on, or, at least, something fun. The anteroom of the unisex restroom reflected the mood; those waiting scrawled verses and sayings on the walls from floor to ceiling—nothing offensive, just humorous. Typical was the one-liner "Mickey Mouse is a transvestite."

The Joslins had played music around Lexington for years. Charlie played guitar and sang in the style of Lester Flatt. "When J.D. first heard me [on the radio]," he said, "when they were living in Cynthiana, he told his dad,

'Listen to that—that guy sounds just like Lester Flatt.' And I did, because I was copying [Flatt] as much as I could at that time."[28]

When J.D. returned to Lexington, they were playing in a country band. Charlie Joslin said, "Bob played mandolin before the fiddle. He was into some fiddling before he quit the mandolin, maybe six months before we went with the Kirby Brothers."[29] Bob tried to play in the exciting but complex style of Benny Martin, who had played with Flatt and Scruggs in the early 1950s.[30] "He bobbed around," Dan Brock said, "like a snake; it was very charismatic in a small club."

Crowe and the Joslins played in various places, but Martin's Place was always in the rotation, as well as the Limehouse, a somewhat more rough-and-ready tavern at the corner of Limestone (also known as "Lime") and Third streets, which had offered music for several years.[31] "The Limehouse was a real 'knife and gun club,'" Harry Bickel said. "There were about half-a-dozen fights [there] one night. It was cold, in the dead of winter, and somebody stole my coat and gloves." Bickel, then in college in Louisville and a banjo student of Crowe's, became an award-winning old-time banjo player, founder of the Buzzard Rock String Band, and host to dozens of bluegrass musicians who played in Louisville.

In its life after bluegrass, the nineteenth-century building that housed the Limehouse served as a storefront church for several years before being given new life as a high-end French restaurant. It became the Atomic Café, a popular Caribbean-style restaurant, in the 1990s, and the area near North Lime has become gentrified around it.

J.D. enjoyed playing Martin's:

> Martin's was a one-of-a-kind place; we had a lot of fun there. I forget when we started playing there, regular. Probably 1963. We played there more than we played anyplace else. Martin's club and the Limehouse was probably the two clubs we played the most. Sometimes, though, we would just take a month off and not play anywhere.
>
> We weren't looking at it as a career. We were just there, night after night, week after week, playing what we wanted to play, and we really weren't looking any further at that time. There was all kinds of people that came in that little club, a lot of UK [University of Kentucky] students, people going to [Eastern Kentucky University] in Richmond, they would

come. We work to a lot of people, now, that are physicians and attorneys, and police officers, and even the UK sports people—a lot of the basketball players—that used to come down there to Martin's.

It was a step down, after playing with Jimmy Martin, of course it was, but at that point in my life, I really never thought about it to that effect. I wanted to keep loose, playing music, and we were just having fun. Everybody knew what it was; I knew what it was.[32]

"I started going down there [to Martin's] every couple of weeks or so," Dan Brock said. "J.D. was not too long off Jimmy Martin. The other musicians were not J.D.'s quality, but it was fun."

Ed Stacy was from Salyersville, in Magoffin County, about ninety-five miles southeast of Lexington. "I started trying to play guitar when I was ignorant—or a teenager! I got an old cheap guitar and kind of learned myself how to play." Stacy had followed Flatt and Scruggs from the time they played at the Clay-Gentry Arena and remembered J.D. watching Earl Scruggs play. "I always kept up with what he was doing," he said.

Ed began going regularly to Martin's when J.D. first started playing there and was often invited up to sing. "Ed had a pretty strong voice," J.D. said.[33]

"They'd take a break," Ed said, "and I'd go back where they were talking and playing, and I'd sing some bass. Finally, they asked me to join the band."

"I knew Ed Stacy," Charlie Joslin said. "He had a good voice, sounded sort of like Mac Wiseman. We hired Ed on upright bass when we started at Martin's Place."[34]

"Charlie and Bob [Joslin] were with him [J.D.], and I started singing along," Ed Stacy said. "I'd never played a bass fiddle in my life. I bought a bass and started learning at home. I'd put a record of Lester and Earl's on and play along with them. After [I learned] I started playing bass with J.D. at Martin's. We played the Limehouse on Wednesdays, and then Martin's on Friday and Saturday."

"Bob Joslin tried to sing tenor," J.D. said. "He didn't sing that high, so we did a lot of stuff in [the keys of] C, G, A, and sometimes D. I really rehearsed those guys a bunch. Bob liked a lot of other stuff—he did quite a variety."[35]

"[J.D.] sang baritone with us on some songs," Charlie said, "but except for that, he wouldn't get near that microphone. Me and my brother, we drank beer all the time, and one time I said, 'J.D., why don't you drink a beer?' and he said, 'Okay, I'll have one.' He drank about half of one, and that's the only time I ever saw him take a drink."[36]

As the word got out about J.D., people who loved his music came to Lexington specifically to hear his band or have a chance to visit with him. Orval was there frequently, when his work schedule permitted.[37]

"I remember people coming in from other towns," Dan Brock said, "and bringing in their banjos. They'd take them apart, and J.D. had to analyze and look at lots of banjos. He was very nice about it, but probably not that interested, unless he wanted to buy one. His benediction was greatly sought after."

"When the college kids found we were there," Charlie Joslin said, "what they would do, ever' one of 'em, they'd order a beer and just sit there and sip on that one. I know they had to pay to go to school and everything, but Mrs. Martin would get so mad!"[38]

"Mrs. Martin was tough," Ed Stacy said. "That's a tough job, running one of those old places and running into all kinds of people."

Ruby Whitaker worked at the Green Lantern, a restaurant and bar on Seventh Street, not far from Martin's Place. "I'd get off at nine thirty or ten, get a cab, and go to Martin's. When I'd walk in that door, Charlie would see me coming in, and would get that little old cigar box and hand it to me. He said, 'You pass this around—you'll get more money than I will.' He was the one who passed the 'kitty' around. They played for beer caps—a nickel for every beer cap and whatever they took up when they passed the kitty."

"Back then," Charlie Joslin said, "there wasn't any money in bluegrass. A man would have starved to death on the road. Bill Monroe would have starved. Me and Bob were both in [heating, ventilating, and air-conditioning] and had a business called Aircontrol."[39] They had "cut a demo at REM Studio," he said. "Cecil [Jones, who sold J.D. his first Gibson banjo, and would later own Lemco Studio] called one Sunday and said, 'Come on out. We need pickers to back up Charlie Monroe.'"[40] Charlie Monroe was Bill Monroe's older brother, with whom he recorded in the 1930s, before he and Bill each formed his own band. At this time, he was semiretired and living in western Kentucky, but would return to performing in the 1970s.

"Sometime in the early '60s, I recorded with Charlie Monroe," J.D. said. "Me, Bob Joslin [fiddle], and Ed Stacy [bass], and Kenny Whalen played electric guitar. We recorded at Bob Mooney's REM Studio on Liberty Road. Charlie recorded one or two albums; I know there were some gospel songs on the one we did."[41] He confessed, "It's hard to remember about Charlie Monroe. Everything he did sounded alike—he had the same rhythm on every song."[42]

There were actually two sessions with Charlie Monroe, and J.D. was on both of them. On August 11, 1962, B. Lucas and Paul Mullins are listed as playing fiddles; Kenny Whalen, Billy Wassum, and K.O. Durham, guitars; and Tip Sharp, bass. Twelve sides were recorded. On December 20, 1964, twelve sides, all gospel, were recorded. Bob Joslin played fiddle; Kenny Whalen and Billy Wassum, guitars; Ed Stacy, bass, and C. McDowell sang harmony.[43]

Tip Sharp, J.D.'s friend from Esco's band, was a disc jockey in Winchester, twenty miles east of Lexington. About 1962, he rerecorded "Bluegrass Covered with Snow" backed with "Just an Orphan," another of his compositions, at REM Studio, with J.D., Ed Stacy, and the Joslin brothers.[44] The 45-rpm recording was later reissued on the King Bluegrass label.

"I went back with Jimmy," J.D. said, "in—I think—'63, and stayed for four or five months. It was about that time we recorded 'Widowmaker' and some others. For the most part, that was myself and Jimmy and 'Tater' Tate on fiddle. Bill Torbert was on mandolin, and Penny Jay [who wrote 'Widowmaker'] played bass."[45]

The "Widowmaker" session was September 17, 1963; J.D. sang tenor, and Penny Jay sang high baritone; studio musicians included Grady Martin on guitar. Other songs were "Thinking Tonight of My Blue Eyes" (Carter Family) and "Red River Valley" and "John Henry," traditional folk songs performed as instrumentals. The *Widowmaker* album, released the following June, contained selections from sessions as far back as 1958; J.D. appeared on half of them.

"J.D. left once," Charlie Joslin said, "and went back to Jimmy Martin. Jimmy came in to Martin's, stood back in the back, and said, 'Don't let anybody know I'm here, or they'll just wear me out signing autographs.' He talked to J.D. and Orval, and J.D. left for about two months with Jimmy. Pee Wee Sweat from Louisville played banjo after J.D. left; when J.D. came back, we let the other guy go."[46]

"Me and Crowe and Charlie and Bob Joslin made a tape in the early 1960s," Ed Stacy said. A tape made at Martin's in 1964 gives a good idea of the band at that time. J.D.'s banjo is, of course, the strongest element, followed by

Charlie's guitar and Flatt-influenced singing. Ed Stacy sang two or three songs a set, playing guitar while "Lightning" played bass.

The repertoire of "what we want to play" was heavily Flatt and Scruggs, with very few Monroe songs (no one in the band had his range or his intensity) and a smattering of Reno and Smiley material. Bobby chose popular country songs, such as Buck Owens's "Love's Gonna' Live Here Again." There were no Jimmy Martin songs on the two sets that were taped, unless Jimmie Skinner's "Don't Give Your Heart to a Rambler" (recorded by Martin while J.D. was with him) counts. J.D.'s melodic rendition of "Devil's Dream" is obviously influenced by Bill Keith's version with Monroe, which had just been released.[47]

Another tape, made the same year at the Limehouse, is similar, with more trios and a few more Jimmy Martin songs; they used the arrangement on the instrumental "Red River Valley" that J.D. had recorded with Jimmy the previous fall. There are fourteen instrumentals among the thirty-two cuts, including a blistering "Cumberland Gap" and an innovative banjo take on "Wildwood Flower." J.D. uses occasional melodic licks and quotes from other pickers, as well as new ones of his own.[48]

Like most part-time bands, people's jobs caused personnel changes, but the Kentucky Mountain Boys remained relatively stable. "Usually," J.D. said, "somebody was around to work until you found somebody you wanted. Back then, most people had jobs, and they were all local. We weren't going to do any traveling; we were just doing it for the enjoyment. Usually, the pickers found you. They'd come in to hear you and you got to know them."[49]

"The way I ended up playing with J.D.," Gordon Scott said, "I started going out and listening after [a friend] told me we had to hear this great banjo player. In the band then were J.D. and the Joslin brothers, with Ed Stacy and 'Lightning' playing bass; they swapped; if one couldn't be there, the other would play. They played every Wednesday, Friday, and Saturday." Scott, from Madisonville, Kentucky, was in graduate school in English at the University of Kentucky, driving a school bus, and teaching guitar, but still had time for music.

"I met Gordon before we started going to Martin's," Hugh Sturgill said. "Crowe and the Joslins went back and forth between the Limehouse and Martin's. Crowe's banjo picking just stood out. J.D. never showed you more than 65 or 75 percent of his tools—he always was a five-tool player. He could do all the chromatic runs in the world, but chose not to do 'em." Sturgill, nicknamed "Turtle" by the band, was a good friend to J.D. and his bands for years.

"We went every night, me and Mitch Johnson and Hugh Sturgill," Gordon said. "We had a folk music trio, and J.D. would let us do a few. He played with us, and this went on five months or so. When J.D. and the Joslins broke up, J.D. called me, and I went over to his house. He knew I knew his material. We rehearsed Monday and Tuesday, then played Wednesday, Friday, and Saturday, and from then on."[50] Initially, the band had Gordon on guitar, he said, as well as "Ed on guitar, J.D. on banjo, and 'Lightning' on bass. J.D. said, 'We don't really need two guitar players.' By that time I had bought an A-50 Gibson mandolin. I wasn't very good, but I practiced and got by. J.D. taught me how to play the mandolin, and I've made a living off that—and he's not even a mandolin player!"[51]

CHAPTER 5
WHY DON'T YOU COME DOWN TO MARTIN'S?

Left-handed Pike County, Kentucky, native Bobby Slone has a self-deprecating sense of humor and described teaching himself to play: "I had the awfullest time there ever was [learning to play guitar], because I played it upside down." When he attempted the fiddle, "I ran off about three dogs that never did come back," he said, but he was playing with the Kentucky Ramblers over Pikeville's WLSI when he was thirteen years old. Later, he went to Bristol, Virginia, on his summer vacation, and played several summers with Buster Pack and the Lonesome Pine Boys on WCYB's *Farm and Fun Time*.[1]

Following several years in Chicago playing country music and western swing—"There was no bluegrass in Chicago," he said—Bobby headed west, and worked with the Golden State Boys, the only bluegrass in California at the time. The group at first included Don Parmley (later founder of the Bluegrass Cardinals), on banjo, and Herb Rice (father of Larry and Tony Rice, who would play with J.D. and Bobby in the Kentucky Mountain Boys). Later members were Vern and Rex Gosdin and Hal Poindexter (uncle of the Rice boys).

In 1962, groundbreaking lead guitarist Clarence White (later famous as one of the Byrds country-rock band) asked Bobby to join the Kentucky Colonels, a hip Southern California bluegrass band. "I left [California] in 1964," Bobby said. "My parents were getting sick, and I came back to Kentucky. That's when I moved to Lexington—I worked for an exterminating company, just to get a job—and wanted to get with J.D. I looked for him for a long time. He was at Martin's. I drove by and could hear the banjo right through the walls, and I said, 'This is the place.' And it was, too."[2]

"Bobby knew I was playing somewhere in Lexington," J.D. said, "but he couldn't find out where it was. I kept hearing about a good left-handed fiddle player, but didn't know how to find him. Finally, one night he just set out to find us. He was driving by Martin's and heard the banjo through the closed door, so he came in and he said, 'It was a sight to behold.' It probably was, with all those wild kids in there and everything. I called him up to do a couple of numbers. From there, that's about it! History was made."[3]

"I had to wade through people sitting on the steps to get in," Slone said. "I sat through about two sets and then got up and played Bobby Joslin's fiddle. [The Joslins] were quitting—they had a business to take care of. In a couple of weeks, I went to work. The band at that time was J.D., banjo; me on fiddle; Ed Stacy, guitar; and a bass player named 'Lightning.'"[4]

"When we broke up," Charlie Joslin said, "we just decided to part; there were no bad feelings. I had four kids and couldn't work but about three days a week when I was playing, so I needed more work time."[5]

"After Bob and Charlie left," Ed Stacy said, "J.D. got Bobby and Gordon, and that's when I started singing lead and playing guitar."

"It was hotter than the dickens that summer [1964]," Gordon said, "with no air-conditioning, and Bobby was living in a trailer park. He was in his underwear, sitting on the couch with a fan on him. He got his fiddle, J.D. got out his banjo, and I got my guitar, and we picked a few. We really took to each other, and J.D. hired Bobby on the spot. J.D. and Bobby knew the same stuff."[6] Bobby Slone would play with J.D. for twenty-four years, the longest tenure of any musician who ever worked with Crowe.

Before *Bluegrass Unlimited* and later magazines and newsletters, bluegrass musicians existed in little pockets around the country, sometimes aware of each others' existence, but with few means of contact—Bobby's experience was by no means unusual. There were good "pickers" in most northern industrial cities, but little mixing outside their own area; even when their names were known, it might take weeks to track someone down—and by then, they might have left that location.

It was even worse for serious fans, because unless the "clubs" advertised (which was rare), there was no way to find bluegrass at all, short of trudging from one bar to another, usually in fairly risky environments. And there was no assurance of welcome, once the right one was found; in the rougher bars, if the newcomer looked or acted different, or behaved in a conspicuous manner, there was always some half-intoxicated fellow patron ready to take him to task. For women, the assumption was that they were there to find companionship rather than music, and refusals could bring ugly results.

However, once the music lover was established as a "regular," there was acceptance, of a sort, but it was often short-lived, as squabbles between musicians and bar owners, invariably of a financial nature, occurred with frequency. Bars changed hands, musicians moved on, or, tired of trying to share their music with an unappreciative public, "hung it up" for a time.

The one area where these difficulties were lessened was Washington, D.C., where there were many fine musicians and dedicated fans who networked among themselves to keep track of who was playing, and where, and in July 1966, they started a mimeographed newsletter. *Bluegrass Unlimited*'s columns "Bluegrass in the Clubs" and "Personal Appearance Calendar," amended by readers to include music all over the country, were, and are, an invaluable resource. Until its circulation grew, however, word of mouth brought people from an ever-increasing radius to Martin's Place—not only fans, but musicians.

"Enis came in to see us a lot," J.D. said, "and we'd get him up to sing with us, mostly Merle Haggard stuff we all knew."[7]

"Art Stamper [an extraordinary fiddle player from Knott County, Kentucky, who lived in Louisville] came in when we were playing at Martin's," Gordon Scott said. "There was one mike, and a weak [speaker system]. Art would stand off the mike and play fills and backup, and when his turn came, he came charging up to the mike—you know the bluegrass choreography—and he was so rambunctious and enthusiastic he'd come across the wooden floor bump, bump, bump, and just fiddle the dickens out of whatever we were playing. He was always loose, more of an old-timey attitude, and a great fiddler."[8]

During a long and important career, Art Stamper played and recorded with Monroe, the Osborne Brothers, the Stanley Brothers, the Goins Brothers, and others, and during the years when he was not traveling would sit in with any good bluegrass band within reach; he was always welcome. "Something inside a musician makes you want to play," Stamper declared. "Bluegrass music is a combination of different things: you've got your blues and jazz, lots of highs and high-pitched sounds. Some of it is lonesome, some is foot-stomping, but there's not that heavy beat that makes country music."[9]

"[Songwriter] Pete Gobel used to come down from Detroit to visit us," Ed Stacy said. "Hargus and Benny Kelly sat in a few times. Hargus was as good a fiddle player as you'd ever want to hear. He played with Jimmy Martin awhile. We'd get 'em up; that Benny could sing 'Muleskinner' and sound just like Bill Monroe. One night, we were playing and Jimmy Martin came in with his band, and we got them up. He [Jimmy] was trying so hard to make us look bad, he just made a fool of himself. Jimmy was just his own worst enemy."

Paris, Kentucky, native Jimmy Hatton was a presence among the Kentucky Mountain Boys without actually being a member. Nicknamed "Brillohead" for the mop of curly dark hair carefully arranged on the top of his head, he played guitar behind the others, quietly, and was available to fill in when the regular guitar player had to take a night off, or left. "He was a better rhythm guitar player than Gordon," J.D. said. "I was teaching Jimmy guitar and he was coming along pretty good. He never could learn to sing, though, he couldn't hear to tune, and you had to tune his guitar for him."[10]

"[Hatton] loved J.D. and his music," Gordon said. "Lester Flatt was his hero, and he played with a thumb pick and a finger pick like Lester. His whole goal was to play as much like Lester as possible."[11]

"How I met him [Hatton], in the early 1960s," J.D. said, "he and one of the people he went to church with just knocked on the door. You know, to get you to go to church with them. We became friends, and remained friends until he passed away. He wanted to learn to play guitar, and I said, 'Why don't you come down to Martin's?' We'd get him up behind us, and I'd tell him the key changes, and that's how he started playing."[12]

"We used to work a lot of private parties during those times," J.D. remembered. "Sometimes they would be after we'd played at Martin's. We'd go to a private party and play until four in the morning. Of course, we loved it. I mean, it was fun; that's what we were having, we were having fun. All those were university parties—they could flat throw a party."[13]

"Those private parties!" Gordon said. "Hippie girls would ask us to play after Martin's; there were lots of college kids at those parties. We would play guitars and sing things by Donovan, Ian and Sylvia, and Gordon Lightfoot. Some people were listening, and some people were not listening, sort of like a wedding reception. J.D. just loved it. We had a lot of fun playing guitars—I'd play mostly rhythm guitar and he'd play lead. J.D. played 'You Are My Flower' and 'Jimmy Brown the Newsboy' on the guitar just like Earl [Scruggs]."[14]

"We would work during weekends," J.D. said, "but doing a day job, we had that too, all of us. At the time, I believe I went in at 7:00 a.m. and got off at 5:00, and then, Friday nights we would play, and sometimes we played Wednesday nights, too, but Friday nights we would play, and try to get home in time to shower and go to work, and then we would have to play again Saturday night, and then, again, I wouldn't get home until three or four on Sunday morning. Of course, I slept most of the day Sunday, as all of us probably did, and then it would start all over the next week. We did that for quite a while."[15]

The band remained consistent: J.D., banjo; Bobby Slone, fiddle; Ed Stacy, guitar; Gordon Scott, mandolin; and "Lightning," bass.

"We played Wednesday, Friday, and Saturday at Martin's place," Bobby remembered. "We played other shows on Sunday and through the week, but usually, we just worked the club. We all had jobs and didn't get out [on the road] much."[16]

Despite Mrs. Martin's strict observance of the law, there were a number of underage kids who found their way in to listen to music. One of them was Virginian Ken Landreth, now a Ph.D. microbiologist at West Virginia University, but in the 1960s, he was a bluegrass music–struck, banjo-playing student at Union College in Barbourville, Kentucky.

An audiotape he made on January 15, 1966, demonstrates what the group could do. Eight of the twenty-two tunes are instrumentals, with "Orange Blossom Special" being repeated, as was "Jimmy Brown the Newsboy." There is "Uncle Pen" from Monroe's repertoire, "Stone Walls and Steel Bars" from the Stanleys, "Just When I Needed You" from Jim and Jesse, "Sunny Side of the Mountain" from Martin, "'Tis Sweet to Be Remembered" from Mac Wiseman, and several Flatt and Scruggs tunes, making up a good representation of popular bluegrass at the time. Hank Williams's "I'm So Lonesome I Could

Cry" and "Wabash Cannonball," solos by Ed Stacy, are the only country songs. The fiddle and banjo are the only lead instruments; Gordon provides a rhythm chop on the mandolin, and Ed does well on guitar and singing but lacks the authoritative Lester Flatt sound Charlie Joslin provided. There is enough audience noise and applause on the tape to make it clear that the boys were well liked and appreciated and that the crowd was having a great time.

"Our crowd was basically UK kids," Lightning Bartlett said. "They were like sardines in that place. The only ones we played for extra [private parties] was UK students."

Crowe, when he first started playing with the Joslins, may have intended just "to have fun," but when the level of musicianship in the band improved, he began striving for better results, and as people left, they were replaced with stronger musicians. His deeply ingrained work ethic and his ear for music prevailed. "I used to rehearse those guys," he said. "It was probably more than they wanted."[17]

His own approach to music was changing, also. The nonbluegrass music to which he listened—blues, rock and roll, country—brought new ideas he could incorporate into his playing. "When I was young," he said, "I tried to sound like Scruggs, but finally, I said to myself, 'This is uncomfortable as hell, and you've got to be yourself. Just get up there and burn it! Play like there was no tomorrow!'"[18]

"If we went to a restaurant," Gordon said, "J.D. would play George Jones, Ernest Tubb, or somebody, on the jukebox. He really loved Jerry Lee Lewis. That was my introduction to commercial country music."[19]

"I was a Blue Grass Boy for one show [in 1965]," J. D. said. "We had taken off from Martin's for a while. James [Monroe] was playing bass, Pete Rowan hadn't been with [Monroe] very long, and Gene Lowinger was on fiddle. Bill called me. He didn't have a banjo player and was playing a county fair at Irvine, Kentucky. Bobby [Slone] and I drove up there, and I played the show and I had a ball. I really enjoyed it. [Later on], Bill and I were reminiscing about past years, and he remembered the time I did that show with him."[20]

A combination of circumstances led to the next musician to join the Kentucky Mountain Boys. Harry Bickel, then a student at the University of Louisville, was interested in all aspects of the banjo. "I first met J.D. in the late winter or spring of 1965," Bickel said. "I would have been nineteen. I was working for Tom Hale instrument repair, doing his pearl inlay. Tom made reproduction banjo necks, and J.D. came to [Louisville]. Tom called me, and said, 'You've got to come hear this guy.' They negotiated the price of the neck [for J.D.'s RB-3 flathead], and Tom said, '[Harry] will be doing all your inlay work.' I asked J.D. if he taught, and would he be willing to swap inlay for banjo lessons."

The pearl inlay in instrument fingerboards can range from simple dots for position markers to intricate patterns of multicolored abalone shell. A steady hand and a good eye are necessary to cut the brittle shell, and inlaying the tiny pieces into rosewood or ebony fingerboards and "headstocks" is exacting work. Inlay is an important part of the appearance of the banjo and is not inexpensive, so swapping was a good deal for both J.D. and Harry.

Harry said, "I'd go up [to Lexington] in the evenings—I've recommended this method to anyone who would try to take music lessons—I'd learn something from an Earl Scruggs record and go and play it for J.D., and he'd show me what I was doing wrong."

His "earliest recollection of [Crowe's band] was Gordon playing guitar, Ed playing guitar, and Lightning playing bass. J.D. had taught me to play 'Foggy Mountain Breakdown,' and he got me up [onstage] and played tenor to it."

"Doyle Lawson's brother-in-law was in one of my classes," Harry Bickel said, "and in lab class, he said, 'You need to meet my brother-in-law,' and gave me his telephone number." Doyle told Bickel that he had "just quit Jimmy Martin. I went to his house, and he was far and away better than me [on the banjo]. I told him I was going to Lexington to see J.D. and he said, 'I just idolize his banjo playing, and I've never met him.' I tried to get him to go to Lexington, and he wouldn't, but one night I went in [to Martin's Place], and there Doyle was—he'd finally gone over, and it wasn't too long before he was in the band."

"Ed had left," J.D. said, "and that's when Doyle came in, about 1966. Harry Bickel would come to Martin's a lot. I think I was giving him lessons, at one point, and he would come to my house. He kept telling me about this guy that played banjo that lived in Louisville, said he used to work with Jimmy Martin. He didn't stay [with Martin] long enough, really, I don't think, to create a name for himself." J.D. told Harry, "'Well, tell him to come up; I'd like to meet him. We've got something in common—both of us worked for

Jimmy.' So, a month or two or three went on, and he never came up, and Harry was coming up about every week. So one night, Doyle came in, and Harry was there, also, and that's when I met Doyle Lawson."[21]

Harry told J.D., "'That's that boy I told you about.' I said, 'I'll get him up to sit in, and that way I'll get a rest.' He wouldn't come up onstage, but afterwards, we got to playing [in the back room], and he could play the heck out of a guitar. That was Doyle and Gordon and me and Lightning, who played bass. We stayed there until three or four in the morning. I [later] asked if he'd come and play, and he was just tickled to death."[22]

Doyle Lawson was born in 1944, near Kingsport, Tennessee, where his father sang southern gospel music. Blessed with natural talent, Doyle took up the mandolin at the age of eleven, influenced by Bill Monroe. Shortly afterward, he began playing the other instruments; it all came easily to him. At eighteen, he started playing banjo with Jimmy Martin. "I had met Jimmy when I was fourteen years old," he said. "I knew I wanted to get a job with either Bill [Monroe] or Jimmy [Martin]. To be honest, I liked Jimmy better."

> In 1960, I heard [Jimmy's] "You Don't Know My Mind" [on which J.D. played banjo], and I don't think I ever heard another recording that had banjo like that; it was the ultimate sound. I was just in awe of J.D. and his playing.
>
> I went with Jimmy [as banjo player] in 1963, and stayed about six months.[23] I won't tell you that I was ready for that job, but I took it. Jimmy was at the top of his game, and I had to work harder than you could imagine. Jimmy and Bill Monroe had a way they taught—they used terms I'd never heard of. Jimmy'd say, "I just wrote this—play the second part." Once I had time to think about what he was saying, and digest it, then it helped, but under all that pressure, I didn't have time to do that.[24]

"I was still with Jimmy when he gave Doyle the first professional job he ever had," Paul Williams said. "We worked real hard helping him—we had a twenty-nine-day tour coming up."

The experience of working with Martin was beneficial, but working for such a demanding man was difficult, and after only a few months, Doyle returned to Upper East Tennessee. Opportunities were scarce, and he knew he did not want to work in a furniture factory, so he looked for somewhere else to settle down:

I was living in Louisville—my first wife had a brother there—and I was working and playing whatever [music] I could in Louisville. Louisville was kind of dry, so right around Memorial Day, 1966, I said, "Let's go down to Lexington and hear J.D." I actually thought he was working at the Limehouse, but there were only about six people in there, and I knew right away that wasn't the right place.

[When I went to Martin's] the place was packed. The kids from over at UK thought that was the place to go. It was hard to get in, and I wound up basically right at the kitchen door. When they took a break, I went back and introduced myself. J.D. said, "Yeah, Harry's been talking about you." I was a little shy, afraid of imposing on anyone, and when he asked me if I wanted to pick one, I said, "No." He said, "Do you play guitar?" and I said I would; I kind of lied, because I wasn't much on the guitar. I never did think about playing rhythm guitar, but I sat in—Jim Hatton loaned me his guitar.

I wasn't all that into singing; I was interested in playing the banjo. In the most part of five years, I learned a lot about banjo picking, watching J.D. and asking him to show me a few things.[25]

"In December of that year," Doyle said, "J.D. called and said Eddie [Stacy] was laid up with hepatitis and could I fill in. I had taken a job playing square dances [in Louisville] with a fellow named Herb Kleinart, and had no more than told him I'd play banjo with him than J.D. called, and I had to tell Herb I couldn't do it. I never was hired on [with J.D.]; I just started playing [guitar] and stayed on."[26]

"He [Doyle] had been with me three or four months," J.D. said, "before I ever knew he could play the mandolin. We were on a break in the back room, and Gordon was trying to figure out something on the mandolin, and kept going over and over it, and he couldn't get it. Doyle looked at him and said, 'If you don't mind, let me see—maybe I can show you how that goes.' Well, Doyle proceeded to take the mandolin, and he could just play the dag-gone devil out of it. I said, 'I didn't know you played mandolin. I thought you just played the banjo and rhythm guitar,' and he said, 'I play a little bit,' you know. And I'm thinking, 'Yeah.' That was actually his main instrument, I think, then."[27]

"Doyle was a sweet guy," Gordon Scott said. "He laid back several months, and finally said, 'I think I can show you how to get that.' He took the man-dolin and was as good a mandolin player then as he is now. I said, 'My God, when you can play a mandolin like that, you ought to be playing mandolin, and *I'll* play guitar!' With the social dynamics of things, I don't know if J.D. really knew how good Doyle was on the mandolin; if J.D. *did* know, he never made that call to say, 'Gordon, you switch back to guitar.'"[28] After that, Doyle played mandolin and sang lead, J.D. played banjo and sang baritone, and Gordon played guitar and sang tenor.

J.D. worked at a farm equipment supplier and helped Doyle get a job there, too. "In the early days," Doyle said, "I was driving back and forth from Louisville and working in a machine shop. That was hard on me; I was afraid I would lose a finger or something. I wound up working with J.D. at Wilson Industrial Supply. [J.D.] said, 'I can help you get on, but don't tell Mr. Wilson that you play music. He knows that I do, but it would be better if he didn't know about you.'"[29]

Bluegrass entrepreneur Carleton Haney produced the first three-day bluegrass festival, patterned on the folk festivals in D.C. and the Northeast, on Labor Day weekend, 1965. Held in Roanoke, Virginia, the festival was thought to be a "last hurrah," an opportunity for fans to see some of the earliest bluegrass bands one last time before they disbanded. Instead, the festival generated such interest and excitement that other gatherings of the sort followed, providing hope and a new source of income for musicians while increasing the fan base.

Dependent upon the weather and locations for success, some festivals depleted their promoters' life savings early on, while others became institutions. Bill Monroe's Bean Blossom Festival, near Nashville, Indiana, has lasted more than forty years, continuing under other management after his death; many have celebrated more than a quarter century. The festival phenomenon reached its peak in the 1980s, with more than five hundred of them worldwide, and shows no sign of stopping.

For bands who, like the Kentucky Mountain Boys, worked in taverns, festivals meant little in the beginning, unless they were free to attend as paying fans, to mingle with other musicians and have a chance to jam in the parking lots. Weekends were big at Martin's, and the boys were obligated to play as usual.

"Jimmy called me about 1966," J.D. said, "and I went back to help finish up the *Big and Country* album."[30] Recorded on the session on November 22 were Vernon Derrick's "Big Country," "Red Rooster" ("She'll Be Coming 'Round the Mountain"), "Crowe on the Banjo" (a fast version of "Bugle Call Rag"), the Jimmie Davis classic "You Are My Sunshine," and "Going Up Dry Branch," written by fiddle player "Buddy" Spicher. These instrumentals would be the last recordings J.D. made with Jimmy Martin.

The album, issued in June 1967, was an all-instrumental one, and J.D. appeared on half of the tunes; one was the 1963 recording of "Red River Valley," which had not been included on the *Widowmaker* album but was on the extended play recording of the same name in 1964.

"I first got to play with J.D. at Martin's," Sam Bush said. Mandolin and fiddle prodigy Bush, from Bowling Green, Kentucky, had ridden up with some other people. "I wasn't driving yet," he said, "and when we got out of the car, J.D. pulls up in a Mustang fastback with mag wheels. That was the coolest, to me. I couldn't be in the club unless I could play a song, and J.D. let me play with the band. Then I had to stay back in the kitchen until I got up to play another song. Gordon Scott and Doyle were in the band, I remember. I don't remember if Bobby was."

"I remember when Sam Bush's dad used to bring him to Martin's," Doyle said. "Sam was not old enough to get in—probably fifteen, sixteen years old, and *man,* you knew right then that kid was going to be a picker—he already was!"[31]

In 1967, J.D. went back to school to get his general equivalency degree.[32] It had been eleven years since he dropped out of high school, and he was working full-time and playing music at least three nights a week; it couldn't have been easy. "Me and my buddy that worked at Wilson . . . went together," he said. "A lot had changed."[33]

The fact that he made this effort says a great deal about J.D.'s character and determination; he did not *have* to do it, but he wanted to do it. Throughout his life, whenever opportunities have offered themselves, he has been ready— and equipped—to accept them. Without promoting himself, he has become greatly admired and respected as a business-minded bandleader. This was not his goal, but he was working toward it, even when he was a part-time musician at Martin's Place.

Ken Landreth made several trips to Martin's Place in the late 1960s. "I was playing with Ray Hoskins and the Cody Mountain Boys," he said.

* Ray was a bass player who had played with Kenny Baker [legendary fiddle player with Bill Monroe] and Bill Grimes. Ray was the littlest guy you've ever seen. He laid the bass down, stood in the cutout [on the side of the bass], and played in that position.

In 1967, [Hoskins] took me up to Martin's Place; I was not twenty-one. I sat there, and Ray played with Crowe. In the band were J.D., Doyle on guitar, Gordon Scott on mandolin, and Ed Stacy. At that time, I was in awe.

Later on, I drove up one Saturday night with [friend] Jerry Correll. I wasn't twenty-one, and Jerry left me standing on the sidewalk in front of Martin's. He went in and talked to the band and came back with a driver's license. I went in on J.D.'s driver's license, so for one night, I was J.D. Crowe.

On August 27, 1967, Frank Schoepf, who had just "discovered" bluegrass music, went from Maryland to Lexington to visit an air force buddy, who had told him, "If you like that music, you'd better come to Lexington; we've got the best damn music in the country." Schoepf recounted the experience:

He took me to this sleazy little place called Martin's. I sat about four feet in front of Crowe all night with my jaw hanging down; I was glued on that banjo. It was Crowe's thirtieth birthday; they sang "Happy Birthday" to him.

I was burned up to get a banjo, and for a month or so, had no luck finding an instrument. I went back to Lexington, and Crowe was playing a different banjo. People told me there was a banjo in the back room that was for sale; I went to look at it, and Crowe said, "I'm going to buy this one I'm playing, but I've got one at home. If I buy this one, I've got to sell that one. If you want to wait 'til we get through, I'll take you home and show you what I've got."

He took me [home] in his GT-500 Mustang and dragged the banjo in. He told me just exactly what it was, a converted 1950 RB-100, worked on by Lee Vance. [That's] one reason I respected him so much—I didn't know from nothing! It sounded really good in his hands; what wouldn't?

That's where I got my first banjo. I got this thing home and had a hard time trying to play it. It had a very skinny neck; I don't know how in the world he played that. Somebody had replaced the fingerboard, and the headstock with the art-deco inlay had been cut into a fiddle shape. It was very easy to identify; one side of the fiddle shape was larger than the other.

Although similar in many ways to the RB-100 J.D. had swapped for his RB-3, this was a different banjo he had never used to record. The banjo J.D. played that night became his second RB-3; he bought it from instrument craftsman Harry Sparks. It was a twenty-hole flathead, and he still owns it.

"I had more fun playing there [at Martin's] than anyplace I ever worked," Doyle said. "We had no aspirations of hitting the road. We played there—it was not a matter that we had to worry about a particular sound. I think it was good music, probably above average. We wanted to play good music, and I think my music was supportive. There was no pressure. With Jimmy, it was about discipline; with J.D., it was a lot of fun, but it was still about discipline, about the music."[34]

For part-time bluegrass musicians, day jobs were a necessity, and just about any job would do, so long as it did not impinge on weekends and was not physically exhausting or dangerous. J.D. and Doyle worked at Wilson Industrial Supply; Bobby worked for an exterminator; Gordon was in school, taught guitar, and drove a school bus; Doyle also taught in a music store; and Ed Stacy drove a beer truck, the most demanding job of them all. The Kentucky Mountain Boys' long hours took their toll, and sometimes the music suffered.

"Lightning was not a bad bass player," J.D. said, "if he'd tried. He'd stand back there with his eyes closed, and he'd get lighter and lighter on the bass. I'd kick the bass and try to wake him up."[35]

"Lightning would almost go to sleep playing bass," Doyle agreed, "and Crowe would yell at him. Eddie was getting well and was going to come back. The band at that time was me, Crowe, Gordon Scott, Eddie Stacy, Bobby Slone, and Lightning. Lightning said, 'We've got too many people in the band. Somebody is going to have to go.' He called the roll, and then he said, 'And then there's you,' and pointed at me."[36]

"What happened," J.D. said, "was that Lightning went. He was just filling in, and he was going anyway. Then Bobby moved to bass. When he played fiddle, Gordon would just fake it or something. Back then, it didn't really matter."[37]

One of the few incidents there occurred among college kids. "One group was talking," Gordon said, "and the others wanted to hear the music. [The would-be listeners] kept trying to make them hush. Finally, a girl from the listener group poured beer on one of the noisy ones. He started to say something to her, then her boyfriend slugged him. *We* went to the back room. By the time the police got there, there was blood and broken glass all over the place."[38]

Gordon explained, "Mrs. Martin was a sweet old lady—sweet but hard as nails. She wouldn't put up with anything in her place. One night, she 'slap-jacked' a guy for dancing."[39]

Doyle described Martin's colorful proprietress:

Ma Martin was about four feet tall, and about as big around, but she wasn't above getting that "billystick" out and giving somebody a whop up aside of the head.[40] One night, Hargus Kelly came in. He had a hard time staying sober—or even getting that way. He would wander in, and I don't remember seeing him unless he had on a suit and tie. The problem was, it would look like you could put a ten-pound sack of potatoes in the seat of his pants. He was standing there with a long-neck bottle of beer. Ma had a fan that she had taken the guard off; the blades caught in the seat of his pants and went, "blop, blop." He dropped that beer, and it just rocked and rocked, but never did turn over. He just picked it up and acted like nothing had happened.[41]

"In 1967," Gordon said, "I graduated and moved back to Madisonville to teach school."[42] He later moved to Florida to work on his Ph.D. "I actually taught at Florida State [University] while I worked on my Ph.D., then taught at a community college, but I always played music." He opened his own business, Gordon's String Music, in Gainesville, Florida, in 1988, and continues to teach, but now his teaching is limited to stringed instruments. His academic teaching, he says, "was fun, but there were too many papers to grade."[43]

"J.D. pretty much shaped everything I've ever done in music since then," Gordon said. "He set a standard of musicianship that was impeccable and exciting and gave me the confidence to do things. We used to sit around and work out harmonies and stuff, and every band I've been in since, I've been the guy that worked out the harmonies. I'd definitely not be doing what I'm doing now in the music business if it wasn't for J.D. Crowe."[44]

"When Gordon Scott graduated," Doyle said, "we had a hard time getting the right people. Then, it was hard to find somebody, especially that J.D., or even I, would approve of. I don't think J.D. wanted to let the music get below a certain professional level."[45]

"Gordon Scott and Lightning left, and I went back to playing bass," Bobby Slone said. "I bought my first upright when I started with Crowe."[46] Bobby was always at least as proficient on the bass as on the fiddle; he has been cited as one of a very few bassists with flawless bluegrass timing, identified as being on the leading edge of the beat, which gives bluegrass its characteristic "drive." It came naturally to him, but he has spent a lot of thought on it, the fiddle, and the way his music could fit best into the music around him. "I think bass in bluegrass should be heard and be solid," he said. "Somebody's got to set the time, and somebody's got to do the duty work. Bass should complement the other instruments; the timing will hold better together. When I play fiddle, I think of myself as a fiddle player; when I play bass, I think of myself as a bass player. I don't think of myself as an outstanding musician. I just try to be professional and play what fits. I think that's what makes a good polished band."[47]

For a while, there were just the four Kentucky Mountain Boys: "Ed played guitar," J.D. said, "and Doyle, mandolin, and me and Bobby."[48]

"Crowe has tapes of me, Bobby Slone, Doyle, and Crowe," Ed Stacy said. "We played more hard-core bluegrass than when we had Charlie and Bob Joslin with us."

> One night, Bill [Monroe] walked in on us. Me and Doyle and Crowe were doing a trio. I was looking at the door—it was so dark in there—and a fellow came walking in wearing a loose Hawaiian shirt, with no hat on. I knew I knew him, but he was right up on me before I recognized him. He said, "Boys, that's as good as I ever heard it done in my life."
>
> Bill was worried about the bus; he had parked it on Limestone, so I called a buddy of mine down at the police station, and told him about the bus [so Monroe would know it was safe]. Roland [White] and James [Monroe] were with him then, and they got up and played.

"One time," J.D. said, "Bill Monroe came in [to Martin's]. He wanted to borrow Bobby to play fiddle. Byron Berline had to leave for the army—it was Byron's last show." Berline left in September 1967; his place with Monroe was taken by Crowe's friend Benny Williams. "Bill sat in, and Byron played. Bobby went with Bill and helped on his next show or two."[49] J.D. and Ed were possibly remembering the same occasion, although Monroe maintained contact with Crowe and visited several times.

"Ed was working for Champion Distributing, and he was having health problems," J.D. said. "I don't think he ever got over having hepatitis, and he had to lift all those heavy crates and things. He didn't want to quit."[50]

"Eddie told J.D., 'I can't keep up with this physically,'" Doyle said.[51]

"The big reason I quit," Ed Stacy said, "they didn't have as hard a job as I did; I drove a beer truck for twenty-three years. Doyle said he and Crowe used to wonder how I did it."

"Bobby Morris at that time [1967] lived in Norwood, Ohio [part of Cincinnati]," Doyle said. "Gordon was gone, and Jimmy Hatton was filling in. Bobby [Morris] happened to come in; he'd been down to the Limehouse. He came up and sat in, and we sang 'Jesse James.' He had a strong lead voice, incredible range, but couldn't sing a lick of harmony."[52]

"I know Gordon had left," J.D. said, "and he [Bob Morris] came to Martin's, and, of course, we always got people up to sit in with us if they wanted to do it, and that's when I met Bob; later on, he joined us, so it was myself, Doyle Lawson, Bob Morris, and Bobby Slone, and I think we worked there at Martin's probably for a year, or over."[53]

London, Kentucky, native Bob Morris had moved to the Cincinnati area in his late teens. "He had played a little bit with Ralph [Stanley]," J.D. said. "Ralph's wife and Bobby's wife used to run around together when they were single. Bob was commuting from Norwood, Ohio, and he was still working for me when he bought a farm [in Kentucky]. Bobby could sing, but Jimmy Hatton was better on rhythm guitar."[54]

During Morris's time with Crowe, "The traveling part of the music business," J.D. said, "we did not do. I think we did go to Columbus, Ohio, a couple of times. What was that famous club? The Astro Inn." He laughed. "A lot of good players had worked there at the Astro Inn. I think a lot of the bluegrass pickers that had bigger names, came in there. You might say it was a little more dangerous than some of the clubs we worked—about like those in Detroit."[55]

The Kentucky Mountain Boys' appearance at the Astro Inn was Saturday, July 6, 1968. Bobby Slone did not make the trip—he had returned to California—and the fiddle was played by Paul Mullins. Bill Yates played bass; he was working with Jimmy Martin at the time, and they dropped in to visit and to sit in for a set. Benny Williams was living in Columbus and played in the Astro Inn house band.[56]

Martin's Place had a lasting impact on some of the most unlikely people. On Valentine's Day 1968, Mabel Ann Benson and Travis DuPriest had their first date there. Both were in graduate school in English literature at UK, and it was the first visit for each of them. "Limestone was, well, an interesting neighborhood," Travis said, "but we were going for the music—and, of course, for the 'first date.' We sat in a booth to the right as you came in to the 'shotgun' bar; I remember it being near the front window."[57]

"I guess we both thought we were pretty lucky," Mabel said. "We all loved bluegrass music and had heard about J.D. Crowe's playing. At the end of each set they would pass the hat around for people to put in what they wanted in payment for the music. Literally: they passed a hat."[58]

The couple continued their educations elsewhere; both received advanced degrees. They were married in 1972. Fr. Travis DuPriest is a retired Episcopal priest and college humanities professor, and Dr. Mabel DuPriest is professor of English at Carthage College in Wisconsin. They have each received many honors but still remember Martin's Place. "We wish Martin's were still around," Mabel said.[59]

"While we were working at Martin's Place," J.D. said, "some of the people that worked at the Holiday Inn—some of the designers and decorators and people like that—would come down to Martin's. Every once in a while one of them would ask me did I ever think about working at a place like the Holiday Inn, and I said, 'Yeah,' but I'd never heard of that kind of music being played at Holiday Inns."[60]

"A guy named Winegardner, I believe," Doyle said, "owned three Holiday Inns in Lexington. We were playing at Martin's, and his daughter came in and just went ape. She told her daddy he needed to have us at his place. He came, and we were packing out Martin's, maybe 125 people."[61]

"He came to Martin's to hear us, and he had to sit on the steps, it was so crowded," Bobby Slone remembered.[62]

"The owner of the Holiday Inns came into Martin's one night and introduced himself," J.D. said, "and asked me if I'd be interested in working at the Holiday Inn."[63]

I think it went in one ear and out the other, because, you know, you hear all these things—a lot of wind from a lot of people that don't mean anything—so I just said, "Oh, yeah, that would be fine," and he said, "Well, meet me at my office."

Well, I did, and that's when I knew, "Uh-oh, this guy's serious about it." And then when I saw where it was, I said, in my mind, "I don't know if this is going to work!" Because it was an awful nice place, like a Vegas compared to where we worked. All the music I'd heard in places like that was a woman sitting there with a piano, or some guy with a guitar, just a solo act, doing real easy-listening stuff—and no string music, at all. We were probably one of the first bands that ever went to a Holiday Inn with that type of music, and then, to stay as long as we did, I don't think that's ever been equaled, and probably never will be again.[64]

J.D. had been the de facto bandleader at Martin's, but with this more serious and certainly more profitable endeavor, his position was formalized. He was the contractor: he hired the other musicians to work for him; he provided the sound system, and, when they traveled, the transportation. It was *his* band, and his name was out front on all the advertising from then on. "We had to get our own sound system," he said, "and it took a while to get everything organized, but we finally did. I think we were to leave in May, and come back after Labor Day, 'cause we worked five nights a week, there, and those months we would leave and go work bluegrass festivals."[65]

"Bobby [Slone] had gone back to California by then," Doyle said, "but we called him, and he came back. We had to get Bobby to come back. When he did, he played bass mostly. He had such a good touch on bass."[66]

"In August of 1968, me, Bobby Morris, Doyle, and Bobby Slone started at the Holiday Inn," J.D. said.[67]

CHAPTER 6
THE RED SLIPPER LOUNGE

Lexington's Holiday Inn North faces a section of interstate highway on which I-64 and I-75 run congruently; incomplete in 1968, both were nevertheless main arteries, heavy with north-south and east-west traffic. One of the largest and most elegant motels in Lexington at the time, the Holiday Inn's size and grandeur made it comparable to some of today's fine hotels, and its "Red Slipper Lounge" was a dark, mirrored cave, dimly lit by crystal chandeliers, with comfortable leather chairs and banquettes and a thick carpet. Sharing a wing and an entrance with the dining room, it was far from the main lobby, connected by halls lined with rooms.

The Kentucky Mountain Boys knew this job was unusual, especially compared to the places in which bluegrass music was usually played. Excited and a little nervous, they bought stage clothes for the first time: black and silver brocade dinner jackets they called "the slicks." Their forte was playing music, and they knew they played *good* music, but whether it would appeal to the uninitiated was a worrisome question. "It was way uptown for us and for bluegrass bands in general," Doyle observed.[1]

"I was a little skeptical," J.D. said, "because I knew what had been in places like the Holiday Inn; they were more upscale than your regular bars.

I was a little skeptical if it would even work."[2] J.D. proposed taking on the job for three nights a week on a trial basis, and Winegardner said that was what he, too, had in mind. For J.D., the new venue signaled a career move of life-changing proportions:

Of course, they had plenty of time to advertise; they did a great job of that. Newspapers, radio, television, and they had brochures in every room, and in the lounge and the dining room, they had little folders on every table, and they did that, I guess, for six months.

When we started, the first Thursday night it was full, and on Friday and Saturday night, it was packed—you couldn't get them in. I think we did that for about three weeks, and then he [Winegardner] approached me about signing a year's contract. Doyle Lawson was with me at the time, and we were both working a day job, and I knew that I, for one, could not play five nights a week and work from eight to five. I tried it for about a month, and it didn't work. So we looked at each other and said, "Do we want to do this, or do we want to work at Wilson Industrial Supply?" It was a good place to work, as far as work goes, but, we said, "Let's go for it!" So we gave our notice and went to the Holiday Inn.[3]

"In 1968," Doyle said, "I quit my day job, and never went back to a day job.[4] One thing [working at the Holiday Inn] allowed us to do was to concentrate on the music—we weren't getting rich, by no means, but we were able to give up the day jobs."[5]

"The idea behind it was to make a living playing music," J.D. said, "but we didn't really know if it would work; we knew we could always go back to doing something else."[6]

From then on, whenever they played, the Red Slipper Lounge was crowded with locals who had enjoyed them at Martin's and others who had been reluctant to go there. Serious bluegrass fans were cheek-by-jowl with the trendy young set who were ready to go anywhere "cool," and they made an enthusiastic audience that spilled out into the corridors. Distant fans planned stopovers at the Holiday Inn on their journeys, and others came for weekends just to hear the music.

"We had a great following," Doyle said. "The crowds were great; usually Tuesday and Wednesday we had a decent crowd, but Thursday would be full, and Friday and Saturday you couldn't get in. They would line up and down the street, into the parking lot, trying to get in."[7]

The first national mention of this new outlet for bluegrass music was an article, "Bluegrass in the Cocktail Lounge," in *Bluegrass Unlimited* in February 1969. Attention was drawn to the difference between this and the usual venues, with a glowing review of the band, its performance, and its choice of material. Among the photographs is one of the Holiday Inn sign, with "J.D. Crow [*sic*] and the Kentucky Mountain Boys" spelled out in movie-marquee letters.[8] This may be the first time Crowe's name preceded the name of the band; in future bands, this was always the case, and now his band is often referred to by his name alone.

Red Allen came to work with J.D. later in the fall of 1968; Bobby Morris could not commute for a five-night-a-week job the way he had when they played at Martin's. "Red was living in Nashville at that time," J.D. said. "We needed a lead singer, and somebody had told me he wasn't working all that much, so I called him and told him what we were doing. He was interested in the job, so he came up and worked with us a while."[9]

Red Allen's raw, powerful voice reflected his eastern Kentucky mountain heritage, and his volatile personality resulted in an emcee style that was often funny, and often offensive, especially to those not used to four-letter words. He saw himself as an entertainer—his hero was comedian Red Skelton—and seemed oblivious to the reaction of a large part of his audience. No one, however, could fault his singing or his rhythm guitar playing, which was as forceful and steadfast as that of Jimmy Martin.

"The album *Bluegrass Holiday* [Lemco LLP-609] was our first effort as the Kentucky Mountain Boys," J.D. said, "and was myself, Doyle Lawson, Red Allen, and Bobby Slone. A good friend of ours who is an attorney, Dan Brock, mentioned, 'Why don't we go in and record?' and I know every time he'd see us, well, he'd mention that. So we got to talking about it and finally decided to give it a shot, so that's how that album came about. We were doing the songs there at the Holiday Inn," he continued, "and the whole crux behind that was to do that album just to sell at the Holiday Inn. That album was never meant to be put out, distributed nationwide. It was going to be sold to tourists and people who came to the Holiday Inn. That's why it was called *Bluegrass Holiday,* because of the area, plus part of the Holiday Inn name."[10]

In discussing the recording session, J.D. recalled, "We did two 45-rpm singles, 'Blackjack' [which J.D. wrote with Doyle] backed with 'You're Not

Easy to Forget' [a Kitty Wells lament Red performed frequently], and 'Pike County Breakdown' backed with 'We'll Meet Again, Sweetheart.'"[11] The two 45s were released on King Bluegrass.

Dan Brock had been a regular visitor to Martin's, "every couple of weeks or so," he said. "It was fun. During that period of time, I got to be friends with J.D." Brock and two associates "went down to the bank and borrowed about three thousand dollars and got J.D. to do [the album]. J.D. wanted to do it, to have a product to sell. They did it at Cecil Jones's [Lemco] studio, and J.D. was pretty much his own producer. The other guys who signed the note at the bank didn't have any input; they had no musical interest and were just looking for a little investment that they didn't have to put a lot of money into."

The twelve sides recorded and issued on the Lemco label include five from Red's repertoire: "Down Where the River Bends," "Philadelphia Lawyer," "Will You Be Satisfied That Way?" "Helen," and "She's Just a Little Cute Thing," with Flatt and Scruggs's "My Little Girl in Tennessee" and "Before I Met You"; "You Go to Your Church," from Jim and Jesse; "Dark Hollow"; and a trio all the way through "Little Bessie," a nineteenth-century "parlor song." The two instrumentals are "Train 45" and "Orange Blossom Special."

"There were a thousand copies in the first issue," Brock said, and "then it was reissued. The second pressing had a new cover." (The first showed a field with white fences, the second a stream rushing over rocks, with J.D.'s name above that of the band.) "We probably gave [J.D.] a hundred records. We got a mailing list from Cecil, and sent out the album to radio stations that played bluegrass. Frankly, not much came of it. There were some reviews; *Bluegrass Unlimited* gave a good review."

The review, in July 1969, granted the album four stars of five, with the comment, "Musically the group is flawless." There is a mild grumble about the shopworn choice of material (chosen deliberately for the audiences to whom it was aimed, which the reviewer could not have known) and a mention of their unusual gig at the Holiday Inn. The final line reads, "Good, hard driving bluegrass, and you still can't go wrong with that." The two 45-rpm records were also reviewed, with the instrumental sides receiving five stars of five, and the songs four stars; Red's singing is applauded, and Doyle's work is called "sterling."[12]

The records were advertised in *Bluegrass Unlimited,* sometimes in full-page ads with photographs, and *Kentucky Song Bag,* a collection of folk songs by Dan and Louise Brock, backed up by J.D., Doyle, and Bobby, was included in the ads. "As the result of the efforts I did voluntarily," Brock said, "J.D. offered to do the *Song Bag.* That was his thank-you."

In the December 1969 issue of *Bluegrass Unlimited, Kentucky Song Bag* was reviewed. "The high point of the album is the fine work of J.D. Crowe's Kentucky Mountain Boys. . . . He churns out some faultless banjo music."[13]

"J.D. played guitar on 'Nine-Pound Hammer,'" Brock said. "It was a nice, clean, uncluttered, unhurried sound right on the money, solid as a rock."

Red Allen, by the time the records were reviewed, was no longer a part of the Kentucky Mountain Boys, having left about the end of 1968. The "Bluegrass in the Clubs" section in the July 1969 issue of *Bluegrass Unlimited* lists Jim Hatton as guitar player with J.D. Crowe and the Kentucky Mountain Boys.

"When Red Allen was with me," J.D. said, "we really used Jimmy Hatton."[14] The band's "weekends" were Sunday and Monday, and Red would drive to Nashville, often finding it difficult to return in time for Tuesday night's performance. It was then that Jim Hatton was most useful; by this time he was a solid rhythm guitar player and glad to help out. His inability to sing put a strain on the others, however, and it was clear they needed a more reliable lead singer. In early 1969, Bobby Morris returned.

"After Bob Morris left [the first time]," Frank Neat said, "Red Allen came to work with Crowe; they recorded that *Bluegrass Holiday* album; then Red left and Bob came back." Banjo manufacturer and player Neat, who later played in a band with Morris, is known as one of the finest craftsmen in the field. He works on J.D.'s banjos and has built banjos designed and sold by both Ralph Stanley and Sonny Osborne, as well as his own "Neat" banjos.

"Somehow," Doyle said, "that record got loose. People started wanting to see us out on the [bluegrass] circuit. After that, we began to get more serious about having some identity that would separate us from the others. We knew we couldn't go out and do covers [of other bands' work], so we started trying to find things that would give us some kind of identity."[15]

"Back then," J.D. said, "some of the people putting on shows were Carleton [Haney], [Roy] Martin, and Jim Clark. Some would call me, and the ones we worked for, we'd go back the next summer. I did most of the book-ing at that time."

Raymond W. McLain's memories of that period are vivid:

Not long after Red Allen left, I went to the Holiday Inn with my father and some other people; we had come down from Hindman [about 120 miles southeast of Lexington]. I was about fifteen, too young to go in, and I just sat on a chair outside the doors. A man came up, and it was J.D.'s daddy. He asked me if I played, and I told him I played banjo. He marched me right in there and sat me on a stool about three feet in front of J.D. He didn't have to go out of his way to do that! He was such a wonderful man, so supportive of that music and just so nice to everybody.

That night made a special impression on Raymond. "You hear that when you're young," he said, "when you have the opportunity to hear someone that is so masterful, you understand something and it just becomes part of you. J.D.'s tone and timing—you just think that's what a banjo sounds like, when you get inspired like that, and feel tone that goes through you like that. Every time I see J.D. now, I think of that first time, and what it felt like." Ray-mond played for many years with his family, first as the Bluegrass State and later as the McLain Family, and now tours with Canadian harmonica player Mike Stevens. He is director of the Traditional Music Center at Morehead State University in Morehead, Kentucky. Raymond and his family appeared on *Circle of Friends,* a second compilation of folk music and bluegrass put together by Dan Brock in 1970 and recorded at Lemco. The Kentucky Moun-tain Boys' tunes were "Rose of Old Kentucky" and "Willie Boy," and they backed up Louise Brock on two folk songs.

"Bless his heart," Doyle said, "I thought the world of Cecil Jones, but we never really had a good recording studio."[16]

Barry Crabtree, from Clay City, Kentucky, was another aspiring banjo player too young to enter the lounge; he sat outside the door. "I told them," his father, Billy Ray Crabtree, said, "'You set that chair so Barry can see J.D., even if he can't see anybody else in the band.' We went every Saturday night."

"They talked Crowe into letting me come down to his house once," Barry Crabtree said. "He tried to show me a few things; it was the thrill of a lifetime."

Barry became a fine professional musician, working with Larry Sparks for eleven years, Wild and Blue, Wildfire, and the Charlie Sizemore Band.

Young Tony Rice was locked out once, too:

> I remember one time, Garland Shuping and I made the trip from North Carolina to Lexington specifically to hear J.D. Crowe and Doyle and Larry and Bobby, and we had no idea that once we got there we wouldn't be able to get in. We had to listen from outside those swinging doors.
>
> That might have been the first time I heard [Crowe] live, but I was very familiar with his musicianship. My father had a copy of *Good 'n Country*, and there were three bands on the album that had turned white from me playing them over and over again. The three cuts were "Bear Tracks," "Cripple Creek," and "You Don't Know My Mind." Even at my early age, when the needle hit the record groove and you heard the first few notes to "Honey, You Don't Know My Mind," there was no question that you were dealing with a totally different force, somebody that knew how to take a 5-string banjo and make it sound really, really, really good.

"I was getting kind of restless," Doyle said, "working at the Holiday Inn night after night. Jimmy [Martin] had been talking to me about coming back. I probably shouldn't have [gone with Jimmy] but I really needed to get away from there. It was beginning to feel like a day job. I think I had a little bit more of a restless spirit than J.D. I was wanting to travel, and J.D. had already done that. He was settled where he grew up."[17]

When Doyle gave his notice, Bobby Slone recommended Larry Rice, a mandolin player he had known in California when he played with the Rice brothers' father, Herb, and their uncle Hal Poindexter. "Larry left [a band called] Aunt Dinah's Quilting Party to come to Lexington," he said.[18]

"Bobby Morris," Doyle said, "by this time, had bought a farm over by Harrodsburg. That was his first love—he loved farming."[19]

"We lived [in Cincinnati] until 1970 or '71," Bobby's widow, Joyce Morris, said, "when we bought a farm in Harrodsburg—Mercer County. After three years, we sold it and moved to Adair County, where we bought another farm. Bob hauled hay and straw to horse farms."

"It didn't take me long to realize I really missed Kentucky, and *really* missed J.D.," Doyle said. "At the end of the year, Bobby [Morris] gave in his notice, and J.D. asked me to come back, front the show, and play guitar. I went out and told Jimmy I was going to leave. He had really had a string of bad luck—fifteen working days got canceled. I'd hocked everything I owned but my wife and kid!"[20]

"When Doyle came back," J.D. said, "Bobby and I went to get him in a rented truck. I told him he'd have to play guitar—I was not going to lose Larry."[21]

The new configuration is listed in the February 1970 issue of *Bluegrass Unlimited*: J.D. Crowe, banjo; Doyle Lawson, guitar; Bob Slone, bass; and Larry Rice, mandolin. This was the makeup of what many people—despite Crowe's later successes—consider to be the best group he ever assembled, with the tightest harmonies and the strongest rhythm.

One of them was teenage mandolin and fiddle wizard Sam Bush, who came up from Bowling Green, frequently with banjo players Courtney Johnson and Alan Munde. He had recorded *Poor Richard's Almanac*, a noteworthy instrumental album, with Oklahoman Munde, and played in a band with fellow Kentuckian Johnson at Horse Cave, Kentucky. "I couldn't even go in that place," he complained. "I could see and hear through those swinging doors, and I stood outside [in the hall] all night."

He continued, "Almost anybody would say Crowe's best band was the New South, but I liked the group with Larry Rice, Doyle Lawson, and Bobby Slone. Doyle was such a rhythm force, and they had the vocal blend as well as the instrumental drive. They just jelled. Larry was one of my favorite mandolin players, and a very solid lead singer."

Young Jerry Douglas, from northeastern Ohio, first saw that band at the Berryville, Virginia, festival:

They were so tight. It was like everybody else played, and they were all having fun, and everything, but these guys were *serious*. It was like, okay, this is the pro leagues, now. When they came on the stage, the whole place just stood on its ear. They were so serious about what they were doing and they were so sure. They were knocking this place out; this was a home run, and [the audience] would barely let them off the stage when they were done. It was by far the most magical and professional moment that I had seen on stage by a bluegrass band. It was like, okay, these guys have played, and what do you follow *that* with?

Budding North Carolina banjo player Terry Baucom had heard J.D. on record. "I fell in love with [Crowe's banjo playing]. My focus shifted. He took what Earl did and added his own little flavor to it, and that "little flavor" was what I just loved. I saw [J.D. with Doyle and Larry] at Camp Springs [Reidsville, North Carolina]—they just stole the show, and were a big hit. I was just a kid, standing there listening."

Baucom has played banjo in many bands, including Boone Creek, Doyle Lawson's Quicksilver, IIIrd Tyme Out, Carolina, and BlueRidge. His banjo style owes a good deal to Crowe, but is more emphatic, more insistent, with an energetic attack. As J.D. interpreted Scruggs through his own personality, so Baucom has interpreted Crowe; he has been extremely influential, especially in North Carolina and Virginia.

Although Doyle returned to Lexington in January 1970, he recorded three sessions with Jimmy Martin as mandolin player and tenor singer. Alan Munde was in Martin's band from October 1969 until October 1971 and played banjo on the same sessions.

"When I worked with Jimmy," Munde remembered, "I was encouraged to play like J.D., [Martin's] favorite banjo player. He liked Bill Emerson a lot, but he always encouraged me to listen and play a lot like J.D. I loved that; never had any problem with that—I wanted to sound like that, too. Jimmy helped me and Doyle, too, while he was there." Munde developed his own highly musical and influential version of a melodic style and would later teach in the bluegrass program at South Plains College in Texas while heading his own band, Country Gazette.

"When I first worked with J.D.," Doyle said, "we had a pretty conventional bluegrass band, with lead, tenor, and baritone parts. When I left for six months with Jimmy, Larry Rice stepped in."[22] Initially on Doyle's return, "Larry was singing tenor to my lead, and J.D. was singing the low part. Our voices—the timbre of our voices just didn't work out right, so we went to a high lead.[23] [He] had a baritone voice, with a good range, medium to low. The best blend was with me on the top end, J.D. in the middle, and Larry on the low end in an inverted harmony. The Osborne Brothers came up with that."[24]

"Me and Doyle and Larry," J.D. said, "we thought about and felt the music in the same way. It was natural and effortless. We rehearsed a lot, or it wouldn't have been as natural and effortless. Larry was young, but his dad had instilled timing in Tony and Larry; Bobby Slone and myself and Doyle were from the old school, and when Larry came, we helped him."[25]

"We worked so hard on our vocals," Doyle said. "I think J.D. would probably tell you we rehearsed more at that time than at any other. Sometimes people would request a song we'd never done together—we knew each other so well, we knew automatically what the other person was going to do."[26]

"That was probably the most precision of four guys," J.D. agreed. "When one of us blinked our eyes, the others blinked. As far as togetherness, that had to be the tightest—Doyle says it too. There wasn't a good solo singer among us, but when you put us together, it worked."[27]

"I enjoyed playing with Doyle and Larry," Bobby Slone said. "I think the tightest group was J.D., Doyle, Larry, and me. We could just breathe each other. We knew what everybody was going to do. It was just so easy. That was probably the most fun; the timing was perfect."[28]

"You can have good bands," J.D. said, "but to have a *complete* band, you have to be able to go on stage and the only person you have to worry about is yourself; then it's *right*. Then you can settle down and play good music and have fun. It's just like one huge sound—everybody is playing the same thing, with a good blend and solidness of everything."[29]

Doyle, who had never thought much of his guitar playing, proved to have one of the best right arms in the business, with solid timing influenced by his two tours with Jimmy Martin, just as Crowe's timing on the banjo had been strengthened during his years with Martin. The two of them created, with Bobby, a pulsing downbeat. Larry, a fine, tradition-based but forward-thinking mandolin player, contributed the crisp upbeat, as well as his share of the melody. Larry had a California sensitivity to songs from outside the usual bluegrass repertoire—and owned an album, *Gilded Palace of Sin,* by the Flying Burrito Brothers, with some songs he thought might work for them.

Badly in need of new material, the boys were open-minded about new songs, and J.D. had always liked to try "something different." They began working out things in rehearsal—and sometimes onstage—that came from sources that ranged from rhythm and blues to rock and roll to country music and the newly named "country rock," and the new songs were incorporated into their playlist as they proved popular with listeners. What made them "different" was the treatment: bluegrass timing and close harmonies and instrumental breaks that offered Crowe and Rice an opportunity to invent new sounds.

The first Burrito Brothers songs they did were "Christine's Tune" (Devil in Disguise) and "Sin City," and they tried Fats Domino's "I'm Walking" and Harlan Howard's "Miller's Cave," as well as Bob Dylan's "You Ain't Goin' Nowhere" and "Nashville Skyline Rag," the latter influenced by Earl Scruggs's recent recording.

They were certainly not the only bluegrass band of the period to explore other forms of music. Younger musicians who grew up with rockabilly and early rock and roll did not hear bluegrass as a form of country music, or in the same way as older ones whose only exposure to music might have been Saturday-night *Opry* broadcasts. Many fans and performers had been introduced to bluegrass through folk music and failed to see the invisible lines that now defined bluegrass as a separate art form. They saw no reason *not* to incorporate the popular songs of the day into their performances. Some of the older musicians saw nontraditional material as a way to reach younger audiences and increase their fan (and financial) base as their country audiences melted away.

Of course, it worked for some of them, but few were as successful as the Kentucky Mountain Boys. Much can be attributed to J.D.'s taste in choosing material that would adapt to his style and to his professionalism in working up the songs in a true bluegrass fashion, rather than simply playing rock and roll with acoustic instruments, as some did.

Other groups pulled away from bluegrass completely, using its roots or its instruments to create personal styles of music that reflected the individualism of the times. Among them were the Earl Scruggs Revue, the Dillards, the Goose Creek Symphony, the Newgrass Revival, John Hartford, and the New Deal String Band.

North Carolinian Gene Knight played banjo with the New Deal String Band until he went into the U.S. Navy in 1970. "J.D.'s playing was a big influence on me," he said. "It just kind of evolved. [We] played the same festivals, and I'd seen him on a fairly regular basis. The effect J.D. had on me was, 'Quit whatever you're doing and stop and pay attention.' [His] stuff with Red Allen and the Kentucky Mountain Boys was fearless, in your face, not fancy but just kind of 'pin-your-ears-back' banjo playing."

The first album J.D., Doyle, Larry, and Bobby recorded with some of the new material was *Ramblin' Boy* (Lemco LP-610). It contained nongenre songs "Born to Be with You" (Don Robertson), "Sin City" (Gram Parsons and Chris Hillman), Dallas Frazier's "So Afraid of Losing You Again," and the title song, by folk singer Tom Paxton. More traditional were "Please Search Your Heart" written by Lawson and Pete Goble, three from Flatt and Scruggs, and a gospel song, "There'll Be No Blind Ones There," by D.C.-area banjo player Pete Kuykendall.

The album, with Crowe's name prominently displayed on the cover, was reviewed in the April 1971 *Bluegrass Unlimited* and received five stars of five. The reviewer noted their experimentation with music from various sources and found that unlike some other groups that might sound too folkie or too much like Nashville, "They always sound pure 'grass, regardless of what they play." He singled out "Sin City" as a song that "doesn't make any sense to me, but they do such an overwhelming version of it I doubt that many will care that they don't understand the words." He concluded with an objection to the number of trios and the singing itself, calling it "lifeless" or "lackluster," yet dubbed the album "one of the year's more memorable" in "a banner year for bluegrass record releases."

"Sin City," as adapted by the Kentucky Mountain Boys, did not make much sense to anyone, but that was because they left off the final verse, which more or less clarified this diatribe against corporate executives. It has, nevertheless, remained one of Crowe's most requested songs.

"In my limited time and efforts to help J.D.," Dan Brock said, "I had told a friend working in New York, and he put me in touch with a guy at Columbia Records in charge of special projects. [David Pochna] was going to leave Columbia but would like to take J.D. on as a special project, and on 20 May 1970, all the guys signed a form."

"We drove up there [New York] and spent the night; Pochna was in charge of all that," J.D. said.[30]

In July 1970, J.D. and the band appeared on ABC's *Dick Cavett Show,* one of the most prestigious of the early talk shows, a first for a bluegrass band.

"[Pochna's] girlfriend worked on that show," J.D. said, "and got us booked on it. Dennis Hopper was on the same show. We performed 'Blackjack' and 'Born to Be with You,' and when we finished, the *band* stood up and gave us a standing ovation, and the studio audience did too. And that was live TV."[31]

The band left New York "that night and drove all night to [a festival at] Lavonia, Georgia," J.D. said. "We got there just half an hour before we were due to go on."[32]

Their association with Pochna did not provide a lot of work, but what they did get was different from anything they had done before. "He wanted to book us in Vegas," J.D. said, "but I knew we weren't ready for that."[33]

"They also did a Winnebago commercial," Brock said. "[Pochna] thought J.D. would be a hit in the Northeast. Marshall Brickman and Eric Weissberg trained under fluorescent lights; they were different from people who'd played in real life." (*New Dimensions in Banjo and Bluegrass* by northern musicians Weissberg and Brickman was released in 1969 by Elektra Records, and subsequently reissued in 1973 with an additional track, "Dueling Banjos," in the wake of the movie *Deliverance*. It offered a view of the music that sometimes differed from "southern" bluegrass.)

Steve Cooley, soaking up whatever banjo music he could find in Louisville and on record, was a "tone" player from an early age and made the same inference: "I'd heard Weissberg and knew his tone was all wrong," he said. "It didn't sound like Earl's or J.D.'s. 'Deliverance' had a sort of pinched tone, not open and fat. It was fine music, but not what I'm all about."

As soon as he was old enough to sneak into Crowe's venues, Cooley studied everything about the physical setup of J.D.'s banjo and the way he achieved his sound, and then adapted what he learned from Crowe with sounds from other types of music into his own style—just as J.D. had done. Cooley played with the Cumberlands and the Bluegrass Alliance and then spent eighteen years with the Dillards, traveling all over the world to perform before crowds numbered in five figures and earning three Grammy nominations. Tired of travel, he returned to Louisville, where he plays banjo and guitar in several excellent local groups.

In 1970, J.D., Doyle, Larry, and Bobby recorded *The Model Church* (Lemco LP-611), a collection of lesser-known religious works arranged and adapted to their style. Released on November 1, 1970, the cover photograph showed

Crowe's name and the title larger than the band's name. *The Kentucky Mountain Boys* was rarely used.

"A lot of people are surprised to learn," Doyle pointed out, "that J.D. did the bulk of the lead vocals in the harmonies on *The Model Church*. If we had just a regular trio, it was J.D. singing lead instead of the baritone that he usually does."[34]

The album received four stars of five in its July 1971 review in *Bluegrass Unlimited*. A different reviewer admitted he has "never cared as much for the Crowe vocals as I have for the group's instrumental work," and found, "They are in need of a more forceful individualized approach in their singing."[35]

While the criticisms of the vocals on these early albums seem ludicrous today, when they are considered classics and studied by those hoping to develop a trio, it is important to understand the strong Monroe-Stanley bias by *Bluegrass Unlimited* and much of its readership during this period. Although it was now a full-fledged magazine, it was still quite a new venture, and perhaps reviewers had not yet learned to differentiate between what they liked and what was good music.

Reviewers may have carped, but audiences were unanimously enthusiastic. During the summer of 1970, the Kentucky Mountain Boys (usually listed as "J.D. Crowe") appeared at some of the biggest festivals from Pennsylvania to Georgia as well as those closer to home, and they were much in demand for the Sunday "Gospel Sing" portions of the festivals.

An article about their performance at Reidsville, North Carolina's Camp Springs Festival, "Breakthrough in Bluegrass Repertoire," appeared in the October 1970 *Bluegrass Unlimited*, with a photograph on the cover. Written by Canadian Doug Benson, who describes himself as a "Monrovian traditionalist of the hardest core," it wholeheartedly praised their performance and saw their adaptation of material such as "Sin City," "She's a Devil in Disguise," and "God's Own Singer" (written by Bernie Leadon, a founder of the Eagles) as "a significant breakthrough, especially coming from a *country* bluegrass group."[36]

The material was not the only thing that changed. The Kentucky Mountain Boys' attire changed, and the "slicks" disappeared in favor of denim jackets with pressed jeans, dress shirts with striped vests, or shirts in various shades of tan and rust, with Roy Rogers–style ties. These gave them a more contemporary look, without giving up uniformity, in a period when many younger bands adopted the ragged, unkempt look of rock groups, while older ones stuck with white shirts and ties, with their leaders in sports jackets. Clothes and hair length as symbols of attitude were a part of the times, and people were likely to make judgments based on appearances.

The whole country was in turmoil in the late 1960s and early '70s, with opposition to the Vietnam War conspicuous in music. Some of the younger bluegrass groups played protest songs, while others chose such arch-conservative anthems as Merle Haggard's "Okie from Muskogee" and "The Fighting Side of Me," creating an additional schism among bluegrass fans already divided into "acoustic" and "plugged-in" camps. The tolerance factor was very small, and critics were not gentle, but the consensus was that new music and ideas were welcome, if they did not step on too many toes.

It was a very narrow fence to walk, but J.D. and Co. managed to do it. They were praised for being fresh and new and for their traditional approach—especially J.D.'s banjo work—because they avoided controversy in their material, which, regardless of its origins, was made to sound as if it had been written just for them.

In the fall of 1970, they decided not to return to the Holiday Inn. With the prospect of travel, they worked at local clubs at which they had no ironclad obligations. The most frequent was Comer's Restaurant, near the University of Kentucky, but there were others. The important thing was to keep working, keep loose, between road jobs.

"We wanted to step up our presence at festivals and things," Doyle said, "and we couldn't do that working Tuesday through Saturday." Doyle also taught at Fred Moore Music when they were in town. "I hated teaching," he said, "but it helped with the income. I taught guitar, mandolin, and banjo, and would give instruction on the basic principles of bass playing. I believe a half-hour lesson was twelve bucks. I would tell the parents when the kid was not interested—the kid would be like, 'Yeah! I'm free, I'm free!' and the parents would be all downcast, like they were trying to live out their lives through the kids."[37]

That winter, through Pochna, "They were on the sound track of a movie about stock car racing," Dan Brock remembered. "It was a B movie that ends up in drive-ins [theaters], and that's about as far as it goes. I don't know what music they used, probably traditional music they didn't have to pay any royalties on."

J.D. described the experience:

> The movie was called *Fury on Wheels* and was about a guy who had "souped-up" his car to where he could beat anybody. The main actor was Tom Ligon; he was on soap operas. In the movie, he hung out at a bar where we played. These young rich people would come in the bar and bet him they could beat him in their nice new cars. They had a bar-fight scene, but wouldn't let us be in it.
>
> It was filmed in Tampa, Florida, and they flew me and Doyle and Bobby down there and back, and paid us $120 a day apiece. They had only wanted me and Bobby, but I told them, "You've got to have three people; you've got to have a guitar." We were there a week; even though you weren't in it that day, you had to be there. The company rented a whole hotel; there were probably three hundred people involved.[38]

After the first of the year, they returned to the Holiday Inn, where the crowds were just as excited as ever, and the lines to get in just as long.

A letter in the March 1971 *Bluegrass Unlimited* described the third annual Florida Bluegrass Festival and called "J.D. Crowe, Doyle Lawson, and the Kentucky Mountain Boys the instant 'hit' of the crowd with their flawless technique and smooth harmony."[39]

By the spring of 1971, Crowe's band was booked at numerous bluegrass festivals along the eastern seaboard, and a poll of *Bluegrass Unlimited* readers showed their impact. The Kentucky Mountain Boys were the fourth-favorite band, after the Country Gentlemen, Bill Monroe and His Blue Grass Boys, and Ralph Stanley and the Clinch Mountain Boys. In the "favorite banjo player" category, J.D. Crowe placed fourth, after Don Reno, Earl Scruggs, and Ralph Stanley. For a band that had been on the bluegrass circuit only one full summer, this was a remarkable jump in popularity; the other bands and individuals had been well known for years.[40]

That summer, they returned to Camp Springs, in Reidsville, North Carolina, on Labor Day weekend, and made a personnel change that would have a lasting impact on the band.

Tony Rice, Larry's brother, had come to Kentucky to work with the Bluegrass Alliance, a Louisville-based band that was one of the first to feature the guitar as a lead instrument rather than as a rhythm keeper. Tony was a "flat picker," who used a single pick to play the melody, as Dan Crary had done before him in the Alliance. From August 1970 until August 1971, Tony was part of one of the on-the-edge bands, burnishing his already abundant guitar skills working with Sam Bush, banjo players Buddy Spurlock and Courtney Johnson, bassist Harry "Ebo Walker" Shelor, and founder and fiddler Lonnie Peerce. In its long history, the band would nurture many fine young musicians—Vince Gill, Steve Cooley, and Jack Lawrence, to name a few—and give a name to the developing concept of "newgrass."

"Anytime I had time to go over [to Lexington] and visit Larry and see him," Tony said, "then I would do that, and hopefully be able to hear J.D. and Doyle and Larry and Bobby together, because at that time, hands down, that was my favorite band. I'm sure I'm not the only person with those sentiments, because in that era, that band—they were cooking."

"The Holiday Inn was a fun gig," Doyle said, "but like anyplace in the world, there were some negatives. Working five nights a week started wearing me down—it was like punching a clock. Being raised on a farm, I was never one that wanted to be closed in, and there was something depressing about it, even though I loved the music. I left [J.D.] in August 1971," Doyle said. "By no means did our friendship end there."[41]

"Doyle and J.D. were very creative together," Hugh Sturgill said. "Doyle was the closest to a partner J.D. ever had."

"When I left J.D.," Doyle said, "I took a job with the Country Gentlemen. They had said, 'We will pay you a salary, or you can just take your chances with us [in a partnership].' I found out they were getting less for a show than J.D. did."[42] That was surprising, as the Country Gentlemen were one of the premier bluegrass groups at the time, usually "closing out" whatever shows they played with other bands.

Doug Hutchens, banjo player, writer, teacher, and, for the summer of 1971, one of Bill Monroe's Blue Grass Boys, remembered learning about the upcoming changes at Monroe's Bean Blossom (Indiana) festival in June:

> Tony Rice was leaving the [Bluegrass] Alliance and going with Eddie Adcock. Eddie had spent a couple of years "under the radar" in California and had returned for the Bean Blossom festival, and had been at several places we played during the summer. Jimmy Gaudreau was leaving the [Country]

Gentlemen and joining Eddie and Tony, and Doyle Lawson was leaving Crowe to take Gaudreau's place [as mandolin player and tenor singer]. Within a few weeks, things changed again. Tony, wanting to work with brother Larry, left what turned out to be the II Generation to go with J.D.

Tony played his last performance with the Alliance at the place where he got the job initially, Camp Springs, Labor Day weekend. He also played his first show with J.D. that weekend as well.[43]

"I remember very well when I made the decision to do it," Tony Rice said. "It really had me in a precarious position, because I'd sort of made the commitment to Adcock and Gaudreau. So I went to Bill Emerson and talked to him about it, and he was the one who told me to follow my own instincts and take the job I wanted to take, which was with J.D. Crowe. So I did."

Bobby Slone had told J.D. about Tony:

The Rice brothers and their family were living in California when Bobby was there. The next I heard of Tony, he was playing with the Bluegrass Alliance. I had gotten acquainted with Tony, and, I don't remember his exact words, but he said, "If you ever need a lead singer and guitar player, let me know." And that stuck with me. But I didn't do that. I have this policy: I will not deliberately hire somebody from another band; they have to quit before I will ever approach them. He told me he was leaving that band, and I said, "Well, when you do, call me." And we left it at that.

When Tony joined me, he said, "I promised the Alliance that I'd play the show with them. Would it be all right with you if I did that, then played your show?" And, of course, I said, "Well, if you can hold up and do it, that's fine with me." So that's how that came about—he walked in there and did a great job.[44]

Not long after Tony moved to Lexington and they returned to the Holiday Inn, two major changes occurred. J.D. had been thinking about a name change for a long time, and the band became the New South. "To me," J.D. said, "*The Kentucky Mountain Boys* kind of labels you to one style of music, and I wanted to change it to something that wouldn't label you—to a name that you could play whatever kind of music you wanted, and the name would still fit."[45]

"We had played a couple of outside dates, somewhere," Tony said, "and Crowe and I were in a Winnebago camper, late one night, and he was driving. I remember him saying he wanted to change the name of the band. To this day, I don't know how he came up with the name the New South, but I do remember that I liked it, liked what it represented. It was a good call on his part."

The second change, not long afterward, was the addition of drums and electric pickups on the instruments. "We went electric right after Tony came," Bobby Slone said. "Mostly, we did that for the monitors, so we could hear ourselves. We needed it for the bar. The Osbornes and the Dillards were having drums, and Crowe kind of wanted to get into that. I played electric bass. The smoke at the Holiday Inn just laid there like a big cloud, like a low-pressure area, and the drums would have a gold coating from the smoke."[46]

"In retrospect," Tony reflected, "that was one of the things very disappointing to me when I did join J.D., was to go into the Holiday Inn and have to put a pickup on my instrument. Well, now, for a while, I tried it without plugging in, and it just wouldn't work, so I went ahead and did that, and it eventually became something that I learned to like, in that I understood the reason for it, but in an ideal world, we'd have been in a totally acoustic format."

"When we added drums and hooked up amplifiers," J.D. said, "it was a look as much as anything. We tried to mix in rhythm and blues and country [music]. That's why our longevity at the Holiday Inn was so long. I always liked to do something a little different."[47]

Initially, everyone in the band got a transducer, a pickup that senses the vibrations of an instrument's strings, but this was unsatisfactory for the banjo. J.D. soon began using a different kind of pickup, manufactured for him by banjo player-engineer Wayne Clyburn, who lived in Cincinnati.

In 1969, while a student at Ohio University, Clyburn had read an article in *Bluegrass Unlimited* by banjo player Bill Emerson, who suggested a need for a banjo pickup that would reproduce the sound of an acoustic banjo. When Clyburn broached the idea to banjo craftsman Kix Stewart, "He responded quite emphatically that it could not be done. That was all I needed to hear," Clyburn said.

> Since the head of the banjo is the vibrating element most responsible for its characteristic acoustic sound, I decided to devise a pickup that would sense the vibration of the head, rather than the strings. The coil and magnet as-

sembly that I devised is located inside the banjo, directly below the middle bridge leg, with the face of the magnet and coil as close to the underside of the head as possible without actually touching it. A thin, flat, rectangular piece of steel is then attached to the bottom of the middle leg of the bridge. When the banjo head vibrates, the flat piece of steel vibrates along with the head and induces an electric signal in the coil that yields a characteristic acoustic banjo sound when fed into a sound reinforcement system.

Clyburn was already a fan of J.D.'s, so when Crowe showed interest in the pickup, "I agreed to give him one," Clyburn said. "At that point, it was my intention to manufacture and market the pickup, so it was advantageous to have someone like J.D. using it. I sold fifteen or twenty pickups as a result of referrals by J.D." Ultimately, the adverse reaction from dyed-in-the-wool bluegrass fans convinced Clyburn not to pursue it as a commercial venture, but for nearly three years, the pickup was in regular use.

"It felt good to 'strange it up,'" Bobby Slone recalled, "but we played regular bluegrass at festivals. We had three drummers [during that period], Donny Combs, Denny Woods, and Jimmy Klugh, mostly in the club in the winter. It put a beat to it, and it was fun. I liked it. Donny was the only drummer who went on the road with us much."[48]

Combs, a Whitesburg, Kentucky, native, had recently returned from sixteen months in Vietnam and was ready to play. His wife was a hairdresser who owned a wig shop, and this was a period during which musicians, particularly, sported a lot of hair. Donny wore a shaggy black wig that gave him a distinctive appearance.

"I'd never played bluegrass," Combs said, "but when [mutual friend and musician] Earl Watkins told me J.D. needed a drummer, I said, 'I'll try it.' I started right after Labor Day, 1971," he said, "right after Tony, but before the name changed to the New South. I was the Kentucky Mountain Boys' only drummer." In point of fact, Jimmy Hatton had played a snare drum on occasion, but to a real drummer, that doesn't count.

"It's a physical thing, playing bluegrass," Combs said. "You have to have good arms and wrists, but after a few nights, I felt comfortable. It's not about the drummer; it's about making the band sound good, filling in some empty places, giving it a little bit of drive. The musicians were so good, I got sort of attached to them." He continued, "When I first started playing [the

Holiday Inn], there was a revolving band stand, or maybe we just turned our instruments around; when we started playing [each night], we were facing the dining room, and about an hour later, they turned the stage around to face the bar. Later, the stage was on the opposite side of the room. I'd always been where people were up dancing, and people came *there* just to listen. I kind of liked that."

Lexington, Kentucky, Christmas, 1950, at home. *Left to right*: Bessie Lee Nichols Crowe, Rosa Marie Crowe, Orval Dee Crowe, and J.D. Crowe. Photo courtesy Rosa Crowe Collett.

Here is a typical scene of the Barn Dance as it appears eac i Saturday night during the broadcast. To our many listeners and friends all over Kentucky, I: diana, Ohio, Tennessee, West Virgi ia, Virginia North and South Carolina who are within listening range of our broadcast, this Barn Dance scene is especially dedicated to the Eureka Flour Co. of Beaver Dam, Kentucky, the sponsors who have made this program possible over the Eureka Network and have brought this wholehearted entertainment into your homes each Saturday night.

Lexington, Kentucky, the *Kentucky Mountain Barn Dance*, ca. 1950. Onstage, Esco Hankins's band, the Tennesseans. *Left to right*: "Jake" Tullock, "Aunt Liz," unidentified announcer, Esco Hankins, Curley Farmer, and "Uncle Josh." *Left side of stage, seated, left to right*: Curly Sechler and the Two Powell County Boys. *Right side of stage, seated, left to right*: Earl Scruggs (in hat), Lester Flatt (with handkerchief), "Jody Rainwater," and unidentified performer. *Standing, far right*: unidentified announcer. *In center of aisle, seated on stairs*: J.D. Crowe. Photo from *Kentucky Mountain Barn Dance Song Book*, ca. 1950, courtesy Frank Godbey.

Lexington, Kentucky, Christmas, 1950. J.D.'s first banjo, a Kay. Rosa Marie Crowe and J.D. Crowe. Photo courtesy Rosa Crowe Collett.

Junction City, Kentucky, ca. 1951–52. Sam Gastin, with Ball Bearing Plectrum Gibson PB-5 with attached fifth string; J.D. would later own this banjo. J.D. with his first Gibson banjo, an RB-100. Note the early appearance of J.D.'s "claw." Photo courtesy Rosa Crowe Collett.

Barn Dance in Mount Sterling, Kentucky, ca. 1953, J.D. with Esco Hankins and the Tennesseans. *Left to right*: Dean Faulkner, "Red" Stanley, Esco Hankins, J.D. Crowe, and George Billings. Photo courtesy Rosa Crowe Collett.

Matoaca, Virginia, High School, 1955, J.D. with Mac Wiseman. *Left to right*: Curtis Lee, Benny Williams (obscured) J.D. Crowe, and Mac Wiseman. J.D. is playing his RB-100; note the "claw." Photo by Bernie Wright, courtesy Frank Schoepf.

Casey Clark's Jamboree, Detroit, 1957. J.D. with Jimmy Martin. *Left to right*: Billy Gill, Frank Wakefield, Jimmy Martin, and J.D. Crowe. Photo courtesy Rosa Crowe Collett.

Mocking Bird Hill Park, Anderson, Indiana, 1960. J.D. with Jimmy Martin. *Left to right*: Herb Hooven; Paul Williams; J.D. Crowe, with his Gibson RB-3, "the Banger"; and Jimmy Martin. Photo courtesy Ken Landreth.

Martin's Tavern, Lexington, Kentucky, 1964. *Left to right*: Ed Stacy, Bobby Joslin, J.D. Crowe, and Charlie Joslin. Photo courtesy Rosa Crowe Collett.

Martin's Tavern, Lexington, Kentucky, 1968. *Left to right*: Gordon Scott, Jimmy Hatton, J.D. Crowe, and Doyle Lawson. Photo by Harry Bickel.

Red Slipper Lounge, Holiday Inn North, Lexington, Kentucky, November 22, 1968. *Left to right*: Doyle Lawson, J.D. Crowe, and Red Allen. Photo by Marty Godbey.

Shoal Creek Park, Lavonia, Georgia, July 25, 1970. *Left to right*: Larry Rice, J.D. Crowe, and Doyle Lawson. Photo by Marty Godbey.

Carleton Haney's Camp Springs Festival, Reidsville, North Carolina, Labor Day weekend, 1970. *Left to right*: Larry Rice, Jimmy Hatton (obscured), Doyle Lawson, J.D. Crowe, and Bobby Slone, posing for unidentified fan. Photo by Frank Godbey.

Todd's Fork Festival, Morrow, Ohio, September 1974. *Left to right*: Larry Rice, Tony Rice, Bobby Slone, and J.D. Crowe. Photo by Janice McLaughlin.

Sheraton Inn, Lexington, Kentucky, March 1975. *Left to right*: Ricky Skaggs, J.D. Crowe, and Tony Rice. Photo by Marty Godbey.

Diners' Playhouse, Lexington, Kentucky, during taping of *Bluegrass, Bluegrass,* a series by Kentucky Educational Television, July 3, 1977. *Left to right*: Bobby Slone, Jimmy Gaudreau, Glenn Lawson, and J.D. Crowe. Photo by Marty Godbey.

Breeding's, Lexington, Kentucky, March 26, 1982. *Left to right*: Bobby Slone, Wendy Miller, Keith Whitley, and J.D. Crowe. Photo by Marty Godbey.

Bogart's, Cincinnati, February 1984. *Left to right*: Randy Hayes, J.D. Crowe, Tony King, and Wendy Miller. Photo by Marty Godbey.

Red Mile Festival, Lexington, Kentucky, May 24, 1993. *Left to right*: Phil Leadbetter, Curt Chapman (obscured), Wayne Fields, J.D. Crowe, and Richard Bennett. Photo by Frank Godbey.

Frankfort, Kentucky, in performance at the Governor's Mansion, KET airdate June 21, 2000. *Left to right*: Phil Leadbetter, Curt Chapman, Dwight McCall, J.D. Crowe, and Rickey Wasson. Photo courtesy of Kentucky Educational Television.

Kentucky Center for the Arts, Louisville, Kentucky, October 2, 2003. J.D. Crowe is inducted into the International Bluegrass Music Hall of Honor (now Hall of Fame) by Sonny Osborne. Photo by Dan Loftin.

Left to right: Dwight McCall, Ron Stewart, J.D. Crowe, Harold Nixon, and Rickey Wasson. Publicity photo by Dan Loftin, ca. 2003–4.

Lexington Public Library Auditorium, Lexington, Kentucky, December 4, 2008. *Left to right*: Ron Stewart and J.D. Crowe. Photo by Frank Godbey.

Appomattox, Virginia, March 9, 2008. Photo by Dean Hoffmeyer.

This mural at the corner of Sixth and Limestone streets, Lexington, Kentucky, depicting musicians who have performed in the area, was unveiled September 20, 2008. Note J.D. Crowe at right, near sign. Martin's Tavern was just north of this intersection. Photo by Frank Godbey.

CHAPTER 7
ROUNDER 0044 AND THE
CONVERGENCE OF 1975

It was several months before Tony Rice felt comfortable with the band:

It was a little rough at first, and in retrospect, I really don't know how [J.D.] had the patience to deal with what he had to deal with, but he did.

The vocals weren't so much the problem, as it was the rhythm section. At that time, I don't think there had been any rhythm section that could touch them in terms of being able to hold a piece of music together from beginning to end. There was something real magical about that combination of Crowe, and Doyle on rhythm guitar and Larry on mandolin and Bobby Slone on bass.

I knew how to play rhythm guitar, but when I went into J.D. Crowe's band, all of a sudden everything had shifted in terms of the rigidity of the timing aspect. It was very rigid. I know precisely where that comes from—that rigidity and that demand from Crowe as a musician came from the school of Jimmy Martin.

Crowe by nature is like myself, in this aspect, that he doesn't like to discuss music. Once in a while, if we felt like there was something that we needed to do, or if things were getting stale, then Crowe would call a rehearsal.

Looking back, I had stepped in and replaced Doyle, whose rhythm on the guitar and drive was that metronomic, and that was one of the things I hadn't had, back in the Bluegrass Alliance. It was a totally different ball game, playing with Crowe. Being the personality that he is, he didn't really have to say anything to express dissatisfaction; it was like an aura that you could feel coming off of him, and sometimes that aura was real, real, real intense. I could just tell, basically, that he was pissed off, but I never felt that aura of anger coming off of him so bad that he was ready to give up.

Richard Bennett, J.D.'s guitar player in the early 1990s, described an incident when Tony first started with J.D.: "Crowe wasn't talking to him, and Tony said, 'Are you mad at me?' and Crowe said, 'No, you're rushing.'"

"J.D. is a perfectionist," Don Combs said. "Every set he played was like a concert. Sometimes, if we couldn't get it, he'd get just a little bit huffy. There were some songs he played that I just simply didn't play, 'cause drums didn't fit. Some songs were *so* fast you'd almost be playing a drum roll."

"It took a lot of work," J.D. agreed. "That kind of thing doesn't happen by itself; there are a lot of frustrations, but if you want to learn to do it, then that's what you've got to do. You've got to learn to 'think alike.' There has to be an effort on everybody's part."[1]

In the December 1971 issue of *Bluegrass Unlimited,* the reader's poll again named J.D. fourth-favorite banjo player, after Reno, Scruggs, and Stanley; the Kentucky Mountain Boys were again fourth-favorite band, after the Country Gentlemen, Monroe's Blue Grass Boys, and Stanley's Clinch Mountain Boys. This was before the addition of Tony and the name change were known to the readership.

Besides his extraordinary voice and lead guitar skills, Tony brought to the group, with Larry, the "blood harmony" that has been so much a part of bluegrass and country music. The trios, while different from those with Doyle, were strong and flavorful.

"Tony sung the high part," J.D. said, "not as high as Doyle, but we did more straight trios. We'd switch [parts] around.[2] Listen, you could be the best picker in the world, but if you don't have your singing you don't have anything. I think singing is half of it, or all of it. When you really get down to it, it's your singing that sells it. A lot of practice goes into that."[3]

"Tony had exposure to and an interest in many kinds of different music," Hugh Sturgill said. Tony had—and still has—a fondness for the music of Gordon Lightfoot, and at least three of Lightfoot's songs soon found their way into their playlist. "You Are What I Am," "Ten Degrees and Getting Colder," and "Early Morning Rain." Tony reflected:

> There was a lot of nights—many nights—after we got off at the Holiday Inn, that Crowe was kind of wired, and I was, too, and so he would stop by the house and we would listen to whatever new albums that I thought he would like, that I could share with him. Gordon Lightfoot, Ian Tyson, old Ian and Sylvia albums, and we'd be listening together, and say, "You know, that would make a darned good tune to play in this genre." I think the idea behind Larry bringing the tunes that he did, some of them *very* contemporary, we did that because we were looking for *anything* that would break the monotony of "Blue Ridge Cabin Home," "Little Cabin Home on the Hill," and "Salty Dog Blues," and on and on.
>
> Crowe is a multifaceted character, and he can be cantankerous—but always in a benign way. When he got in those moods of being cantankerous, something usually got done, and there were also times when he would be very diplomatic about having some sort of inside discussions with the band.
>
> We had quite a few squabbles, but it never amounted to anything—the brotherhood with him was always there, from the start. There was a respect there.
>
> There are some facets of musicianship that the only word for is *mysterious*. Outside of the ability to hold a piece of music together, a lot of the rest of it will fit in that category of being "mysterious." I had the ideal view of the man and his music, and how he would execute whatever he intended to do. If I hadn't played with J.D. Crowe, my own standards maybe wouldn't be the same. He had no tolerance at all for anything that was inferior.

With the drums, Bobby's electric bass, and the amplified instruments, the band could now hear themselves over the crowd noise. Some diehards complained, as they had done when the Osborne Brothers electrified, but Crowe was satisfied—for the time being. They could stop worrying about *sound*, and enjoy playing *music*.

The band, by this time, had adopted Tony's shiny knitted shirts, long sleeved and snug fitting, as their stage dress. They gave them a more updated look that went well with their electrified sound. It was clear to the least-informed observer that these were not "good ole boys" playing "foot-stomping" music, even if it *was* bluegrass.

Obviously, this did not come about easily, or quickly; there was an effort on the part of each musician to contribute to the team effort; solo breaks were the opportunity for individualism, but they still had to mesh with the other instruments.

"In bluegrass," Don Combs said, "the drummer uses the same chop as the mandolin player; if either one is off, it can really cause some problems. You'll hear it and think, 'This is the beat,' but if you just cut it in half, you'll not work yourself to death."

Don Rigsby, who played mandolin with Crowe in the 1990s, felt as though "the mandolin's main role is to play snare [drum] and the bass's role is to play the drum kick. The guitar fills in all the gaps, and the fiddle is not a rhythm instrument at all, but has to play in meter."

"Donny Combs," J.D. said, "one hot night, was three sheets in the wind—not drunk, just having a good time—got hot, and his wig slipped down over his nose. He took that thing off and threw it out in the audience, and said, 'I'll never wear that damn thing again!' And he didn't."[4]

When Larry had to have a cyst removed from his wrist, Sam Bush filled in for him. By that time, the Newgrass Revival had been formed out of the Bluegrass Alliance, and Sam, Curtis Burch, Courtney Johnson, and Butch Robins were playing rock-bluegrass fusion music.

"Newgrass was not working then, so I agreed," Bush said.

I had not started amplifying my mandolin, and they were all plugged in. I know I was there for two weeks, five nights. I played Larry's mandolin, plugged in, and I realized I enjoyed the plugged-in part, but best was playing with one of the greatest musicians for feeling, timing, and drive. J.D.'s not about playing hard or fast, it's just the intensity of what you do, the total feeling. Of all the great banjo players I've had the opportunity to play with, Crowe is the gold standard of timing and drive.

When I stepped up and did Doyle Lawson's "train whistle" [on the mandolin] on "Train 45," J.D. came in [on the banjo], and it was like being hit in the back. It was the moment of truth. There was no messing around, no child's play. It plays faster than it sounds.

In April 1973, the New South recorded their first album, for Starday, in Nashville, with Nashville sidemen chosen by J.D. Bobby Slone was not on the recording. "Bobby was very shy about going into the studio and playing electric bass," J.D. explained. "He hadn't been playing one that long, and he told me if I could, get someone else to do so."[5]

Titled *J.D. Crowe and the New South,* the album (SLP 489) was produced by Merle Kilgore and was a mixture of some of their most requested songs: "You Can Have Her," "You Can Share My Blanket" (by Lexington song-writer Steve Brines), "How Come You Do Me Like You Do, Do, Do" (by swing-era bandleader Gene Austin), "Devil in Disguise," "God's Own Singer," "Ten Degrees and Getting Colder," "(That's What You Get) for Loving Me" (Lightfoot); Larry Rice's "My Heart Talks to Me" and "Come on Down to My World," and Paul Simon's "Leaves That Are Green," the last two taken from a Lemco 45 rpm (LEM-321). The album was not released until June 1977, depriving the New South of anything to sell at performances or to use in booking; the Lemco albums were out of print.

Larry Rice left the band in the fall of 1974 to play with Dickey Betts (formerly with the Allman Brothers), and Ricky Skaggs, from Lawrence County, Kentucky, replaced him. He was freelancing in the D.C. area and thinking about starting a band.

I started with J.D. in November of 1974. I had been with the Country Gentlemen for a couple of years, and with Ralph Stanley for a couple of years before that. Keith Whitley and I had talked about putting together a band. I got a phone call from J.D., and he wanted to know if I'd come and play mandolin. I'd been playing fiddle with the Gentlemen, so my mandolin chops had faltered, and I'd been singing baritone, so my voice had dropped down a bit. I didn't even own a mandolin.

I told J.D. that Keith and I wanted to put together a band, and he said, "Well, can you come and stay until you do?" I'd been wanting to do something different, and it would be back in my home state, and that was cool.

So I came down for a weekend, just to play, and kind of go over with Larry some of the things he did, and learn some of the songs. It was quite a job, but it was one of the best moves, musically, I ever did, getting to be a part of the New South group, and the New South album. That was an awesome thing; I think that's a landmark record.

After using several borrowed mandolins, Ricky was able to buy a 1924 Lloyd Loar Gibson F-5 mandolin. "I'd never had a real good mandolin," he said, "and this one had a real narrow neck, like a fiddle, and I loved that. I still have it, and it's a wonderful instrument. J.D. and the band were playing electric when I came, and I liked it better acoustic—I know Tony liked it better. Back in those days there wasn't any real good pickups; maybe a few that sounded okay, but I think we all liked it better acoustic. I feel like it was more natural sounding if we unplugged."

"Ricky wanted to [work with Crowe]," Tony said, "but I knew he wasn't going to stay unless the band went back to acoustic. Ricky, by that time, was on the same wavelength that I was, in that he had never played in any musical configuration that had timing and drive that was that precise."

Tony and Ricky talked with J.D., to see if he would be willing to go back to acoustic music in order to keep Ricky in the band. "I don't remember that being a problem," Tony said. "I think [J.D.] might have been ready for it, anyway."

When Tony's grandmother died, J.D. again asked Sam Bush to fill in. "J.D. called me at 4:00 p.m. at Courtney's house," Sam said. (Courtney Johnson lived about 125 miles southwest of Lexington.) "He said, 'Can you get up to Lexington?' and I said, 'I'll go home and take a shower and throw my mandolin in the car.' J.D. said, 'You don't have time to go home and take a shower. You don't need no damn mandolin, either. I need you to play guitar.' I wasn't even in clothes that *I* might wear onstage; I'm sure I looked pretty skuzzy." The crowd was not large, but Sam said, "I had a *ball*. It was the first time I ever played with Ricky—at least I got to show him I could play bluegrass. I had really long hair, and Ricky was emcee. He said, 'Tony looks a little different tonight.'"

"In the New South," Ricky said, "there were lots of different harmony structures. All the years I'd been with Ralph, I either sung the 'third' [part], or I sung the 'high tenor,' which is a high fifth, an octave above baritone, so that was pretty much all I had done in harmony. Coming to work with J.D. and Tony, I had to learn things like 'Sin City,' where there was a high lead, and they were singing two parts below me. I was hearing people moving under me [vocally] that I hadn't heard before. It took a little bit of getting used to."

Crowe was a good teacher, more by example than by instruction, and it did not take long to smooth the rough edges. "That's one of the great things about working four shows a night—you can hone up your skills!" Ricky said. "People always talked about how tight we were. When J.D. would kick something off, Tony's going to come in where he's supposed to be, the mandolin was there, and Bobby—it was so well put together because we had played all those shows. It was a surprise—a shock—to me that it wasn't long after we started playing that J.D. said, 'Oh, by the way, we're supposed to go cut a record.' I wondered, 'Why cut now? Why not wait until I've been in the group for six months?'"

The contract was with Rounder Records, a small, independent company known for its quality products, but hardly a competitor in the business. It began in 1970, with three young people who wanted to record music they liked. Ken Irwin, Marian Leighton, and Bill Nowlin started small, reissuing obscure recordings in their *Early Days of Bluegrass* series, and recording regional musicians who maintained close ties with the roots of their music. Criteria, Ken Irwin said, included the following: "Would it stand up over time? Could we break even? It was not until later that we could make money." Their first venture into recording a popular band out on the national festival circuit was the New South. Of the beginnings of their relationship, Ken said:

We had seen [J.D.] at festivals fairly early on and in 1974 approached him at Gettysburg [Festival] about a banjo record we're still hoping for. Later on in the festival, he and Hugh Sturgill came over and met with us. We had set up a table and were selling records. We felt at the time we were too "small potatoes." We had worked with Del McCoury, but at the time, he was very regional, and so was Don Stover. [We'd recorded] a number of older bands, such as the Bailey Brothers, and old-time acts, Olabelle Reed, and [the] Highwoods [String Band], but not anybody considered a national act at that time. We were very surprised they came over and said they'd be interested; J.D. didn't want to be with Rebel [Records], who was the reigning label at that time.

I was at the sessions, but wasn't very active; I had not developed a lot of the skills I have now. J.D. at that time was a legend in our eyes, and I didn't feel I had much to contribute. We were still coming out of being fans—we still are fans—that was the primary role we had at that point, and we were nowhere near as involved as we became later on. We learned very much on the job.

> They came in very well prepared. I remember being surprised when
> they brought in drums and piano. We had nothing to do with that.

J.D., following the example set by Jimmy Martin, enhanced his five-man
group in the studio with whatever musicians he deemed necessary, a pattern
he has followed ever since.

The album referred to variously as *Rounder 0044*, "the brown album," and
"the Old Home Place album" was actually named *The New South* and was
recorded in two sessions in January 1975. Dobro player Jerry Douglas, then
with the Country Gentlemen, was on the sessions. "Tony and Ricky and I
had worked together on a couple of records," Jerry said, "and they talked
J.D. into letting me play on this record, and after that, I knew I was going
to join this band, but they had to talk J.D. into it. I don't think J.D. was too
crazy about Dobro players up to that point."

"I felt," Ricky said, "that Jerry had learned how to play fills and backup
to enhance the music; the Dobro wasn't just a solo instrument to him. J.D.
agreed that we would have Jerry on two cuts, maybe three cuts at the most.
Once he came in and kind of proved his worth, I think J.D. was really loving
the sound that we got with Jerry, and I think Jerry ended up being on six or
eight cuts." To Ricky's delight, J.D. invited Douglas to join the band. "I was
really glad; I felt that was part of a new sound that would be pleasing to a
whole lot of people."

J.D. said:

> I knew the lineup that consisted of Ricky and Tony and Bobby Slone and
> Jerry Douglas and myself, if we couldn't get it together and play, then
> there's no hope, 'cause the talent was there. Those guys are just phenom-
> enal. Tony'd been with me about three and a half years at that time; he
> had learned all the material and was very comfortable, and Ricky, when
> he came in, was no problem, 'cause he knew a lot of the material that we
> did. It was a group where you didn't have to worry about anybody but
> yourself, and that don't happen a lot in this business.[6]

"Bobby's influence," Tony said, "in a way, was equally valuable to J.D.
Crowe's at that time; he was an integrated part of a really precision rhythm
section, and there had been very few bass players—if any—up until that time,
who could feel that comfortable being that good at it, and never let it waver."

"'Born to Be with You,'" Jerry Douglas said. "[Bobby] just enshrined himself in the bass players' hall of fame, when he kicked off 'Born to Be with You.' How in the world did he do this, and he's left-handed, reaching across, slapping?"

"Jerry Douglas is probably one of the finest Dobro players that ever was, or probably ever will be," J.D. said. "When we recorded the album—the Old Home Place album, or *0044*, as a lot of people know it—Jerry was still working with the Country Gentlemen. So we borrowed him for the session. Meanwhile, he had told me that he was going to be leaving the Gentlemen, and he was interested in joining the New South. So when he did, he joined the New South."[7]

The record was a mixture of traditional material—Flatt and Scruggs's "Some Old Day," "Sally Goodin,'" and "Cryin' Holy," and "The Old Home Place," by the Dillards' Dean Webb and Mitch Jayne; modern folk songs, Lightfoot's "Ten Degrees" and "You Are What I Am"; "Rock Salt and Nails" (Bruce Phillips) and "Summer Wages" (Ian Tyson); current country songs, Earl Scruggs's "Nashville Blues" and Rodney Crowell's "Home Sweet Home Revisited"; and rhythm and blues with "I'm Walkin'" (Antoine "Fats" Domino).

By the time it was recorded, the band had left the Holiday Inn, after a remarkably long tenure, "from 1968 to 1974," according to J.D. "There was a change in management, and the new guy wasn't sympathetic to our kind of music, so we went to the Sheraton Inn for a period of four or five months. We were all really happy—we'd been [at the Holiday Inn] so long, and we were ready for a change."[8]

"I think the Sheraton had made a better offer," Tony said. "I remember very well that I was glad to get out of the Holiday Inn and go over to the Sheraton. The crowd was less rowdy, and it was usually full."

Being in the same place night after night, playing a lot of the same music, can wear down even those who love what they are doing, and sometimes it was monotonous and repetitious, as Tony Rice explained:

> There were other times when everything jelled, and in that moment when you feel the feedback from the audience, you feel that it's almost a closed circle, when you get an audience in there that's that good. We were lucky in that we had more of a listening audience than you might think. There were times when it got really rowdy, but you could always feel that energy coming off a listener. You really knew when you were playing to a crowd

of people who were not there just for the spectacle of the event, but they were there to hear music, and they knew what they were hearing, and they liked it. In those moments, everything shifted gears, and the monotony of it disappeared.

"We worked [at the Holiday Inn] five years, every winter," Bobby Slone said. "You get so you can't impress yourself a bit, you can't feel the music good. People say you can get really tight playing in bars—and you can, if you're playing three or four nights—but six nights is just too much. You play to the same audiences over and over, and you play so much you're tired." Changing places brought a fresh perspective. "You can do the same material, but if you have a different audience, you can enjoy playing. [The Holiday Inn] was really good for us because at that time, we were one of the few bands working. All the time I've worked with Crowe, we've worked regular. It's not good for the music, but it's good for other things—it pays your bills."[9]

"I think we were lucky," Tony said, "that we had what we did [at the Holiday Inn]. In those days, as an occupation in the music business, and in the musical world that we lived in, that was the ideal situation. This was a really good paying job. It was a lot of work; I mean, there were times when we were doing four sets a night, six nights a week, and that was a lot, but it was really good, steady pay, and you could depend on it every week." As a bonus, "In the summer months we would go and play the festival circuit and a few concerts."

"For ten years after we left the Holiday Inn," J.D. said, "there were people calling to see if we were there. They'd been there, and would stop every time they went to Florida."[10]

Some of those early fans probably *still* think Crowe is at the Holiday Inn. Those who do not really follow bluegrass have no idea of his international importance, of the countless banjo players—and other musicians—who have been influenced by him and his bands, or of the esteem in which he is held all over the world. To them, he is just part of their young days and the good times they had at the Holiday Inn. While he was there, though, they were enthusiastic and supportive and willing to stand in long lines to see him.

Not only bluegrass fans but visitors from outside the bluegrass world came to the Holiday Inn, and Crowe remembers most of them. "Maria Muldaur, Stephen Stills, Clarence White, Chris Hillman, Rick Roberts—all the Burrito

Brothers—they'd play Eastern Kentucky University and then come see us,"
he said.[11]

"Some people would come purposely," Doyle said.

> Jeannie Shepard, the country singer; she married Benny Birchfield, who did
> that great third part harmony with the Osborne Brothers. [They] used to
> drive up from Nashville during the week, and sit there just to listen to the
> music. There were some Southern Gospel singers used to come through
> and just stop and listen to us sing. They would sit in a corner and order
> coffee, but they were always respectful, never got out of the way.
>
> Curly Sechler used to pull trailers, and he would stop and spend the
> whole evening there, drink coffee, and listen to us pick. George and John
> Shuffler used to come up. George was working with Ralph Stanley and if
> they were doing a gig in Ohio and had a little free time, he'd run down to
> the Holiday Inn. Clarence White came in one night; he was working with
> the Byrds. He and Bobby had worked together in the Kentucky Colonels.[12]

Fiddle player Paul Mullins came down from Middletown, Ohio, and Art
Stamper came over from Louisville. They both sat in numerous times, adding
to the excitement for fans and easing the monotony for band members.

"I had been a fan of the Byrds, then the Flying Burrito Brothers," Frank
Becker said. Becker is a lawyer and photographer in Lexington. "Gram Parsons had left," he said, "and Chris Hillman took over. When they played at
Georgetown College [about twelve miles north of Lexington], some friends
and I bought out the whole first row; it was their second to last concert. J.D.
was one of their idols, [especially] Chris Hillman. Two of them went to the
Holiday Inn with me; J.D. Crowe recognized Hillman from the stage and
asked them to come up and play with them, and they did four songs. It was
just great."

Others who came to the Holiday Inn were "Don McLean, but before he
got famous," J.D. said. "The Goose Creek Symphony—the drummer sat
in with us. The Supremes came in—I don't think they stayed too long. Of
course, Jimmy Martin, Tom T. Hall, Faron Young—his fiddle player played
the whole night—and Gordie Tapp of *Hee Haw.*"[13]

"The Country Gentlemen used to come in and sit in with us," Don Combs
said. "Doyle was with them then. And I remember John Hartford coming in."

"Hank Williams Jr., when he was just starting out, was a bluegrass fan," J.D. said. "He was trying to learn to play the banjo. He had a tape of 'Big Country' in his bus, and we went out there and played until 4:00 a.m."[14]

Frank Schoepf had continued to visit Lexington to hear Crowe, and one night he and Larry Smith (who had played banjo with Del McCoury) were in the audience, and requested "A Letter to Tom," a gentle nineteenth-century "parlor song" brought to bluegrass by the Country Gentlemen. "I knew they did it once in a while," Schoepf said. "There was a noisy bunch at the bar that got louder and louder. They were coming out of a trio, right before a little banjo thing, and Crowe, who never says anything, leaned into the microphone and *screamed*, 'Shut up, God damn it!' The people at the bar were 'Meadowlark' Lemon and another one of the Harlem Globetrotters, and they were really *big*!"

The new Sheraton Inn, at I-75 and the Athens-Boonsboro Road, just east of Lexington, had a stage in their large dining room—more than twice the size of the Red Slipper Lounge—and a bright, elegant atmosphere, with waiters bustling through with flaming platters and champagne buckets. The crowd was even more of a mixture than that at the Holiday Inn: established fans, overnight guests, and those who came to dine, but everyone seemed to enjoy the music.

They had their share of visitors there, too. One was mandolinist David Grisman, who had played traditional bluegrass with Red Allen and was developing his innovative "Dawg" music. He sat in and spent time with Tony. And, of course, Orval Crowe. "I knew Orval quite well," Tony said. "I liked him. He would usually wander in a couple times a week [when we were playing]. If there was ever a proud father, then it was Orval Crowe. He was a very good soul, and I really miss him a lot."

Another visitor was completely out of their sphere. "Aaron Rosand [classical violinist of great reputation] came here in the 1970s for the first time," said George Zack, retired music director and conductor of the Lexington Philharmonic Orchestra.

He stayed at the Sheraton, and after we had finished rehearsing, we went over there to get something to eat. [The New South] started their routine show, and everybody was talking and eating. I realized that Aaron wasn't listening to us; he had turned around and was listening to the band.

"These guys are really good!" he said. "They're not just playing chords; they're playing the music." I didn't know J.D. personally, but had met Ricky, so I took [Rosand] up during a break and said, "Would you like to meet one of the greatest violinists in the world?"

They were excited, even more than Aaron, and he was pretty excited. "Would you like me to join up for a few?" he said. He was exhausted, from travel and rehearsing, but he got up and played with them. They were totally enamored with each other. It went on so long we had to ask them to take Aaron's food back [to the kitchen] and keep it hot.

"I think those guys are going to hit it really big," Aaron said. Every time Aaron came here, he tried to make contact with Ricky or Crowe, but was never able to.

Rosand also made an impression on the New South. "George Zack brought Aaron Rosand to see us at the Sheraton," J.D. said, "and George brought him up and introduced us. We had a good time after the show, and he invited us to come and see him the next night in concert, and we were right there, too. I thoroughly enjoyed that show. That's probably as pretty a tone as I've ever heard come out of a violin."[15]

"We were guests at his concert," Tony said. "My music library was fairly diverse, and I knew of Rosand and his reputation. One of the thrills of my life was to see him walk out on stage, with nobody plugged in, with that many musicians, and him being able to stand there and play that violin where you could hear every note of it."

"He had an affinity for bluegrass," Ricky said, "and loved the old-time fiddle tunes and that kind of thing. He is such a brilliant violinist, and I was so impressed to meet him, and to see his Guarneri violin and his $50,000 fiddle bow. We went and saw him at his concert, and were just blown away with his musical ability."

Jerry Douglas visited the Sheraton, too, "just to play with them some in the middle of the week," he said. "At the same time, they had to go into the TV studio at KET [Kentucky Educational Television] to explain their instruments and play a little. Everybody had on their [stage] shirts—like rayon, a stretchy, shiny material—it was just the times, it was the '70s. [The television show] came out soon after that. I was still playing with the Country Gentlemen, and we came over to Rosine, Kentucky, to play a Bill Monroe festival. Some old fellow came up and said, 'I saw you on TV the other night, playing with J.D. Crowe.'" Jerry interrupted him, "Whoa! Hush! These fellows don't know I'm about to jump ship!"

"The tape," Tony said, "was exceptionally good; the performances were exceptionally tight, and the audio and the video were remarkably good; I think, even to this day, it would be considered a priceless item in the aspects of music reproduction. Of course, we had the weird hair and the weird shirts at the time."

"It was amazing to play with J.D.," Jerry said.

I knew I had gone to another level. This guy whose taste and time and tone were impeccable, rivaled by none; he wrote the book on those things.

J.D. Crowe, in his very subtle way, would give you a lesson. He sort of spoke in parables. He wouldn't tell you, "Don't do it like that," but he would say, "Think about it like this, and listen to what I do and give me your interpretation of what I'm doing." Not in those words, but that's the point that he was always trying to get across—so it's a cohesive piece, and doesn't go off on these different tangents, and you hear the separation in the notes so you know when he's cut off a note, you know when he's letting a note ring, and you can eventually figure out the reason why.

Crowe is known for his timing, first of all, and there's no other tone like that. If you look at the parts of a banjo and how they work together, the head of the banjo is so important, and that's what I hear when I hear him play, I can almost reach out and feel the tension on the head of that banjo. It's explosive. You think it's going to just burst at any time—a big hole is going to show up in the front of his banjo, because it's so, so loud, and the impact of his thumb when it comes down on that fourth string is like—he's done that to me before, he's come up behind me and thumped the head on his banjo when I'm tuning, and just scared me to death. He likes to do that—he likes to play tricks on people. He'd play the practical jokes, but he never hurt us, because he wouldn't put the cigarette load *that* close to your face.

That spring, Tony was able to acquire Clarence White's herringbone Martin guitar; Clarence, his boyhood hero, had parted with the guitar some years previously. "Bobby knew the whole story," Hugh Sturgill said. "Clarence had hocked it to a friend for seven hundred dollars when he went with the Byrds and went back for it later. 'I helped you for friendship,' the guy said, 'and I haven't seen you for a year. I wouldn't sell it back to you for any amount of money.'" When Bobby told him the story after Clarence's death, Hugh loaned Tony the money to fly to California and buy the guitar, which he still owns. Although the guitar was in terrible shape, requiring extensive repair and frequent overhauls, it was important to Tony because of Clarence, who was his boyhood hero, and it is now equally important to guitar fans, because of Tony.

"We left the Sheraton Inn in April of '75," J.D. said, "and started doing road concerts—festivals, clubs, and concerts—as we had done every summer since 1971."[16]

"The New South had a new van," Hugh Sturgill said, "and worked every weekend until they went to Japan. At that time, Larry Sparks, the Seldom Scene, the Country Gentlemen, and the Osbornes went on last [at festivals]. By July, nobody wanted to follow Crowe, and they would think up the most ridiculous reasons why they had to leave a festival early."

"We went to Berryville, Virginia," Jerry said, "and played that festival and blew the place away, just like [Crowe] had when I saw him there four or five years before that. And we went to Japan in September, and we had such a great time, 'cause it was the peak of our popularity and the peak of bluegrass popularity, really, in Japan."

"The Japanese tour was a great trip," Ricky said. "It was really so much fun, it was amazing. We would play thousand-, fifteen-hundred-seat theaters, concert hall–type venues, and the places would be packed. I was really blown away with how many young people came, how many fans there was over there, whether it was the same ones night after night that would follow us around, or if it was different bunches of people every time."

"It was the first time we went to Japan," J.D. said.

We were all excited about that. I'd never been to Japan, and I don't think any of the other guys had. On the way over, we played McCabe's Music Hall in Los Angeles, and Paul's Saloon in San Francisco.[17]

[The Japanese people] will do anything they can to make you welcome. When you get off the plane, they meet you with a limousine and take your instrument. Now, I'm real particular about my banjo. "Do not worry, do not worry," I was told, and I didn't. The only time I saw it was when I was playing. They carried it from hotel to dressing room, and would even open the case, but they wouldn't take it out of the case. You don't have to turn your hand for anything.

The audiences in Japan are fantastic. We played, and I know a lot of them did not understand what we were saying, but they understand the music. Then, of course, quite a few of them *could* understand what we were saying. We always had interpreters; I guess five or six people with us all the time—mainly to keep us out of trouble. The audiences were really great over there; I've never played to audiences as lively and excited as they were.

Japan is a fun place to be; there's lots of fun things to do. We saw gardens—we were over there when everything was in full bloom, and really beautiful. We really didn't have a heck of a lot of time.[18]

The tour, lasting about ten days, kept them busy, "and we worked eight days out of the ten."[19]

"I remember the language barrier," Ricky said. "That was quite a feat for a boy from eastern Kentucky that demolishes the English language to begin with, me trying to talk to a Japanese person. I remember one thing that was funny; it was really, really hot over there. The rooms had no air conditioners. I remember Tony getting to his room and picking up the telephone and saying, 'Ahh, hello, Tony Rice, United States. Room hot, room hot.' And they said, 'Ahh, Mr. Rice, open window, open window!' We had a ball, it was just a great time, and we played a lot of great music. I had no idea they were going to be recording a lot of the shows."

"It wasn't as radically different as you might think," Tony said, "because [bluegrass bands] had been there before us. There was an interest [in bluegrass] there that was really running rampant at the time. The venues, the hotels, and the travel were just like being over here, but the interview segments and signings were like a zoo; it made you feel like a rock star in the United States. That was the only thing that was different—they were all good gigs."

"They'd want a piece of your clothing," J.D. said, "a pick, an autograph. We still talk about how scary that was. They were all just coming at us and wanting *something*. They had to get us out of there in a hurry—you could get injured. They didn't mean to, of course, and it's kind of fun, one time, but I'd rather not have that. I like it a little bit more calm."[20]

"We had to run from the stage to the car," Jerry said. "People were actually trying to tear our shirts off. It was like being the Beatles, and we were a bluegrass band! But we were J.D. Crowe and the New South, the most revered band that there was, in Japan, and that was the difference. I was nineteen years old and experiencing these things on such a high level that I could never repeat that again. I'm glad it happened then, with my friends. You really learn a lot from every band you're in, but that was a landmark, for me."

Thinking back, Ricky observed:

The Japan trip was bittersweet for me. It was like our farewell tour, 'cause right after we got back from Japan, Tony left to go with David Grisman, and Jerry Douglas and I decided that we'd just go ahead and put together a band, Boone Creek. As hard as that was, I knew I had J.D.'s blessing, because that was our deal going in, that I would stay until I put a group together. I would probably have stayed a little longer, if Tony had stayed, my singing partner. I felt like our duets were just so good and I loved singing with him, and the trios were awesome, with J.D., and there was just so much about it that I loved. But with Tony being gone, if I was going to start over again, putting together a band, I'd rather do it for myself.

Ricky and Jerry's departure took Tony by surprise:

I had no idea, when I gave notice to Crowe, that Ricky and Jerry were going to leave and form their own band. I think they thought that the five of us together was such a unique sound that if one person left, it would have interrupted the spirit of what was there. I think, in retrospect, that everybody was ready for a change. The New South, in a short period of time, kind of did what it intended to do. Everybody's sentiments, though unspoken, were basically the same, that individually, we were ready to move on to other pastures.

I know for a fact that Ricky and [Jerry] wanted to do a new format that was very much vocal oriented, and by that time, I had had my fill of singing. Even though I was in perfectly good voice, I wanted to take a break from it. I know that J.D. was ready to move the New South into its own new identity, which was more contemporary, not necessarily to pander to the commercial country market, but he did want that sound.

I remember it was Labor Day weekend, because I had been with the Bluegrass Alliance from Labor Day 1970 to Labor Day 1971, and with Crowe from Labor Day '71 to Labor Day '75, when we played our last show as a band.

"Our last song," J.D. said, "was 'Sin City,' and Tony was standing there with tears running down his face. While we were walking offstage everyone felt pretty sad about the situation, but things have to change."[21]

"What took some of the sting out of the emotion," Tony said, "was that I had already done some extensive rehearsal with David Grisman, and was ready for a change. His music was radically different—it kind of became part of my soul. It wasn't a situation whereby I was leaving one traditional bluegrass band and going into another."

"I felt sorry for J.D." Jerry said. "All of us leaving at the same time. I don't think Ricky and I really wanted to go! We just thought, it's going to change so drastically when Tony goes, if we're going to step out, this is the time we need to do it. We talked to Crowe about it, and he was always like, 'You need to do what you need to do.'"

"I remember," Tony said, "that there was no anger. I don't remember any negativity at any time. The only one I remember being angry was Bobby Slone, because I think Bobby was so locked into that niche, and you could understand his frustration. I knew that him and Crowe were going to remain together, but I didn't know what musical direction Crowe was going to be headed in, and I know Bobby didn't." Tony was relieved that "Crowe was really supportive, and familiar with what I liked about Grisman's music with Richard Greene and John Carlini. Crowe's reaction was basically what mine was: he was in awe of what he heard coming out of a mandolin, a violin, an acoustic guitar, and an acoustic bass. This was something that nobody had even dreamed of doing before, and the music instantly grabbed your attention. Crowe was very encouraging."

"[J.D.] never reacted in front of me," Jerry said, "but I have to think that it hurt, deeply hurt." He continued:

> I really respect him for not throwing in the towel and yelling at us. I think that it was better that we all left at once, though. If we had dribbled this out, like Tony left then Ricky left then I left, he would have been rebuilding. The worst thing you can do as a bandleader is to have to be training people all the time, teaching them your music, the way you do things, the way business is going to be, and it's a real drag. So we did him a favor. J.D. got the chance, then, to start a whole new band, and have a completely new sound. The band wasn't built around the guitar anymore; he didn't have to give away breaks, and there was a lot more banjo coming out of that band [after we left].

"When they left," J.D. said, "I wished them well, and of course, they did well. We all knew what we had at that time, but everybody likes to 'do their own thing,' as they call it."[22]

"When I think about what we did," Ricky said, "in the short amount of time that we had, and then Boone Creek and the two albums we did, how many young groups we influenced with those three albums. That was a very influential time."

CHAPTER 8
THE NEW SOUTH:
BLUEGRASS, COUNTRY,
AND MORE

The album the New South had recorded in January was released in September 1975, as *Rounder 0044,* and created an immediate furor. The cover art was different from most bluegrass albums, and J.D.'s hand, in the band picture, was making what is commonly referred to as "a rude gesture."

"We had a slide one inch square," Ken Irwin said. "It was the only one in which everybody was smiling. That's what we made our decision on. I don't know if the band [seeing the small slide] knew about the finger, but obviously, it showed up when it was a foot square."

"We were kind of on a deadline," J.D. said. "It was cold, we had gotten aggravated, and were just acting the fool. When we got through, that was the best shot. I said, 'We'll send it to Rounder, and if they approve, we'll use it.' Well, they did. I got to thinking about it and called Ken [Irwin] and said, 'On this album cover, what we need to do is print ten thousand albums and change the cover.' I had this bright idea of making it kind of a [collector's item]. I know for a fact that some of those albums, they were paying as high as thirty-five or fifty dollars for, because it was out of print—so it worked."[1]

As soon as people opened the album, however, they forgot the cover, and many of them forgot what they had earlier learned about bluegrass music. The timing, the force, the tightness of the vocals, and the talent of the musicians blended to deliver a new kind of bluegrass that would have a pervading influence.

Dave Haney, in his article "Rounder, 15 Years on the Edge," reported, "The New South album inaugurated a polished, uptown but tradition-based style of bluegrass that attracted a whole new crop of musicians and listeners."[2] Haney, a bluegrass musician himself, is presently professor of interdisciplinary studies and Appalachian studies at Appalachian State University; his graduate-level course in Appalachian studies, Bluegrass Traditions, includes heavy emphasis on *Rounder 0044*, which he calls "the recording that changed bluegrass." "[The New South] made the kind of innovation that Flatt and Scruggs had done," Haney said, "by absorbing all kinds of cultural influences, not setting out to change [others], but saying, 'We're playing this music and that's how it's going to sound.' These people realized their link to traditional bluegrass, and made that connection intelligent. They had a different kind of timing, and all bands since have used that timing."[3]

"The New South idea aimed at a broader market," Ken Irwin said. "They were thinking they were going to be something very different, in terms of sound and how they were going to be viewed. [The name] 'New South' was a statement of that: southern, but new."

"The New South sound," Sam Bush said, "is probably the sound more young bands have copied than any other in the last thirty years. Younger people have listened to and copied Crowe more than they have Earl Scruggs. Like Mark O'Connor took Benny Thomasson's fiddle style and ran with it, it's the same thing Crowe did with Scruggs. J.D.'s got all sorts of other influences than Scruggs."

"When you saw the '75 band," Barry Crabtree said, "or heard the album, that pretty much changed bluegrass for everybody; it was a whole new sound."

"That album kind of reenergized things," Gene Knight said. He was teaching banjo in a music store when 0044 came out. "I'd be back in the practice rooms, and they'd put on that amazing cut of 'Sally Goodin.' I couldn't keep my mind on what I was doing. There are a lot of people I've admired, and still admire, but J.D.'s still the man. He knows when, where, and what *not* to play is just as important as knowing what to play."

Rounder 0044 transformed not only bluegrass but Rounder Records itself. As Ken Irwin indicated, "It was extremely important in developing Rounder as a recording significance in the bluegrass industry. We were considered by the bluegrass community at the time to be a bunch of hippies, but when J.D. recorded for us, it gave us legitimacy in the bluegrass audience. J.D. became, perhaps, the first act a number of labels would have loved to have, and he chose Rounder; his stamp of approval was of more significance than money."

A review of *Rounder 0044* appeared in the November issue of *Bluegrass Unlimited*. Musicians and performances are lauded and the arrangements are called "faultless," but the Gordon Lightfoot and Fats Domino songs are singled out as "forced and relatively synthetic," and there is a homily on the future of bluegrass "being within the context of relatively traditional, or traditionally oriented, material."[4]

Wikipedia, the online user-supported encyclopedia, reviewed *Rounder 0044* as "a landmark in Bluegrass music," and said, "This one album changed the nature and direction of bluegrass music [so that everything since must] be viewed in light of this album."[5]

Twenty-five years later, the album (now a compact disc) is still influential, and J.D. Crowe and the New South are still playing and recording material from whatever sources they choose.

In re-forming his band, J.D. first asked Harley Allen, son of Red Allen, to play guitar, and Taylorsville, Kentucky, native Glenn Lawson, a Bluegrass Alliance alumnus, to play mandolin. When Allen did not work out, Glenn moved to guitar, and Crowe looked for another mandolin player. "I never wanted to play the mandolin," Glenn said, "but Lonnie [Peerce] told me the Alliance needed a mandolin player, and when [J.D.] asked me to play guitar, I was really glad. Then Jimmy [Gaudreau] came and we started rehearsing. Jimmy was a monster musician."

Gaudreau, originally from Rhode Island, had experience with the Country Gentlemen, Eddie Adcock's II Generation, and later with Keith Whitley in Country Store. "Word came through the bluegrass grapevine that Crowe was in the market for a tenor-singing mandolin player," he said. "When I started with [J.D.] it was like jumping on a freight train. Crowe went to the Jimmy Martin school of bluegrass, and has that Martin drive. He wants that thing like a freight train all the time, moving on down the track."

"I remember working with a metronome when I first started," Glenn said. "[Crowe] made everybody learn that timing. My thing was always vocals; I actually learned what precision timing was. You can't do anything in music without it. [J.D.] doesn't teach in any traditional sense, but you can learn a lot. You've got the right eyebrow raising up if you miss something, and you've got the glare. It was the biggest learning experience of my life. Our personalities did jell, and we got really, really good. Maybe that's why four sets a night didn't seem so hard."

J.D. said about all the band members he has trained, "They probably learned from me like I did from Jimmy and them. It's not verbal instruction, just watching the people that have done it before and have been through the experience. You don't know it's happening; it's a natural process of learning."[6]

"I always let the lead singer do what he's more relaxed with and does better," Crowe said. "I've never made any new singer coming in try to sound like the ones who had left. That's virtually impossible; you cannot do that. The people in the band at that time, I knew were a little different, so we worked out what we could do best as a group."[7]

"I was more of a folk singer," Glenn said, "and the music took a turn in that direction. It was a real switch for Crowe, and some people didn't like it. Pickers didn't like it, but a lot of people loved it. A lot of college kids in the clubs we played were really grooving on us. Some of the songs we did regularly were 'San Antonio Rose,' 'Lonesome Feeling,' 'Hickory Wind' [Gram Parsons], 'Brand-New Tennessee Waltz,' 'Gone at Last,' 'My Window Faces South,' and 'You Can Share My Blanket' [by Lexington songwriter Steve Brines]."

Most of these were not from Crowe's previous repertoire, nor were Jimmy's specialties, "Red Rocking Chair" (from Charlie Monroe) and "Sea of Heartbreak" (recorded by Don Gibson). Of course, they performed instrumentals, classics, and some of Crowe's standards, but this seems a deliberate separation from the material played and recorded by the 1975 band.

Although the band worked well together, some audience members were upset. "I came in after Ricky and Tony, one of the greatest bands ever," Glenn said. "People took a lot of pains to come up to me and say, 'You're not Tony Rice.' The first year or so in that band, I took a lot of flack; Crowe was playing the 'Crowe-Bro' [a resophonic instrument with a 5-string neck] and was into exploring whatever there was to do. People just didn't like it; they wanted to come in and hear that driving 5-string. [They] would come up and tell him to put that thing down. I think even J.D. suffered a little bit."

Nothing, however, kept away the crowds. "We worked all the time," Jimmy said, "four sets a night in various Holiday Inns. We worked the Ramada Inn in Frankfort, and the Holiday Inn and the Great Midwestern Music Hall in Louisville. We'd work about a month, then go somewhere else."

Terry Baucom remembers living and working in Lexington when he played with Douglas and Skaggs in Boone Creek. "Crowe and them were playing the same places [we played]. When I was off, I went to see them and sat in [on fiddle], and really observed [Crowe] closely. Most of the time, we'd be playing and they'd be playing right down the street. We'd have fifteen minutes off and we'd go see them; they'd have fifteen minutes off and come see us. This went on the whole time I was in Lexington. It was a good time for bluegrass."

"We opened a Holiday Inn in Louisville that seated three hundred people," Glenn said. "We played there three nights a week and packed it out every night. In the winters, we played the Holiday Inns and Arnie's Pizza Lounge in Lafayette, Indiana."

Steve Cooley said of Louisville's club scene, "The Storefront Congregation was open at that time." It and the Great Midwestern Bluegrass Music Hall often hosted the New South; in summers, bluegrass festivals all over the country welcomed them. Crowe's popularity and drawing power had not diminished, and the new band appealed to a different crowd as well.

"Jimmy Gaudreau and Glenn Lawson were probably the most entertaining band J.D. ever had," felt Hugh Sturgill. "They carried on an intelligent conversation with the audience, and could tear up any bar crowd."

"J.D. loved the comedy," Glenn said.

I remember nights when we had them rolling, and he enjoyed that, and let his hair down. Some of the most fun I had with him was when we did those comedy things, and then would hit the good music really hard.

Entertainment was a big part of what we did with Crowe. We had a ribald song, "The Mailman," we did with a glass, which gives you a kind of Rudy Vallee sound. It was not good for festivals, but worked well in clubs. We laughed a lot, we really did, but with J.D., the serious thing was the banjo, and his music. No matter what we did, we'd always go back to that.

One joke got old, Crowe and them loading my cigarettes. I was shell-shocked, they loaded so much. One night in Maryland, I got offstage and lit up and exploded right in front of the audience. I was furious—it almost made me stop smoking.

Jimmy agreed:

Crowe was a prankster. After a while, it's not so funny. So we would go out and find our own cigarette loads. J.D. would say, "You'll never get me!" and we took that as a challenge. J.D. smoked those Hava-Tampa Jewels; I bought some, took a penknife and opened up the cellophane wrapper [loaded it], and sealed it back. Sure enough, it exploded, and he was not too happy about it. "I'm gonna get my pipe!" he'd say. So we threw a load in his loose pipe tobacco. "How did you do that?" he asked, and I said, "I didn't—you did!"

During the festival season in 1976, we were still traveling by Dodge van; it was another couple of years before the Winnebago. Even in the summer months, we did some inn gigs. There were no holes in the calendar. [Working with Crowe was] a great move for me musically. It sharpened my chops to work with a banjo player of that caliber.

That summer they worked a festival in Canada, where J.D. served as a judge in the World Banjo Competition. The winner of the junior division was thirteen-year-old David Talbot, who had grown up in Ontario and learned to play from his father's Flatt and Scruggs records. Isolated from mainstream bluegrass, he heard Crowe for the first time. "When the New South came on," he said, "and Crowe started playing, it was like something had hit me in the side of the head. I told my dad, 'This is just like those Flatt and Scruggs records.'" He bought *Rounder 0044* and the current issue of *Banjo Newsletter* with Crowe on the cover and still describes the weekend as "magical." Talbot moved to Nashville in 1998 to play banjo with Larry Cordle's Lonesome Standard Time, was a cofounder of the Grascals, and works for country superstar Dolly Parton. He cites Crowe as one of his major influences, after Scruggs.[8]

In February 1977, J.D., Glenn, Jimmy, and Bobby recorded for Rounder *You Can Share My Blanket*, with a full complement of Nashville sidemen. The title song and "The Hurting When You Go" were by Brines, collaborating with Sam Bush on the latter; "Hesitating Too Long" and "Are You Sad Tonight" were written by Glenn Lawson; and the rest were "As Tears Go By" (Mick Jagger), "Ten Miles from Natchez" (Graves & Lambert), "Did She Mention My Name?" (Lightfoot), "I Don't Know You" (J. Dawson), "Hickory Wind"

(Gram Parsons), and Don Williams's "Gypsy Woman." "You Can Share My Blanket" and "Did She Mention My Name?" were also on a 45-rpm single.

Bobby Slone returned to fiddle on the album and played fiddle onstage from then on, with a succession of electric bass players. "We played the first show in Missouri," he said, "with me back on fiddle. I was nervous and wanted an upright bass in my hand so bad! Some of those songs we'd played for ten years, I'd never played on fiddle. I felt like everybody was looking at me and waiting for me to tear loose on fiddle, and I knew I wasn't going to do it. After about three months, the shaking went off a little bit."[9]

At the Berkshire Mountains Bluegrass Festival in June, a recording was made of several bands; the New South did "I Don't Believe You've Met My Baby," a Louvin Brothers song, with Bobby on fiddle and newcomer Mike Gregory on electric bass.

By that time, two albums taped at Tokyo concerts during the 1975 tour had been released (Towa TWA 106-S and Trio PA-6326) and were available in the United States as imports. *Rounder 0044* had sold out its initial pressing and was reissued with a different jacket, this time named *J.D. Crowe and the New South* instead of simply *The New South*. King Bluegrass was purchased by Rebel Records, and *Ramblin' Boy* was reissued as *Blackjack*.

During the summer of 1977, an eight-program television miniseries, *Bluegrass, Bluegrass,* was taped at a dinner theater in Lexington, Kentucky, by Kentucky Educational Television. Bands, chosen from those living or appearing nearby, ranged from Ralph Stanley to the Newgrass Revival; capacity crowds were knowledgeable and excited—this was something rare for bluegrass.[10]

The series was a great success, with several encore presentations, and was picked up by other PBS stations across the Southeast. Other bands on the series included the Highwoods String Band, the Falls City Ramblers, the McLain Family Band, Stoneycreek, Boone Creek, and J.D. Crowe and the New South.

"At that time," J.D. said, "I was leaning more toward progressive bluegrass, if you want to call it that—actually, it wasn't bluegrass—I just call it 'American music,' combining several elements. You could probably call it 'country grass.'"[11]

Reviewed in the August 1978 issue of *Bluegrass Unlimited, You Can Share My Blanket* (Rounder 0096) was damned with faint praise: bluegrass was warned to be wary of Nashville "slickers," lest they "sell you choruses and orchestras," and although the de-emphasis on banjo and fiddle was deplored, the overall sound was praised as "crystal clear and very full," and the songs were described as "fresh." The album was described as similar to the 1973 New South Starday album, which had finally been released in 1977.[12]

After two and a half years, Glenn left the band. "My last show," he said, "was in Johnson City, Tennessee. Everything just clicked; I was just loose and doing what I did, and when we got offstage, J.D. said, 'That's the way it's supposed to be,' and I said, 'I'm giving you my notice.' It was a heck of a time in my life as a young man," he continued, "playing with a precision band and traveling. I felt like I was on top of the world, and generally had a great time doing it."

Glenn was replaced by Keith Whitley, from Sandy Hook, Kentucky, who had been on stage most of his life. As teenagers, he and Ricky Skaggs worked with Ralph Stanley; later, Keith was Stanley's lead singer twice, separated by his venture in Country Store.

"Keith started the latter part of 1978, in the fall," J.D. said. "We were playing in Maryland, and he played his last show with Ralph and rode back in the camper with me. He stayed with me for four years.[13] I remember Keith telling me, while he was still with Ralph, 'I'd like to do something a little different, and why I'd like to join the New South is because you guys do different things.' I thought that was a good compliment."[14]

Keith's warm, rich country voice was distinctly different from any of Crowe's prior lead singers, and, as previous singers had done, affected the overall sound of the band and the choice of material. He was also a gifted mimic and could imitate Lefty Frizzell (one of his heroes), Merle Haggard, and Lester Flatt. Lester enjoyed the parody, and the two of them could sometimes be found talking backstage, Keith sounding as much like Lester as Lester did.[15]

Keith told the story of traveling on the interstate one dark night after Lester's death, and, spying Earl Scruggs's bus in the other lane, saying over the CB radio in Lester's drawl, "Earl, I'm back." It was never reported whether Earl heard him, but the story demonstrates Keith's sense of humor.

The band's stage attire took on a western appearance, following the current "look." Their high-crowned hats had deeply curled brims and were accompanied by vests and boots. Keith and J.D. sported neatly trimmed beards.

"Keith Whitley," J.D. said, "probably is one of the finest singers I've ever listened to. He was unique; he kind of patterned his style after Lefty Frizzell, Merle Haggard, and George Jones, with a little Johnny Paycheck thrown in. Keith was a singer's singer—he could sing any style, it didn't matter what it was, and he could do it so good that whatever style he was doing was just as good as any other style. He was a phenomenal musician. I just wish he had had a chance to become the legend he could have been, had he stayed another ten years."[16]

Keith's voice was full of emotion; it was easy to believe that whatever song he was singing was out of his own heartbreaking experience, and, wrapped around by J.D.'s fluid banjo backup, his singing could touch the most hard-hearted listener. Although the emotion was natural ("Crowe is a very emotional banjo player," David Talbot said, and "it comes out in his playing"),[17] the effect was achieved through professional skill and technique.

"If Keith is singing a song," J.D. said at the time, "I'm backing up; then, if Bobby comes in to back up on fiddle, I'll back off and back up what [Bobby] is doing, just to fill in. You'll hear nothing to take away from the singer or whoever's out front, so that what you hear is nothing but a good rhythm pattern. Just a nod and we know what's going on. You always have to be aware of what's going on; that's what makes some bands such a pleasure to play with."[18]

From his earliest years, J.D. has preferred backup to instrumentals. It was Flatt and Scruggs's "whole band sound" that drew him in; Scruggs's banjo was only part of that sound, and Scruggs's backup was as important as his breaks.

"Backup makes a singer want to sing," J.D. said. "If it's another guy taking a break, it makes him want to play. What you do is complement them and make the whole thing sound better."[19]

"[J.D.] is possibly the most rhythmic banjo player there ever has been, or ever will be," David Talbot said. "He never plays the banjo to forsake the rhythm of not just the banjo, but the rhythm that he produces in his playing is always totally supportive of the overall band sound." During a mandolin solo, Talbot observed, "Crowe goes into this really wonderful rhythmic vamping, where he'd go back and forth between the two chord positions in the same chord. It's like a drum. His playing is very much a drum for the group, too, in terms of the rhythmic power of his playing. The power and rhythm of his playing is unequaled; that's just one of the things that gives his band a real edge."[20]

"In J.D.'s sound," Ken Irwin said, "timing is extremely important, then drive and tone. Beyond that, there's a lot in terms of him as a band leader; in terms of repertoire—I think he's very underrated in that—and in terms of his choice of musicians; and his views of what bluegrass is and his willingness to make music he feels is appropriate to a particular song." Moreover, "Once he's decided on a singer, it's all about the singer and the song: whatever enhances or makes that song better should be used, and whatever doesn't should be left out." Ken added, "J.D. also has incredible taste. There's not a single solo you'd say, 'I wish he hadn't done that.' I think he brings taste to his band and his band members. Everybody talks about his timing and tone, and they tend to leave out his taste."

Bobby Slone, describing the band during that time, said, "With the band we've got now, we're more capable of doing anything we want—Keith has such a good voice."[21]

"I love [traditional bluegrass]," J.D. said, "but I am a firm believer that if two or three bands [on a program] do nothing but straight 'grass, and the last band comes out and does a variety of material, I know from my experience that although the others will be enjoyed, the [band] that does variety will go over better."[22]

In 1978, the Holiday Inn North, in Lexington, had a new manager, who wanted to bring back bluegrass to what was now the Post Lounge. Six bands would come for a month each during the winter, with housing provided. The New South, after an absence of four years, was scheduled for December and was greeted by a large banner reading, "Bobby Slone for President." Buttons with the slogan "I love Bobby Slone" were passed out to a room-stretching crowd who were thrilled to see Crowe's return.[23]

It was a well-deserved tribute. By this time, Bobby had been with J.D. for fourteen years, always smiling, dependable, and approachable. Fans who were shy about speaking to J.D. could count on a pleasant few words with Bobby, and probably some sort of a joke.

"Bobby Slone," J.D. said, "there is not another one like him. One of the finest guys, musicians, personality-wise, you couldn't have a better guy as a band member—or anything, for that matter. He's just so reliable; never any problems. We never had a problem. Bobby was very serious, but he was also a prankster." Of Bobby's influence, J.D. asserted that it "was probably more than any of us realized, because he was the one that was really stable. I know I used to talk to him about things, and I think all the guys in the band at one time or another talked to Bobby about things other than music. He was just the kind of guy you could go to and discuss things with, and nothing else was ever said about it."[24]

"Bobby was the guy we'd go to, to complain about anything," Jerry Douglas said, "and Bobby would just go, 'No, no, don't worry about it; Crowe's a fine man; he knows what's going on. You'll never meet another guy who's going to be better to you than J.D. Crowe.' He was J.D.'s champion. He would stand silently in the background, knowing everything that was going on, and was always the first one to point out anything funny that was getting ready to happen with J.D. or Tony, who were the two guys who were always sort of digging a hole for themselves as we would go around [taking breaks]— especially Tony, not J.D. so much, because he was on another level."

"[A friend] and I used to watch J.D.," Gene Knight said, "and see if we could catch him making a mistake. If J.D. kind of backed himself into a corner, he could always find a way out."

"Bobby had been through all of these bands with J.D.," Jerry said, "and had seen everything, so he was just watching us, the young Turks, fall on our faces, but he'd be the first one over to pick us up. I love that guy—Bobby Slone is one of the sweetest people I've ever met."

Early in 1979, J.D., Keith, Jimmy, and Bobby recorded *My Home Ain't in the Hall of Fame* (Rounder 0103). Ohioan Steve Bryant, who had been in Boone Creek, had replaced Mike Gregory on electric bass.

Again a departure from traditional bluegrass, the music is supplemented by steel and drums and includes a fair number of country songs. The title song, from Merle Haggard, is followed by "(I'll Be Your) Stepping Stone" (recorded by George Jones), "She's Gone, Gone, Gone" (Harlan Howard), "Railroad Lady" (Jimmy Buffett), "Sin City," Flatt and Scruggs's classic "Will You Be Lonesome Too?" (by Alton Delmore), "Lady" and "Showboat Gambler" (Dan Seals), "Tennessee Blues," and "My Window Faces the South."

Setting aside Keith's haunting, smoky vocals and several powerful trios, this recording could be used as a tutorial for banjo players. Crowe plays some of his most subtle and eloquent backup, and his breaks on the slow numbers have a gentle, gliding touch that is a far cry from a banjo's usual percussive impact.

Charles Wolfe, in his book *Kentucky Country*, said the song "My Home Ain't in the Hall of Fame" has become "an anthem, not only for Crowe, but for like-minded young experimentalists" who have "little respect for the so-called 'Nashville sound.'" Wolfe reported, "Some critics have compared Crowe's band to the so-called Outlaws (Waylon Jennings, Willie Nelson) in country music, men who aggressively and purposefully set out to change the music."[25]

Those who have followed Crowe's work closely know that he had no intention—even no interest—in changing anyone's music but his own. As he has reiterated, "I just like to do something different."

Relegated to the "Additional Releases" section of the reviews, normally the spot for new bands, or those who have not quite gotten it together, *Bluegrass Unlimited*'s May 1980 review of *My Home Ain't in the Hall of Fame* dismisses the recording as a clone of *You Can Share My Blanket* (which, when reviewed, was called similar to the 1973 Starday *New South* album [SLP-489], despite the fact that the two—or three—albums had different personnel, different kinds of material, and different treatments).[26]

Frets' brief review referred to it as "progressive bluegrass" and praised the "well-blended vocals and tight picking."[27]

In the "Callous Thumb" section of the October 2002 *Banjo Newsletter*, it was noted that *My Home Ain't in the Hall of Fame* had been reissued on CD, with "legendary vocalist Keith Whitley." The recording "combined the band's love of bluegrass with classic honky-tonk and western swing influences," with "Whitley bridging the gap between Crowe's various influences beautifully and effortlessly."[28]

The *All Music Guide* review of *Hall of Fame*, shown on the Billboard Web site, states, "[The] sound on this 1978 recording was completely different from most of what was then being called 'progressive bluegrass.'" It explains, "Basically, this is a honky tonk album with a banjo and a few bluegrass numbers. Many of these arrangements work beautifully. The combination of Crowe's brilliant banjo picking and Whitley's even more brilliant singing is pretty much unbeatable."

"In 1979," J.D. said, "the New South, consisting of myself, Keith Whitley, Jimmy Gaudreau, Bobby Slone, and Steve Bryant, went back to Japan, and worked some of the same venues we did in '75. The reception was very close to what the first one was—it was great. There was a live album recorded at the time, and I remember thinking, 'I sure wish that this turns out with a better mix than the first time,' and, thank goodness, it did. I was very pleased with it. It was strictly live; there was no overdubs and no editing, nothing; it was exactly like it went down."[29]

Rounder 0159, recorded on April 18, 1979, in Tokyo, was released in 1987 as *Live in Japan* and given a highlight review in the January 1988 issue of *Bluegrass Unlimited*. "One of the most satisfying live albums that I have heard," the reviewer said. "All-out bluegrass music played by people who know not only how to do it, but what it's all about. [They] play . . . with expertise, finesse, and carefully controlled abandon."[30]

That summer, Jimmy left the band to join Glenn Lawson, Béla Fleck, and Mark Schatz (both from the band Tasty Licks) to form "Spectrum." Jimmy's replacement was Pennsylvania multi-instrumentalist and tenor singer Gene Johnson, who had been with Cliff Waldron, Eddie Adcock's II Generation, and Night Sun, before leaving the road.

"When Crowe called," Gene said, "I asked, 'Who's singing lead now?' and Crowe said, 'Keith Whitley.' I wish it had been almost anybody else! I thought about it for two weeks; I always enjoyed being around Keith, but I had a wife and two kids and there was not a lot of money in bluegrass, going back on the road. I knew I wasn't going to move down there; I would be going back and forth." He continued:

> Most of the time, I drove down the night before—probably a seven hours' drive. If we only had a few days between [jobs], I stayed at J.D.'s, Keith's, or Bobby Slone's house a lot. If there was time to spend a few days at home, I did that. When I stayed at Keith's house, a lot of times I'd sit and play with him.
>
> I knew all the time Keith had the voice to make it in Nashville; it's amazing how many people there are in Nashville who played with J.D., people who have been through his band. It was surprising how much

country-tinged music we did in J.D.'s band, with Keith's singing. That's a credit to J.D.; he can entertain a bluegrass audience with a variety of music. With a singer like Keith around, I tried to stay away from singing lead as much as possible; I was always into harmony. I got a lot of response from "Sin City," a song where the tenor is the lead, and I would sing it strong and leadlike.

I remember certain nights when everything would click. That's all the encouragement Keith needed to sing his heart out. He'd give you a little side look, a little look in his eye like "Is this as good as it gets?" and then you just couldn't play long enough.

The good nights were the majority; it's hard to pick out any particular ones. We played the Birchmere every three months; it was one of those places we liked to play. There were good audiences, a lot of pickers.

Crowe's got the drive that makes it fun to play with him. I don't know what it is he does, exactly, but something about his timing really encourages you to play well and makes it easy to play well. Everybody knows Crowe's got the tone, but what he can do for you when he's laying it in behind you, you can't beat that. He's still my favorite banjo player, and I've played with a lot of great ones.

Gene didn't smoke, but the jokes with cigarette loads went on. And on.

In the frigid, snowy winter of 1979–80, the New South returned to the Holiday Inn for a month, but that was the last season of bluegrass there. Brian Powell was the bartender in the Post Lounge from 1978 until 1982:

After bluegrass, they brought in "Outlaw Country," bands I couldn't stand, and I left. I was there when they voted bluegrass out, and I was the only one who voted for it. At that time, [Holiday Inn] had a slogan, "No Surprises."

Crowe was a kind of quiet type. We'd get to talking after [their] show, and he was real friendly after he had accepted you—but not from the stage. One time, we were talking about [the suitability of] playing and singing gospel music in a tavern, and Crowe said, "It's the only place some of 'em are going to hear it."

"[He] brought me a gallon of moonshine in a plastic milk jug on New Year's Eve. I said, "Crowe, is this any good?" and he said, "It must be. I run my lawn mower on it." He was pretty much a teetotaler at that time.

In the summer of 1980, "I got a phone call from Tony," J.D. said, "and he said, 'Hey, man, I've got to do a bluegrass album [for Rounder]. Would you

be interested in picking the banjo on it?' and I said, 'Yeah, where're we going to do it?' and he said, 'We'll do it out here in California.' So I said, "Well,
who else you got on the gig?'"[31] Tony chose for the session Crowe, Doyle
Lawson, Todd Phillips, and legendary fiddle player Bobby Hicks, who, at the
beginning of his long and illustrious career, had played and recorded with
Monroe in the 1950s.

"We were all playing acoustic music," Doyle said. He explained:

> Probably Tony was a little further out than the rest of us. They said J.D.
> was playing "country 'grass" and I was playing "contemporary music,"
> Tony was playing "alternative music," and Bobby Hicks was playing with
> Ricky Skaggs when [Skaggs] had his country career going. Everybody had
> a different label, but all of our roots were deep into bluegrass. Tony called
> and said, "I want to do a bluegrass record, right straight down the middle,
> traditional bluegrass, because I want people to know where our love is,
> and where our roots are."
>
> J.D. and I met and flew out together, and on the way, we made a list of
> songs, and when we got there, Tony had a list, and we started weeding
> them out—"Who knows this one?" and "We know this one; we know that
> one." We ran through them once or twice, and went to the studio and
> recorded them.[32]

Tony's idea for the session was, "Rather than isolate everybody," he said,
"we would sit real close, facing each other, where we had eye contact and
nobody overdubbed anything."

"The atmosphere in the studio when we were doing those albums was
great," J.D. said. "The feeling, the being together. We had worked together
so much we could read each others' minds. We could make eye contact, so
we all knew what was going on. A lot of it was live, and was done in one
take, maybe two takes. When you know the material, and you've got good
musicians that know the material, you should not have to do it more than
one or two times."[33]

"It was going to be a Tony Rice record," Ken Irwin said. "They got there
and started working, and Tony saw it was more than that—everybody contributed significantly, and it should be shared. Doing all those older songs
with top-quality people and an updated sound, in the process of making the
record, Tony saw it as a series."

Tony agreed:

> I decided that it didn't sound so much like a Tony Rice bluegrass album as
> it did sound like a *band*; since there wasn't a band, you couldn't give the
> album a band title; what I came up with was *The Bluegrass Album,* because
> that's precisely what it ended up being.
>
> The concept of the first two volumes was to go back to 1945, with Flatt
> and Scruggs and Bill Monroe playing together on the *Grand Ole Opry* and
> on those old Columbia 78s. Think about it, nobody had done that since
> 1946—that sound had not been re-created by anybody. Period. Nobody
> had even come close. I thought it would sure be nice if somebody could
> resurrect this lost era of bluegrass music that the last two generations of
> bluegrass musicians don't even know exists. It's unbelievable how many
> musicians do not know how good that sound was.

A brief, unusual review of the first volume appeared in the March 1982
Frets Magazine, concentrating on the top-notch personnel and using an anal-
ogy of great golfers; it is complimentary but not specific.[34]

"I felt pretty good about the recording," Doyle said. "I thought it was
really good. I'd never sang with Tony until then, but Tony was such a great
lead singer it was very easy to sing with him, and the timbre of our voices, I
thought, meshed well, they had a good blend, and Crowe's an unsung hero
when it comes to baritone singing. He can fit his voice and blend it in where
you hardly know it's there—except when it isn't, and then you say, 'Well,
what's missing?' That's quite an ability, to be able to do that."[35]

"I wasn't on the first [*Bluegrass Album*] and kind of wondered," Jerry said,
"but then I listened to the record, and thought, 'I'm so glad I'm not on this
record, and I know why they didn't ask me to be on it, and I'm glad they
didn't, because this covers an era that had no Dobro in it, and to me, it would
be sacrilegious to put it there.' As they went on into the Flatt and Scruggs
era that probably had Josh Graves on it, it would be natural that a Dobro be
involved, and that was fine with me."

Eventually, there were six "Album Band" albums, each of them paying
tribute to a certain facet or period of early bluegrass music. "The order that
the Bluegrass Album Band records are in makes perfect sense," Jerry said,
"as the material progresses and gets into different areas of human strife, and
then the final one, the instrumental one."

"We did the instrumental album," J.D. said, "because Tony's voice had just given out on him, and he was not able to sing anymore, like he used to. We just decided to do an instrumental album, because we knew that would be the last one. That was also a fun project, 'cause I got to hear two of the best, greatest fiddle players that ever was, Vassar Clements and Bobby Hicks."[36]

"I had no idea that [the Album Band recordings] would have the impact that they did," Tony said, "in terms of the attention that they brought. It's almost like the first of those six volumes spawned a new regeneration of 5-string banjo players that sought after that J.D. Crowe dynamic range, and that kind of drive, and that tone, and that deliberation. All of a sudden you've got a few hundred fiddle players overnight [trying to play] like Bobby Hicks, with that power—the same power that J.D. Crowe played the 5-string banjo with."

"Neither I nor any of the other guys had any idea," Doyle said, "that that recording would make such an impact at that time. That surprised me, because I thought *everybody* had listened to the first-generation people. The kids would come to us and ask, 'Did you write that song?' and I would say, 'No! I didn't write "Blue Ridge Cabin Home!" If you like what we did, go back and listen to the real deal.' All we were doing was paying tribute to guys that blazed the trail, and to show people that our love was for authentic bluegrass music."[37]

Album Band sessions took place in California, Virginia, and Nashville and spanned the years from 1980 to 1996. During this period there were several concerts that brought the musicians together, but between those, they were all playing their own music. The New South flew to distant jobs, but until 1982 traveled the eastern half of the United States in a Winnebago camper Crowe purchased in 1978.

"J.D. wanted to customize [the Winnebago] to how we used it," Gene Johnson said. He continued:

> Since I'd been a carpenter, I said, "I'll do it for you." I put the whole thing together with pretty heavy screws—I noticed later that those screws were sticking out [through the metal sides], and we had a kind of porcupine. It made things quite comfortable, though, with more bunk room; you didn't have to just sit and endure the ride. There was a lot of humor to be had [in the band], a lot of funny stuff when we traveled in the camper.

We all drank way too much during those times. On reflection, we could have been more helpful, but I never saw Keith drink more than anyone else, unless he was depressed, and then he was into a bottle. That causes stress for everybody in the band, when you don't have someone to replace him—you can't go on without a guitar.

I remember when I first met Keith, back when he was about fifteen. He had a pretty high voice—he was a tenor, and a couple of years later, his voice was quite a lot lower. Somebody had told him if he'd drink straight whiskey and smoke cigarettes, it would lower his voice. I wish they hadn't done that—it took his life.

I left [The New South] in early 1981 strictly for monetary reasons. David Bromberg offered me a job with good day pay and all road expenses. That was the one thing about playing with J.D.—it cost me an arm and a leg to drive down.

Gene eventually moved to Nashville and became part of "Diamond Reo," which celebrated its twentieth anniversary in 2009.

Gene was followed by Campton, Kentucky, mandolin player Wendy Miller, who had been eight years with Larry Sparks, toured France with banjo player Mike Lilly, and worked three years with the Russell Brothers. Wendy had heard Crowe at the Holiday Inn and remembered people saying,

"Let's go down to Lexington and listen to J.D. Crowe." That says something right there. It was always just "J.D. Crowe," not the band.[38]

Crowe's just an incredible musician, and it was fun to stand beside him and try to keep up with him. He used to challenge us; man, he was burning it. But it was great; good years, playing beside Keith Whitley's singing and J.D.'s banjo playing.[39] Keith was one of the best singers in the United States, and the talent just flowed from one side to the other. It was unbelievable. I thought the world of Keith and J.D. Playing with somebody of that stature gave you a good feeling, 'cause you knew it was going to be a good show. [J.D.] sort of breathed fire into you.[40]

With J.D., when you walk on the stage, you're gonna get J.D. Crowe; he's the best—he's incredible. All you've got to worry about is doing your part. I always admired him—he could kick off a song that maybe we hadn't done in a year or two, and get exactly the right timing and the right tempo, never miss it. It just seemed like it stayed perfect in his memory. Sometimes we'd do an old Jimmy Martin tune, and Crowe would kick it exactly like you'd heard it on the album thirty years ago, so you wouldn't have to practice it—just play it like it was on the record. That always amazed me. I think that's the mark of a great musician, the feeling for music, getting it right in your mind before you do in your fingers.[41]

The New South's next album, *Somewhere Between,* was recorded in 1981, with J.D., Keith, Wendy, Bobby Slone, and Steve Bryant, plus studio musicians on electric guitar, steel, drums, and piano, and the Jordanaires (famous as Elvis Presley's backup singers). "There'll probably be some of our old fans that'll be disappointed," J.D. said at the time, "because we're not doing hard-core 'grass. I'm going to do some different things."[42]

"I always knew Keith wanted to do country [music]," J.D. said later, "and I knew he could, if he just had the breaks, and I knew how hard it was to get that, in Nashville. So I kicked a few things around in my head about producing an album—back then we called them 'albums'—with him singing more country-ish songs. I went to Nashville, and talked to some songwriters and got some songs, and he came up with some songs that he liked, and we got that album together." J.D. concluded, "That was probably the thing that helped him get his contract with RCA. There again, I knew what was going to happen. I hated to lose him as a lead singer, but I knew where he belonged, and if I could be of any help to do that, that's what I wanted to do."[43]

"Most of *Somewhere Between,*" Wendy said, "was concentrated on getting the lead [vocal] down. There wasn't a lot of banjo picking or mandolin picking on it, 'cause it was mostly a showcase for Keith, a little different, had a country touch to it."[44]

"I only played banjo on two cuts," J.D. said, "and that was my own doing, because I was featuring Keith as the soloist, and [the album is] a cross between country and bluegrass. It showed his versatility as a singer, for one thing, and I thought that maybe this would help him, if he got to a place where he wanted to be, and people really cared about him, and Lord knows I did, and so did everybody in the band. We did all we could, but it didn't work." Unfortunately, "Some people are bent on self-destruction, not, maybe, that they wanted to, but that's just their fate in life. True, it's a sickness, and there's not really a lot you can do about it, just help them along. There's no cure, unless you want to be cured."[45]

"Keith was so well respected as a singer," Wendy said, "even when he was still doing bluegrass, that the 'who's who' would come into the studio to see him. We had only cut about three songs on the album, and the next week, the phone call came from RCA, and then, of course, it was only a matter of time. He played on [with the New South] for a while after that."[46]

Released in 1982, *Somewhere Between* (Rounder 0153) included Lefty Frizzell's "I Never Go around Mirrors," Tom T. Hall's "Another Town," and the title song, from Merle Haggard. Others were "Dance with Me, Molly," "Long Black Limousine," "Where Are All the Girls I Used to Cheat With?" "Family Tree," and "To Be Loved by a Woman" (Billy Joe Shaver). "I Would Have Loved You All Night Long" (Glenn Martin) and "Girl from the Canyon" (Gordon Lightfoot) were also on a 45-rpm single.

Somewhere Between had the country flavor Crowe had sought, but it was the honest, straightforward sound of the country music he loved as a boy, and a far cry from the overproduced, contemporary "Nashville sound" so prevalent at the time.

CHAPTER 9
BURN OUT, TIME OUT, AND SECOND WIND

Steve Bryant was gone by the time the album picture was taken. "[He] left after I was there about a year," Wendy said, "and went to Nashville as a studio musician. I recommended Randy [Hayes]—we called him 'Cosmo'—and he did a great job."[1]

Hayes, from Waneta, Kentucky, had worked with Wendy in the Russell Brothers. Primarily a guitar player, he also played bass and drums and had a strong tenor voice. "About every note I learned was from [Steve Bryant]," he said. "He was one of the best bass players out there. I had to re-form what I played to fit; this was different—different music, a different feel, and playing with the world's best banjo player. I learned a lot from Crowe about music in general," Randy continued.[2] "I went into the band knowing who [Crowe] was, and I had great respect for him. I just did what he said."[3] In 1981, when Hayes joined them Wendy was with Crowe, and "Keith had been there about four years. They had just finished *Somewhere Between,* and were tweaking it. I could feel the tension when Keith cut that album," Randy said. "Ricky [Skaggs, a country star at the time] never once offered to help Keith, and Keith didn't want his name mentioned."[4]

"We held the album up three months," J.D. said, "on account of we couldn't get the Jordanaires. They're semiretired, but we got them."[5]

Somewhere Between was reviewed in the April 1983 issue of *Frets*, with a warning that this was not a bluegrass album, or a "country-oriented" one, but "actually pretty good country fare," on which Crowe's "banjo takes a back seat."[6]

The *Columbus (Ohio) Dispatch* called *Somewhere Between* "an album of country music so traditional sounding in instrumentation and harmonies, it turned a lot of heads."[7]

With Keith's country career a real possibility, everyone tried to keep him straight; they worked constantly and stayed busy between shows. "Nobody on the bus drank in front of Keith," Randy said. "There was no alcohol on the bus or anywhere."[8]

The first year Randy was in the band, "We [only] had two weekends off," he said, "[and played] good gigs, like the Birchmere, which was one of my first shows. Every trip was fun."[9]

"We clowned around all the time," Wendy said, "but when we went on the stage, it was business; we entertained." He continued:

> People had paid good money to come and see us. Crowe has got quite a reputation for being an incredible musician, and all of us tried the best we could to play up to that level. We worked hard to get it right, and if we didn't get it right, it might be three days later, or the next weekend, we'd know about it—in a nice way. Crowe had a nice way of letting you know about it; he'd laugh about it and tell you what you'd done.
>
> But we'd get in the bus, and it was a lot of fun. We done so much traveling, and were on the road so much, and you just can't get along without having some fun. You pass the time by laughing, and we did our share of that.[10]

"Crowe and Bobby Slone were the biggest nuts," Randy said, "always playing pranks, laughing, and cutting up. Bobby Slone was the funniest man I ever met in my life; he didn't have to say anything—he was just funny. We had a ball. When the music started, then Crowe got serious."[11]

"Bobby Slone," Wendy said. "You could not play, you could not travel, you could not be around a more gentle, absolutely great, decent, human being than Bobby Slone. You could play with him on every stage from here to Maine or California and never hear a word that displeased you. He's just a kind human being. Bobby was always there when anybody needed him; he was just a dear friend to everybody. You could always get a laugh out of Bobby, and he could always make you laugh. You could say that Bobby and Crowe were the catalysts that made [that band] work."[12]

"When J.D. hit the stage," Randy said, "it was just totally professional; he wanted it as good as it could get, and that's pretty much what everybody gave him. That's what sets him aside from other bluegrass bands."[13]

Wendy agreed:

> He had built a level of expectations that he was going to live up to, and he still does today. He plays so clean, his timing is so perfect, he still plays with all that confidence, and he's got so much talent that it won't let him do anything but the best.
>
> Keith was a lot like J.D.; he really wanted to get it right. He was a great guy to work and travel with; he never lost his temper. I could see that he was reaching for another star, and it finally happened.
>
> I've always thought that J.D. gave him that [chance] when he recorded *Somewhere Between*. We didn't talk about this, but he was a great country singer, and I think [J.D.] let Keith stretch his talent when he gave him the opportunity to cut that album. I know that album propelled Keith into country music, because it wasn't but a week or two before RCA called. Somebody "bird-dogged" that tape to them, and they offered him a contract right there.
>
> The contract didn't happen right then, but they wanted to hold Keith. [When they finally let him record] his first few records hit the charts. He had the talent, but it just wasn't to be.[14]

West Virginian Paul Adkins was the next lead singer for the New South. "I had been traveling with them," he said. "J.D. knew Keith would leave. I learned the routine and helped sell records and drive the bus."

"The night Keith quit," Randy said, "we called Paul right away and went straight to Canada."[15]

"I was very fortunate when I started with Crowe," Paul said.

> He had just gotten his first bus. That was a big commitment for J.D., as it would be for anybody. I actually helped do the inside, the bunks and

headliner. It was great to have a bus to travel in and hang out in during festivals. My first tour was two weeks to Canada; [J.D.] called me in the middle of the night. It was way up there in Ontario—you could almost see the Northern Lights.

J.D.'s timing was impeccable, right on top of the beat. My guitar just played itself. J.D.'s only the best. I think that's the general consensus among people who like good, head-on banjo—especially among banjo people. I feel so lucky and very humble about getting to play with that caliber of musician. It made me a better musician.

"Most shows we done," Wendy said, "you could look out in the audience and see every banjo player in the area come to see J.D. and get one more of his licks."[16]

"People would ask me," Paul said, "[because] J.D.'s expression onstage is so serious, 'Is he hard to play with?' I never had more fun than traveling with J.D.; every trip was an adventure. Orval traveled with us a couple of times. What a good fellow! The apple don't fall too far from the tree."

"Paul Adkins was a good singer, easy to sing with," Wendy said. "I thought a lot of Paul. I think he fell in love in Washington, D.C. and wanted to live in that area. He started a band called 'Borderline,' and they put out some really good bluegrass, some good stuff."[17]

"I stayed with J.D. about two and a half years," Paul said, "and introduced the guy who followed me, Tony King. He was like all the rest of us, just 'eat up' with Crowe. He recorded some songs I brought into the band. One was played a lot on the radio. It was *Ride the Train*, from an old Alabama album. It was funny, 'cause J.D. didn't like Alabama material."

"Tony King was fun to work with," Wendy said, "and was a really good guitar player. He was a good singer, but, to me, there was something missing. When you lose Keith Whitley—I'd been so used to singing with Keith, and [we] were from the same part of the country. Maybe we talked alike or sung alike. But Tony was a good guy to work with, and Tony was there after I left."[18]

North Carolina native Tony King came to the band in October 1983. "My audition was a weekend," he said. "[J.D.] flew me up, and we played in his living room. When I got the job, I already knew all the Crowe stuff. After being such a fan, finding myself playing in his band was a dream come true."

He, like J.D., had wanted to be an electric guitar player, but "when I heard Tony Rice, it was over. I sold my electric guitar and bought an acoustic guitar—an old 1934 Herringbone, almost the same as Tony's."

Tony King had played lengthy stints at tourist venues in Gatlinburg, Busch Gardens in Williamsburg, Virginia, and the 1982 World's Fair, but "[playing with J.D.] was my first job in a real live band. I'll always love him for giving me the chance. Crowe's a perfectionist. It was learning at the feet of the master, and I appreciate and cherish that. He was real demanding—you know what timing is when you play with him—and you *had* to listen to him. He knows what's right, and he'll tell you. I probably couldn't do what I do now without the level of musicianship in that band."

"Tony King," J.D. said, "was a good parts singer and a good musician."[19]

Tony didn't smoke, but "I got good at loading cigarettes," he said, "especially Wendy's. I learned to poke them through the cellophane with a toothpick, or to open the wrapping, load them, and seal it back with Super Glue."

In 1983, a show at George Washington University's Lisner Auditorium reunited original and current members of the Country Gentlemen and the Seldom Scene. With Crowe's reassembled '75 band (with Todd Phillips on bass instead of Bobby Slone), the three bands recorded live for Sugar Hill. Six songs were included from Crowe's show: "I'll Stay Around," "I'm Not Broke but I'm Badly Bent," "Fireball," "Why Don't You Tell Me So?" "Freeborn Man," and "Train 45."

The double LP was issued as *Bluegrass: The Greatest Show on Earth* (Sugar Hill SH-2201) and created a stir. *Frets'* review in May 1983 was ecstatic, calling it "a must-have record," and saying, "The musicians . . . turned in some of the best performances of their careers." It also said, "You could run through every superlative . . . and still undersell this extraordinary [album]."[20]

"The Album Band was in the studio," J.D. said, "when Ricky called and said we had been nominated for a Grammy—the *almost* New South [for "Fireball" on the *Greatest Show* reunion album]. I didn't think we did anything that outstanding or different. 'Fireball' was a Josh Graves Dobro instrumental we liked to close the show with sometimes." Frankly, "We were surprised to be nominated and even more surprised when we won [the Grammy for] Best Country Instrumental Performance.[21] Chet Atkins and people like that were nominated. I always regretted that Bobby wasn't on it; he really deserved to get the Grammy, because he was one of the New South. I think Bobby was sick and could not make the trip."[22]

With three volumes of the Bluegrass Album series completed and very popular, a tour of the "nonband" was planned to spread the word in person. "The Bluegrass Album Band tour," J.D. said, "the first one, the main one, was 1983, I believe. We did about eight or ten days. That was a lot of fun; that was a good time, and the crowds were great."[23]

Some of the fun might have been tempered a little; the neck of J.D.'s banjo (the Banger) was broken in transit. He borrowed Alan Munde's banjo for one show in Norman, Oklahoma, but he still had to get through the tour.

In 1982, he had played an RB-75 belonging to Bob Rodgers, from Arkansas; it was all original, with a twenty-hole, flathead tone ring. Rodgers recalled:

> I received a call from J.D. wanting to *borrow* it. I was not attending the show, but sent the banjo [to Fort Worth, Texas] for his use. The [Banger] was sent back to me, minus the broke neck. [J.D.] later had a new neck made for the [Banger] and brought the [Banger] back to me for my use. I kept the [Banger] for over a year, taking it out in public two or three times. Three people knew whose banjo I had. That banjo stayed under the bed most of the time I had possession. Had I lost his [Banger], I would have moved out of the U.S.
>
> [J.D.] was caretaker [of the RB-75] for seven or eight years before I sold him the banjo. I think he became owner in 1990.

The RB-75 was J.D.'s main banjo for quite a while, then took turns with the Banger and his other RB-3. "I play them all," J.D. said "I'll play one a year, put it down, and play another a year, kind of rotating them. It's nice to be able to do that. They all record good; I'll record with just whatever I'm playing at the time. I might use two banjos on the same record, one on a session, then go back and finish up with another."[24]

Banjo player Terry Baucom is also a fine fiddle player and was working with Doyle Lawson's Quicksilver at the time of the tour.

> [Bobby] Hicks was on call with Ricky [Skaggs], and Doyle said, "You go on the whole tour with us, and when Hicks can't make it, you play." Hicks done half of it, and I did the last half. Me and J.D. roomed together. Some of my best times were there, a banjo player playing fiddle with *the* banjo

player. It was quite a treat; I was glad to be a part of that. People just packed the places; they went "off," which made you play better.

[J.D.] just plays so good, his timing and everything, he just pulls you up to a different level. It just picks you up and makes you want to play, like playing with a good guitar player who really understands rhythm. Fiddle-and-banjo playing with Crowe is like a whole band standing there.

Crowe's so easygoing, and, like me, he don't talk a lot out, but we'd get back to the room and talk all night about banjos. We'd talk about setups and this pot or that, and tone. Crowe always kept the best banjos, and would say, "Here, check this out."

During the tour, the Album Band went to Nashville and appeared on Ralph Emery's program, *Nashville Now,* on TNN.

"Ralph Emery," J.D. recalled, "asked Tony, 'What is "flat picking"?' and Tony, in his very infinite wisdom, looked up and said [holding up his hand up with a pick in it], 'This is a flat pick.' That's it, that's all he said. And I thought, 'What a great comeback!' That said it all."[25]

The next album the New South cut was *Straight Ahead.* J.D. and Tony King were on the entire album; Bobby played fiddle on three cuts, and Wendy was still around for three cuts, supplemented by Sam Bush on mandolin; Steve Bryant returned to play bass on half of the album; Jerry Douglas guested on four cuts; and Randy (on various cuts) played bass and drums and sang tenor and lead.

The album was well titled; it was more bluegrass than anything Crowe had cut since *0044,* with more banjo, more harmonies, and some fresh material. There were some old songs, "God's Own Singer" and "Helplessly Hoping"; some *really* old songs, "Walter Hensley's "Stoney Mountain Twist" and "Sugar Coated Love" (recorded by Carter Stanley with Monroe in 1951); with "Say You Lied," "You're No Longer Mine," "Miner's Lady," "Ride the Train," Tom T. Hall's "Belleville, Georgia," and Doyle Lawson's "Runaround."

The day he and Jerry Douglas went up from Nashville to Mach 1 Studio in Central City, Kentucky, to record several tracks for *Straight Ahead* stands out in Sam Bush's memory:

Wendy had left the band before the album was finished. It was a great day, one of the few times my dad was in the studio when I recorded. He loved J.D.

J.D., Bobby, and my dad were in the control room. They were using a two-inch, twenty-four track recording tape; there is a switch you can throw that isolates one track. They put my track totally out of time—I know I did it right—Crowe was laughing; we all laughed. I was about to start the next song, and this guy comes in, in full police uniform—Central City Police. He said, "Are you Sam Bush?" I said, "Does it sound that bad?" and he said, "You need to come with me."

All of them were in the control booth, just crying with laughing. J.D. wouldn't let me listen to any of the tracks. He said, "It's okay, I know how you play." That whole day, I never heard any of my playbacks in sync. I never heard one *note* I played in sync.

Straight Ahead (Rounder 0202) was issued in 1986 and received a glowing review in *Bluegrass Unlimited*. "J.D. Crowe," the reviewer said, "didn't have to claw . . . to the top of the heap. He just strolled up there . . . and everybody else got out of the way." He praised the singing and "up-front" banjo, which he called "the voice of the band," and said, "It is Crowe's backup that moves the band and guides the sound."[26]

"Terry Johnson, from around Cincinnati, took Wendy Miller's place," Curt Chapman said. "He was a good tenor singer, and a pretty good mandolin player. He was a big practical joker." Curt played in the New South with Terry in 1988 and '89.[27]

Terry started in June 1985 and had not been in the band long before Randy left to join Keith in Nashville. "[Playing with Crowe was] probably the most fun I'd ever had," Randy said. "J.D. was one of the best guys I'd ever known, and he was just so much fun to be around. The only problem with me was that I played electric bass, and some of the bluegrass people weren't fond of me."[28]

When Randy left, Bobby moved back to bass, and the New South was a four-piece band for a time: J.D., Tony, Terry, and Bobby.

"Bobby would drive the bus most of the time," Tony said. "He'd drive all night; I don't know how he did that. I wasn't too good at driving it. One night, they had to take it away from me. I was going up a hill and had to double-clutch it. There were people behind us, and it nearly got away from me. Finally, it turned into a money pit, and after that, J.D. would hire a Cadillac or a Lincoln, and we'd all pile into it."

In the fall of 1986, Tony King left to play with country singer Holly Dunn. "It's harder to make a living in bluegrass," he said, "but I still love it." He later played with Vince Gill, then worked two years as part of Matthews, Wright, and King before joining Brooks and Dunn, with whom he performed for fifteen years. "Most of the contacts I made in Nashville were due to playing with J.D.," he said. "Everybody knows who J.D. is, and everybody respects him. It's amazing, what kind of pedigree it gives you to have played with J.D. I'm still proud of being in a band that had those guys in it; it was an honor."

Tony was replaced as lead singer and guitarist by Robert Hale, from West Virginia, who had played with the Reno Brothers (Don Wayne and Dale) and Eddie Adcock. "I played with Crowe the first time for about two and a half years," he said, "until he decided to take time off. Being around Crowe was a dream job for me, 'cause I'd grown up listening to him. I learned a lot from him; he instilled a lot of confidence in me. He's not a guy to sit down and tell you what to do. One of the best things he ever told me was, 'You don't have to be Tony Rice or Keith Whitley. If I didn't think you were good enough to be here, I wouldn't have hired you.'"

"Robert is a good singer—a good musician and a good person," J.D. said. "He has a good personality onstage."

Curt Chapman had been in Southern Blend, a popular and accomplished bluegrass group from Richmond, Kentucky. He gave his notice, "and when I walked in my house from that," he said, "Crowe was on the telephone, asking me to fill in [with the New South] on the *Mountaineer Opry* in West Virginia."[29]

> My first show was in November 1987, and I was in the band through 1988, when J.D. took off. Robert Hale and Terry Johnson were in the band; Bobby had played fiddle on a couple of shows with Keith, and that's why they called me [to play bass]. Bobby came back on fiddle the very next show.[30] That's the way it was all through 1988, until Crowe retired.[31]
>
> After that show, I called him in the next day or two, and said, "If you need a bass player, I'd like to audition for the job." He said, "I've got another show; let's see how it goes." I never asked again, and it got to be kind of a joke. That was the longest tryout period—thirteen, fourteen years, something like that. The only [band member] who stayed any longer was Bobby Slone.[32]

Going from Southern Blend to playing with J.D. was like going from a real good band to a band that's the way it's supposed to be. Just being around J.D., you know immediately that he knows exactly what he's doing; he's a master of his craft, there's no doubt in your mind, from the time he hits that first note, you know he knows that banjo up one side and down the other, knows everything there is to know about it.

Drummers I played with had told me I had good timing, but when I started with J.D., I learned how to play *right* timing. Playing in a country band, or a rock-and-roll band, there is a different groove that you have to be in, and it's hard to go from that to play bluegrass, because you've got to be on the edge of that downbeat without rushing, and you've got to know when to pull back, but still be on the edge. When you feel it, you know you're there, and if you don't feel it, you're *definitely* not there. That is J.D. Crowe timing.

Right after the Christmas holidays, J.D. called and said he was going to take time off. He was burnt out and needed a break.[33]

"About 1989," J.D. said, "I disbanded for a while. I wasn't out of the music business; I just didn't record as the New South after *Straight Ahead*."[34] The stress, he found, "was driving me crazy—the people I had to work with. Stress will do a lot of things to you; I will not put myself back in that position."[35]

"Crowe was getting tired of the road," Wendy Miller said. "He was too young to retire, [but] from 1980 to 1985, we were constantly on the road in that big bus. We didn't fly a lot, and spent an awful lot of time on the road. Through an acquaintance in Huntington [West Virginia], J.D. got a contract to do a mail route for four or five years."[36]

"You have to do something," J.D. said. "I was a mail contractor. A lot of people think I was walking, delivering mail in the city—no, thank you, I did not want that! I had a route, about 350 miles a day, with about five stops, and I did that for about six years. In that time period [1988–94], I was able to play some, record some, and I had some people that would drive when I wanted to be off. The only thing about it—the route had to be run; somebody had to do it."[37]

"I rode with him and drove [the route] several times," Curt said. "Bobby did too."[38]

"A lot of people had the misconception that J.D. just quit and went to carrying mail," Doyle said. "That was not what it was at all. He bid on a mail route; he had a truck and somebody to take care of the route if he didn't want to do it. It was not like he was throwing newspapers up against the door of a house. It wasn't that at all. He'd really just gotten weary of the whole thing and wanted a break. I'd always tell him, 'You need to come back; we need people like you. You're not ready to quit.'"[39]

The mail route gave J.D. freedom for other pursuits. He had time to be with his family and to work in his garden, and there was always golf. While waiting for the mail route to develop, he took a part-time job delivering parts for an electrical contractor. All of these were comparatively restful, and the feelings of stress began to diminish.

Banjo player and electrical contractor Wayne Ritchie, when he was underage, first heard Crowe at Martin's. "I met Crowe when I got out of the navy and could go into those places legally," he said. "I went at least once or twice weekly [to the Holiday Inn] for a long time. Jim Hatton and I worked together at Kentucky Utilities."

Ritchie started his own company in 1980 and had little time to play, but he became a capable, confident banjo player. "Crowe influenced me," he said. "He showed me things. J.D. was getting set up with this contract to carry the mail. He drove my little old Nissan pickup and delivered parts. For a year and a half, two years, '85 to '87, I got to hang out with my hero—when he worked for me, he had a key to my house."

When Bill Riddle walked into the Holiday Inn in 1972, he had no idea who the musicians were:

I don't think I was even twenty-one years old. During one of their breaks, I walked up to the banjo player and asked about lessons. "I do a little teaching at Carl's [music store] downtown," he said, so we made arrangements.

The first thing he said to me was, "You've got to get another banjo." He was so good, he'd have to watch his hands and slow it down to show me how to do it. I took lessons a couple of semesters [before returning to Louisville], and J.D. was so friendly and down to earth, it was a couple of years before I realized how important he was.

[Sometime later], I was back in Lexington, doing construction, and Wayne Ritchie was the electrical contractor. J.D. came driving up, delivering parts. People in other kinds of music are always trying to *be* somebody, and here was J.D. who *was* somebody, just natural, friendly, and comfortable.

Riddle now owns the Atomic Café, a popular Caribbean-style bistro, in the building that once housed the Limehouse.

"After I kind of got out of the music business for about six years—I didn't quit completely, I did some special things—but I had always had it in my mind that I would go back into it, but it would be at *my* time," J.D. asserted. "I started thinking about that, but I wasn't in any big hurry about it, because I was really tired, burnt out with the whole scene. I didn't want to be around music or pickers at that time—nothing personal, but that's just the way I felt."[40]

There were many "special things" that J.D. participated in during his time off. The fifth Album Band album was recorded in 1988 and '89, and the "Rounder Records All-Star Bluegrass Band" did a Kentucky Educational Television *Lonesome Pine Special* in Louisville in 1988.

On February 16, 1989, Orval Crowe died after a lengthy illness.[41] A good and loving man who never met a stranger and never made an enemy, his life was characterized by Sonny Osborne: "He was a fine, fine human being."

Among various "reunions"—usually with substitutions—was the May 1990 Kentucky Mountain Boys' reunion at Dobson, North Carolina, which brought together J.D., Doyle, and Larry Rice, with Ronnie Simpkins on bass. The July 1992 KMB reunion at Denton, North Carolina, reassembled J.D., Red Allen, and Doyle, with John Bowman on bass. A series of 1991 "Pickin' Parties" at Riverbend in Cincinnati Vienna (Virginia), and Baltimore featured reunions of the '75 band: Rice, Skaggs, Douglas, and Crowe, without Bobby Slone.

Bobby Slone had become a staff musician at Renfro Valley in 1989 and was no longer available for long trips. He liked being off the road. "It's like fifty-five miles for me, down and back," he said.[42] He was a good fit in the situation there, being adept at several styles of fiddle playing: "I feel more comfortable playing swing when I play country [music]. It's probably what you start out on; swing is easy for me; it comes real easy. I love bluegrass fiddle playing, and I'll get it one of these days, maybe. Some country players can't play bluegrass fiddle, and there are some bluegrass fiddlers who cannot play swing or country. It's got a lot to do with how you feel it or how much you like it."[43]

"Bobby's a survivor, a great musician," Wendy Miller said. "He's been in music for forty or fifty years and is still playing good. He adapted his fiddling to the [country] style, and they think the world of him down there."[44]

On May 9, 1989, Keith Whitley died of an overdose of alcohol, saddening the entire world of country and bluegrass music and ending what had promised to be an exceptional career. He was thirty-three years old.[45]

"I got hurt about it," Bobby Slone said, "but I got mad at first. For him to do that to himself, when he'd always wanted to be a star, and then he got that close to it . . ."[46]

"I was not surprised at all," J.D. said. "I was shocked, but I had always told him, 'If you don't straighten up, you won't live to be forty-two years old.' And he didn't. You cannot live like that and abuse your body that way. About his death, in my opinion, I really don't think he knew that he had drank as much as he did, in his condition, because once you reach a point, you don't realize how much you're drinking. His heart just quit, and he went to sleep."[47]

J.D. continued to play occasionally, including sitting in on shows with Jimmy Martin and reunions with Martin and Paul Williams. Shows with collections of top-flight musicians followed, such as the April 1991 "Superpickers" at the Birchmere: J.D., Tony Rice, Sam Bush, Jerry Douglas, Stuart Duncan on fiddle, and Mark Schatz on bass.

The Masters of the Five String Banjo tour took place in the fall of 1993; a changing cast of banjo players demonstrated various styles, backed up by Laurie Lewis (fiddle) and Dudley Connell (guitar). "I did three shows in California," J.D. said. "It was the easiest thing I ever did. There were all these banjo players; I'd heard of them, but had never heard them play. Will Keys was there, and Carroll Best, from North Carolina, a guy from Ireland, and a guy from Africa who played a different instrument related to the banjo. I did one tune by myself—that was weird. Dudley and Laurie did about ten or fifteen minutes. Then there was a finale when everybody took a break and showed the various styles. It was neat. People really enjoyed it, and I enjoyed doing it."[48]

"One day," Curt Chapman said, "[J.D. and I] were on the golf course, and I was hoping he'd want to get back into it. He said he'd like to get a bunch of guys together and just play when we wanted to."[49]

"When I came back," J.D. said, "I had made up my mind I was not going to do as much, I wasn't going to be playing as many dates, I was not going to put the pressure on myself like I had before, and it was just going to be a little easier. I decided, 'I'll just do so many dates a year, and that's it.'"[50]

"I'd say Bobby Slone is the reason I got to play with Crowe," Richard Bennett said. Bobby had called J.D.'s attention to the young singer and guitarist while Keith was in the band and again when Richard visited *Renfro Valley* to jam. Richard was a lead picker, in the vein of Tony Rice, and an accomplished singer.

"Bobby wanted me to come down and hear him sing," J.D. said, "so I went down and heard him play, and thought, 'Well, this might work out,' and talked to him about doing lead singing and playing guitar, and he was very interested."[51]

"Crowe called me," Richard said, "the end of '89, about New Year's, and asked, 'Would you like to come up to my house for the weekend and play some music?' We played together, just two [instruments], and did a lot of Flatt and Scruggs stuff. Crowe said, 'I guess we'll get a bass player and a mandolin player, and we'll do some jobs.' So that's the way I was hired."

Richard, growing up in Johnson City, Tennessee, had been surrounded by fine musicians and was playing guitar at the age of eight, "for whatever I was worth at that age," he said. He had heard Crowe on Jimmy Martin albums, then those with Doyle and Larry. "I was starting to listen to Crowe's trio, which was completely different than anyone else's, in its vocals, and the drive of the music." He was overwhelmed when *Rounder 0044* came out. "That's the best music I'd ever heard," he thought, and borrowed a copy. "I used to go to sleep at night with headphones, with that record on continuous play. I just loved it. That was my biggest influence ever, as far as Crowe's recordings—and it still is today. I like that better than anything he ever put out. That's when I started noticing Crowe's approach to music; I think he hit a plane there, a whole different plateau that no other band had hit, so vocally powerful and instrumentally powerful. That was the kind of band I wanted to be in."

The first mandolin player and tenor singer was Wayne Fields, Richard recalled, "and we started developing the trio that Crowe wanted at the time. We worked really hard for a year, finding material and working it up. That was a really neat time in my life, a lot of playing one-on-one with Crowe, and his thoughts on music. My favorite trio was Wayne, J.D., and me. It was something to do with all that rehearsing."

Wayne Fields, a banjo player, argued with Crowe when he was called to Curt's house. "What do you need me for?" he said. "You don't need a banjo player." What they needed was his unusually strong, brilliant tenor voice. "Crowe brought a little mandolin," Wayne said. "I just went over and started singing. Crowe had a lot of patience with me. I thought I knew Crowe's material, and thought I knew something about singing—until I started with Crowe. He knows every aspect of bluegrass music, knows every singer's part. *Everything.*"

Originally from Hazard, Kentucky, Wayne moved to Lexington when he was fourteen. "My heart was always in bluegrass," he said, "but I never was around pickers who could play." While in high school, he played rock and roll.

He was working in his father's service station on Newtown Pike one night and took a call from the Holiday Inn. "A guy had a flat tire," he said. "I walked in, and there were Crowe, Slone, Tony, and Larry. I sat down probably thirty minutes, thinking, 'Dad's going to kill me.' I was like twenty or twenty-one. [After that] I went out every night. I was fortunate that J.D. was giving lessons and signed up. I just naturally took it that *everybody* was that good.

"Crowe picked out my first banjo," Wayne said. "I was always so nervous and scared around Crowe—I still get jittery around him—but he was always nice to me. There were so many times I wanted to talk to J.D. but I wouldn't, because I would be imposing, or too forceful in myself."

In 1975, Wayne took Noah Crase's place with the Boys from Indiana. He also played with John Cosby and the Bluegrass Drifters, and they won first place in the 1984 International Band Championship sponsored by the (fan-based) Society for the Preservation of Blue Grass Music in America (SPBGMA), and with Southern Blend.

"We rehearsed about a year when I started with Crowe," Richard said, "and our first gig was in Kingsport, Tennessee. I was playing at Pigeon Forge five days a week, and I dropped it and came up here to Kentucky and played weekends. Wayne, Crowe, Curt, and I started doing dates. Then, a short time later, Phil started."

"We were playing a different style of music," Curt said, "more straight-ahead bluegrass, with more Flatt and Scruggs–style stuff, a lot from *0044,* just more bluegrass."[52]

"On 'The Old Home Place,'" Wayne said, "when you get to 'The plow in the field' part, nobody made it sound right except J.D., Tony, and Ricky. It was a 'crossover' part, when the baritone jumps to tenor, and Tony goes down to the baritone note. They were so good at a lot of that crossover—they used it on 'Some Old Day.' If you never sat down and studied it, you don't realize what they're doing."

Practice sessions were held at Curt's house. "Betty Rose [Curt's mother] had a big lot of food. After about forty-five minutes, we'd take a break and eat like it was Thanksgiving Day. Before eating, it was all business; afterward, J.D.'d say, 'Let's have some fun.'"

"We'd be sitting there rehearsing," Wayne said, "and J.D. would say, 'Fields, do some backup. I'm tired of doing all the banjo backup.' Crowe hadn't been playing for a while. He'd get his second wind, and then he'd really start picking and sometimes pick until three or four in the morning. That was my opportunity as a musician, to sit across from my idol and watch him pick."

"When Crowe was taking a break," Richard said, "Wayne would ask if he could play Crowe's banjo, and Crowe would say, 'Sure, go ahead.' Wayne would play, and Crowe would just watch him. That's the only guy I ever saw him do that with. Crowe would say, 'He's got it.' That's the best compliment you could ever hope to get out of Crowe."

Dobro player Phil Leadbetter had worked with Grandpa Jones and with Vern Gosdin and had performed before President Gerald R. Ford at the White House, but he was working a day job as a nurse in Nashville and hated it. "It was raining," he said. "I'd had a bad day at work, and I just felt like it, so I called J.D. like I was looking for Richard Bennett. He said, 'Richard told me about you—you're a Dobro player. I never really liked Dobro with Flatt and Scruggs because Josh [Graves] robbed Earl of a banjo break.' But he invited me to his house to pick."[53]

I had carpal tunnel syndrome and got him to hold off until I had surgery. I asked him, "When's the first job?" and Crowe said it would be about two months, so I had both hands done at the same time.

The first show I played with J.D. was in May, 1992, at the Red Mile [Trotting Track in Lexington]. We'd rehearsed once. I still remember how scared I was coming in there. I took a tape recorder, and told my wife and friends to get pictures in case he fired me—I wanted to prove I had played with him. He never told me I was hired until I'd been in the band about six years.

People you go to school with want to pitch for the Yankees, or somebody; I always wanted to pitch for J.D. Crowe.[54]

It was not really that J.D. didn't like Dobros; it's just that he liked Earl
Scruggs's banjo better. "When I first heard the Dobro [with Flatt and Scruggs],"
he said, "I despised it, because it took away from Earl's banjo breaks, and I
wanted to hear the banjo."

In J.D.'s opinion:

> The difference in Dobros and fiddles is just whatever you want to hear. I
> like both of them; I just can't afford to carry six people. I like the fiddle
> probably a little better, because Dobros and banjos clash a lot. You've re-
> ally got to watch that; when you've got two instruments that's played with
> fingers, with a roll. They can get in each other's way. That's what I thought
> about when Josh Graves joined Flatt and Scruggs, but they worked it out.
> At the time, I couldn't understand why they [hired Josh], but later on, I
> figured out why, and it was a great move.[55]

Phil was a great move for Crowe, too; the band was complete, with J.D.,
Richard, Wayne, Phil, and Curt. "There was a lot of difference between
before and after [Crowe's hiatus]," Curt said. "I was a little more confident
in what I was doing—it was more of a building process."[56]

The band took on more work, with Phil doing a lot of the booking.[57] That
meant more travel, which was not always smooth.

> If you want to get J.D. mad, just get lost. He can go off so fast and he can
> calm down that fast, just like turning a light switch.
> We played a show in a gymnasium in the western part of the state. [The
> sound system had] little bitty round mikes with little wires sticking out. We
> played that show, and J.D. could not hear, and he was so mad. . . . He took
> off that RB-75 and looked like he wanted to throw it down, but he knew
> what he had in his hands and he didn't. He just put it in the case and stood
> there looking at it. Then he reached in his pocket and got his wire cutters.
> He pulled up the strings right above the bridge and cut all of them.
> He said, "That's why I quit playing. You know, I don't have to do this
> for a living." And I said, "I sure don't. I'm just doing this because of you."

"I knew going in I wasn't a mandolin player," Wayne said. "The deal was,
I'd stay until he found a mandolin player–tenor singer. We worked up all the

songs for *Flashback*, in a little over a year. Then Don [Rigsby] came along, and [J.D.] had to hire him. [He] was playing at Olive Hill [Kentucky]," Wayne said. "I got Richard and said, 'You need to hear this guy.' They started picking, and that was it."

"[Phil] Leadbetter said J.D. was looking for a tenor singer," Don said. "J.D. only knew me as a fiddle player. I told him I was really a mandolin player. I remember singing with J.D. for hours for the audition. He called me the next Sunday; it was kind of like Elvis had called—pure excitement. He was already one of the most influential people in this business."

Don had grown up in a Stanley Brothers atmosphere in eastern Kentucky, but that changed in 1975. "My older brother brought home *Rounder 0044*, and I was captivated. I really liked that stuff before I became a player—the New South was the thing. Ricky and Keith were local heroes where I came from, and that gave me a connection, and just made me love [their music] more. The whole band sound was what always gripped me." He eventually played with Charlie Sizemore, Vern Gosdin, and for two years with the Bluegrass Cardinals.

"My association with J.D. Crowe was a transforming thing for me, musically. J.D. was all the things I had learned, combined into one person with tone, timing, and taste. He was an excellent teacher. He could explain things; he'd get this look of concentration on his face when he was trying to explain. He knew what he wanted, and how to get it, and he was very patient. We did a lot of playing in B flat," Don said. "That's the Crowe key, because the banjo sounds so good there."

"One thing about playing with Crowe, it's consistent good music," Richard said.

He's not going to play anything less. You're going to play the kind of sound Crowe wants to play, and you're going to learn a lot about dynamics, whether it be instrumentally or vocally.

His playing has so many elements that a lot of people might not hear that aren't used to listening for that. It hits peaks, and then it goes back into a straight plane that he likes to keep, and that straight plane is what you have to be able to play and sing to play with Crowe. He kind of teaches you in his roundabout way those peaks, the extra icing on the cake.

"You've got to be able to hear timing and feel it," J.D. said. "You've got to hear a groove. There's as much timing with singing as with instrumentals—more—you've got to phrase your words, even in your solos, and stay in the structure of the timing beat that you have. Somebody once said, 'Trying to teach somebody timing is like trying to teach them to taste.'"[58]

"Until I came with Crowe," Richard said, "I didn't realize that vocally, timing is just as important as it is instrumentally. I learned that through playing with Crowe. He's the first guy I ever played with in my life that taught me that rhythm, and he's taught many of them that."

"You can teach them music," J.D. said, "but you can't teach them that gut feeling that comes from listening to a lot of music when you're a kid. To me, music is *feeling*. Without *feeling*, it's just not the same. When it's so strong you can feel it, then it's good."[59]

"My mandolin playing took a big jump forward," Don said, "and got a lot better—everything improved. I got to play in places and for people I'd never dreamed of. That was the point where I decided to [make music my career]."

CHAPTER 10
THE *NEW* NEW SOUTH

When the *new* New South went into the studio, they took with them some new material and some old songs, but it all came out as bluegrass, Crowe style. Well named, *Flashback,* the CD reflected various periods in J.D.'s recording life, with Richard's Tony Rice–influenced voice and guitar; Don's refined mountain tenor and crisp mandolin breaks; Phil's smooth, always appropriate Dobro; Curt's solid bass; and, of course, J.D.'s crackling, authoritative banjo, the "drum" of the band, beneath and on top of it all.

Richard Bennett wrote or cowrote four new songs: "Waiting for You" (with Curt Chapman), "If I Could Go Back Home Again" (with Wanda Barnett), "'Til My Dying Day," and "Still Loves This Man."

There are two from Flatt and Scruggs's repertoire, "I'll Just Pretend," with its lovely fiddle passages beautifully rendered by guest Randy Howard, and "Bouquet in Heaven"; Jimmy Martin's "Mr. Engineer," a showcase for Don's voice; and Merle Haggard's "Ever Changing Woman." "Long Journey Home" and "When the Angels Carry Me Home" are familiar, but the treatment makes them fresh and new. "Nashville Skyline Rag" and "Sledd Ridin'" are two of J.D.'s rare instrumentals.

Flashback was recorded at Mach 1 and Magnolia studios; J.D. used the RB-75 throughout.

"I had never recorded in that type of situation before," Curt said. "Until *Flashback,* I'd played electric bass. At Bean Blossom I'd picked up 'Tater' Tate's big blond bass; J.D.'s ears pricked up. I knew he liked that sound, and I'd have to get an upright bass. I hadn't been playing long when we recorded, and I marked the neck, so I wouldn't waste studio time."[1]

"Randy Howard was a great fiddle player," Phil said. "I had never heard him until he walked in [the studio] that day. He really did some good stuff; it was just amazing. He probably did ten different breaks on some things, but he would say, 'Aw, I can do it better.'"[2]

"*Flashback* was a lot of fun to do," J.D. said. "I enjoyed it. It was a project like all New South projects—we just wanted to go in and make a good product. All the guys in the New South when we recorded it—and Randy Howard, who played guest fiddle on the album—contributed a lot and worked hard at it. Overall, I think it came out rather well."[3]

Flashback (Rounder 0322) was nominated for a Grammy for "Best Bluegrass Album" in 1994, and the same year Crowe won "Banjo Player of the Year" at the (professional) International Bluegrass Music Association (IBMA) convention. Despite the eight years during which he did not record with the New South, his work and influence remained strong in the minds of his peers.

There were enthusiastic reviews in *Bluegrass Unlimited:* "J.D. has done it again. A tight, well-rehearsed band . . . hot instrumental work, with J.D. leading the way. Very close . . . to earlier efforts." The singers and new material were praised.[4] And *Bluegrass Now*: "Pure bluegrass delivered with comfortable familiarity . . . everything here clicks so well. All are highly qualified musicians, fully able to mold each song into a tightly knit performance."[5]

These, word of mouth ("Crowe's back!"), and the Grammy nomination prompted a huge demand for bookings. "*Flashback* really opened a lot of doors for us," Phil said. "We played the *Opry* while the album was hot, and *Music City Tonight,* with Crook and Chase. It reached number one on the *Bluegrass Unlimited* chart, and the song 'Waiting for You' was number one, too, so we had double number ones. A lot of people was just ready for J.D. to get something out—he hadn't had anything out since *Straight Ahead.*"

"We were playing more than J.D. really wanted to," Richard said. "At one point, it may have gotten out of the comfort range. That project could have catapulted into another recording, if we had stayed together and there had been the material. Thousands of people told me, 'I don't know what's happened, but since this band came together, Crowe's talking more into the mike.'"

Richard saw to it that every show was recorded, and the band listened to the tapes while they traveled:

> I was the audio guy in the band, so we'd always have something to listen to and stay awake. It was valuable to tape those things—like investing in books. J.D. was complimentary if he liked something you did, and if you did something wrong, he'd let you know. One way or the other, you were going to hear what he thought about it.
>
> I learned this playing with Crowe: you've got to be natural. If it flows, it flows, and if it don't, you're doing something wrong. Onstage, he did it all with eye contact, whoever was a little off, he'd look at them. Most of the time, though, he was having fun, and he wanted you to have fun, too.

They also listened to old country music and Flatt and Scruggs tapes. "I remember all the times we'd be driving down the road," Richard said, "and J.D.'d say 'This is how solid you need to be, every instrument.' And [about a Scruggs lick], 'I still can't play that.'" Other "on-the-road" pastimes, such as stopping at Waffle Houses and White Castles, continued, and cigarette loads, by now, were constant. "Crowe would load my cigarettes, and I would load his cigars," Richard said. "He used to load my dress shoes with toilet paper, too."

Curt was a frequent victim. "J.D. looks very serious onstage, and he *is* serious when he's onstage, and about what he's doing," he said. "Other than that, he's probably one of the biggest practical jokers you've ever seen. At that time, I was smoking, and I didn't get a lot of rest, because I never knew whether I'd have lips after I lit the next cigarette—he was big on the cigarette loads [and] everything from trick soap that would dye your skin white or red or black in the shower to pepper gum and whoopee cushions. Nobody escaped."[6]

"Curt," Rickey Wasson said, "was about to go to the crazy house. He'd hear someone clap their hands, and he'd hit the floor, afraid his face was blowed off." Singer–guitar player Wasson played with Crowe in the 1990s and from 2001 to the present. "You never leave the table [in a restaurant] until you're through," Curt said, "or you're likely to get salt in your tea. People put flowers or little toy cars in Phil's Dobro or wet paper towels in your shoes."[7]

J.D. kept close watch on his briefcase filled with tricks and his stash of cigars, but he got caught occasionally, much to the delight of everyone else. "When J.D. had the mail route," Phil said, "he had a little Nissan truck with a little camper on it. [After returning from a gig], maybe 2:00 or 3:00 a.m., me and Richard would drive around a while, then put that camper on sideways or across the hood. He finally put a chain and lock on it."[8]

"One time, we were driving all night, dead tired," Curt said, "and J.D. went to sleep in his lounge chair. Me, Richard, and Phil duct-taped him to his chair. Crowe left his banjo [one time], and I took the back off and filled the banjo with dry paper towels. He ran his thumb over the strings, five minutes before we went onstage; there was an initial look of surprise, and then he knew."[9]

"A member of the band had gotten to feeling pretty important," Don said, "and wasn't riding with us. J.D. was pretty upset, and riding back, J.D. decided to address the issue. He told all of us, 'You might be the best band in the world, but you better remember the reason you're out here is because of this damn banjo.' When J.D. said that, he didn't say it to crush us, but it stung. He is the catalyst; other people might contribute, but he is the constant."

"There's a story about Chet Atkins, sitting in a music store playing guitar," Don recounted. "Someone said, 'Chet, that guitar sounds great!' Chet put it on the stand and said, 'Now, how does it sound?'"

Wayne Fields played one last tour with the New South in July 1994. "Curt called at 5:00 a.m.," Wayne said, "and said they were ready, and had to leave at 6:00 a.m. Curt told me, 'Don's laying in the floor with back spasms and can't go.' So I called in and got things set up at work so I could go. If it had been anybody else in the country, I'd have turned them down."

Richard left in 1995:

The reason I left, Crowe had slowed down, and we weren't working much. I had an offer from Lou Reid and Terry Baucom to go on a one-year tour that was pretty heavily booked up, and I needed to work more than we were working. I left on really good terms. I always dreaded leaving, because it felt like home. Musically, it was a nice home; the people I was surrounded by were like your brothers, so it was really sad for me.

Once I got with Baucom, and started working with him, his respect and admiration for Crowe's style of banjo playing was so incredible that it's almost like Terry sometimes didn't even want to play his banjo. He wanted to listen to tapes of Crowe and I playing together, or whatever tapes of Crowe I had, because he admired his playing so much. He told me one time, "There is no other guy that I know of on the banjo that can get the tone that Crowe gets. It's just not possible. And that pull—the way that J.D. pulls the banjo." Baucom is a huge fan of Crowe's, as we all are.

"When I was working for [J.D.] he was semiretired," Don said. "We played twenty or twenty-five dates a year. It was hard to make a living when you've got a family. If he'd been playing as much then as now, I'd probably still be with him." By that time, "Richard had left, and Greg Luck was playing guitar. We were kind of in a rebuilding phase. [J.D.] didn't make it hard for me to leave his band except by being so nice. It was all business to J.D.; he didn't take it personally. I told him it was the hardest thing I'd ever had to do. I left in May of 1995."

North Carolina multi-instrumentalist Greg Luck, who followed Richard as lead singer and guitar player, grew up listening to Flatt and Scruggs and the Osborne Brothers. He had played with Redwing, the Lost and Found, Lynn Morris, and the Bluegrass Cardinals before joining J.D. His sincere, warm voice was totally different from Richard's, but blended right in, with more of a country flavor:

When I first started, Don Rigsby was still in the band; he went with the Lonesome River Band, and Darrell Webb came in on mandolin for about six months, then Dwight McCall.

Snuffy [Smith] knew me and knew J.D. real well, and I think that's where my recommendation came from. When I got to play with J.D., it was like the music I'd cut my teeth on and grew up listening to, but with material as good as you could ask to play. I never got to play as much good material as with J.D.

If you're going to play bluegrass, that's the high-water mark for play-ing bluegrass. I didn't think I'd ever get the chance, but sometimes good things happen. I wanted to play rhythm like Tony and sing like Keith, and if I could have, I would have.

When [J.D.] is playing banjo, if you're thrashing on the guitar, you're going to stick out like a sore thumb. J.D. never said, "You're doing this wrong . . ." The only thing he'd say was, "Make sure that the timing in your vocal phrasing is dead on with the timing in the song, and be sure to hold your words out at the end of each line. Don't cut it off too fast."

J.D. kind of shows you without trying to tell you, or to demean you in any way. He's smart enough not to surround himself with people who don't hear timing the way he does. J.D.'s a real good guy, too. He's paid his dues, and if he wanted to have an attitude, he could, but he doesn't. It was so fun to play with somebody with the status of J.D. and have them not turn out to be an asshole.

We traveled in rented vans most of the time. There was always something going on. Curt was involved in a lot of [the practical jokes] but mostly on the receiving end. There was never a dull moment; I don't think a stick in the mud would last long in that band.

In the fall of 1995, to celebrate Rounder's twenty-fifth anniversary, three of Rounder's top bluegrass acts participated in a lengthy bus tour. J.D. Crowe and the New South, Laurie Lewis and Grant Street, and the Del McCoury Band performed twenty-eight times in a month. "The other bands on the tour were very complimentary about Crowe's sound," Greg said. "When J.D. would get tired of talking to us all the time, he'd go and find a janitor and talk his ear off, somebody who didn't treat him like he was a legend. The janitor didn't know he was J.D. Crowe, and neither one of them cared."

Dwight McCall's first show with the New South was August 10, 1996, in Alexandria, Kentucky. He had experience with Cincinnati-area band Union Springs and then with the Country Gentlemen. "I was living in Cincinnati and driving to Virginia," he said, "eight and a half hours to Charlie [Waller's] house. I called J.D. and asked if he could use me. The hardest thing I ever had to do was tell Charlie Waller I was leaving. We were playing a *ton,* Thursday through Sunday, and I wasn't going to be able to keep up with it."

The son of singer and guitar player Jim McCall (best known for his work with Earl Taylor and the Stoney Mountain Boys), Dwight was possessed of a high, precise, powerful voice, but "I never wanted to sing," he said. "All I ever wanted to do was play banjo. I never picked a note until I was sixteen, then played with Dad and Walt Hensley in the Dukes of Bluegrass. They needed a mandolin player, and the only reason I played mandolin was because I didn't have a banjo. Dad didn't even know I could play."

Dwight knew all the New South material when he joined the band. "J.D. said he never had anybody who knew his material as well as I did, so that was a nice pat on the back. When I first went to rehearse with them—he was my hero, man—I was shaking all over, but there was no pressure."

In 1996, AcuTab Publications released a book of banjo tablatures of the songs from Rounder albums *Flashback* and *Rounder 0044,* approved and worked on by J.D., with additional information and many photographs.[10]

The Bluegrass Album, volume 6 (Rounder 0330), was issued in the summer of 1996. It was probably the closest thing to a J.D. Crowe instrumental album that will ever be recorded, although he was on half of Jimmy Martin's *Big and Country* album (Decca DL 74891), released in 1969; appeared on a Joe Green fiddle album (County 722) in 1969; played on *Tony Rice—Guitar,* a mostly instrumental album (King Bluegrass KB 529) in 1974; and shared banjo duties with James Bailey on Doyle Lawson's *Tennessee Dream* (County 766) in 1977.

J.D. explained:

> To be an instrumentalist, or to play an instrument that is known for instrumentals, I never really got into a lot instrumentals; I play them, probably because I have to, or maybe that's what they expect you to do, but if I listen to two instrumentals, that's all I want to listen to. I was always more into the "band concept" that, to me, is where it is. I think I have played shows where I didn't even do an instrumental, because I really don't want to do them. You hear the banjo—it does kick-offs, the banjo does breaks; I just have a thing about that.[11]

A concert the New South played on April 18, 1998, in Columbus, Ohio, is a case in point; it really impressed the reviewer, who called Crowe's band-leading "team-oriented," and likened him to rock guitarist Eddie Van Halen in ability. He marveled that Crowe did not play an instrumental until the seventh song of the performance, a thing he says Van Halen would never do "in this lifetime," thereby giving his band, who "continued [Crowe's] tradition of excellence," the opportunity to play "an equally important role in the performance," making the concert "all the more memorable." He said that band members were equally adept at harmony singing, playing backup, or "blazing away on lead runs that seemed to increase in speed, complexity, and clarity."[12]

The New South's next album continued that excellence and proved again that they could take their music back to the time when country and bluegrass were closely related and still stay contemporary. With no extra instrumentation in the studio but the fiddles of Buddy Spicher and Glen Duncan, and Rickey Wasson on guitar, *Come on Down to My World* (Rounder 0422) presented the New South in a spare but eloquent display of their talents. Greg's warmhearted, homespun voice; Dwight's clever mandolin breaks and intense tenor (featured as lead on four songs, including his own "I Don't Know"); Phil's Dobro taking the place of pedal-steel guitar; J.D.'s usual breathtaking banjo; and superb fiddling (including "twin" fiddles) combine with admirable material to produce an exceptional recording.

The title song, written by Larry Rice, and Dallas Frazier's "I'm So Afraid of Losing You Again" had been staples of New South performances for years, as had "White Freightliner." Merle Haggard's "Back to the Barrooms," nostalgic "Grandpa's Shoes," and the old gospel rouser "I'm Goin' That Way" are rooted in country tradition. "Careless Love," done here as an instrumental so clear you can almost hear the words; "My Blue Eyes You Left in Tennessee"; J.D.'s own "J's Tune"; "Come Back Sweetheart"; and Rebe Gosdin's "You Didn't Say Goodbye" are pure bluegrass.

The May 1999 *Bluegrass Unlimited* review of *Come on Down to My World* stated, "Crowe and company do a terrific job. . . . Often [Crowe's] vision results in some of the best contemporary bluegrass of the day. Another worthy outing for a great banjo picker and his band." The reviewer singled out individual performers for praise.[13]

Come on Down also garnered a review in *People Online*: "A bonanza for bluegrass fans. There's a nice, loose feel to this CD. . . . The obscurity in which they've labored seems undeserved."[14]

"That album was a good experience for me," Greg said. "People come up to me and say, 'You're the 'Back to the Barrooms' guy, aren't you?'"

Greg moved from Nashville, where he had been living, back to North Carolina and left the band; it was just too far to drive. He was followed by Rickey Wasson, a native of Stanton, Kentucky, as lead singer and guitar player.

Rickey had played other instruments from an early age, but settled on the guitar when he was about sixteen:

> I was mostly interested in lead guitar, mostly George Shuffler stuff. The first time I bought a Crowe record, it had Tony on it, and I thought, "There's no way I can do that!" but when I heard it later, I thought, "That's so cool!" It grew on me; it was a new style of bluegrass.
>
> When I was seventeen, about 1984, we formed Southern Blend. They had already played and sang together, and they helped me with my singing. [We] were together a little over ten years, and quit in 1995. I always tried to play J.D.'s style of music because of Wayne [Fields], and I learned so much from those guys—harmony singing and playing, and when not to play. I had a lot of fun; it made what I'm doing now a lot easier.
>
> When J.D. called me to fill in on a show in Texas, I'd done 75 percent of his songs with Southern Blend. Greg had had a wreck and messed himself up; in Texas, I sang "Lefty's Old Guitar." It's told from the perspective of the guitar, rather than a person telling a story. It just blew J.D. away. I've knowed that song for twenty years, and it was pretty neat to get to record it.
>
> I filled in at the end of 1997, when [J.D.] was going through some band changes. He called me [to work] in January of 1998, and I started the first of March 1998.

Rickey also filled in with Alison Krauss's band during that year.

Richard Bennett had filled in on occasional Album Band concerts since 1994, when Tony Rice's voice was failing. "It was always short notice," he said, "and if promoters had a hard time with me being there, Crowe made sure they treated me well, and not just as some guy. Crowe always went to bat for me. Not a lot of guys would do that, or even take the time."

When a trip to England and Ireland was planned for April 1998, J.D. asked Richard and Jimmy Gaudreau to fill in on guitar and mandolin, respectively, with Phil and Curt. Rickey and Dwight were new to the band, and even though Richard and Jimmy had never played together, they were both professionals who knew J.D.'s music. According to Richard:

> The first night there, we were in Ireland. Everyone got their instruments and clothes from some dude who showed up at the airport. Jimmy and I were rooming together, and actually almost asleep, and there was a knock on the door. J.D. said, "Hey, you two, come here; I want to show you some-

thing." From the look on his face, we thought he'd found maybe a snake in his room, or something like that. He said, "Look at this!" and opened up his banjo case and pulled out his banjo neck. It was busted off, and it was one of his old Gibsons. He was really upset, which is understandable. We went to sleep, thinking, "God, what are we going to do?"

The next morning, Crowe called the promoter as soon as he got up. A guy showed up with a banjo for Crowe to play that night, a Gibson RB-250, with a fifth string slide instead of spikes.

While I'm up there singing in this really neat auditorium—it's like from the sixteenth century, and immaculate, so the sound is just completely incredible—this happened both sets, I'm singing, and in the background I can hear, "This son of a bitch! I cannot tune this son of a bitch!" This went on all night. And the funny part of the story is that the guy that brought the banjo is sitting right in the front row.

Beginning with *Bluegrass Holiday*, J.D. had produced his own albums, except the Starday *New South*. Only he knew the effects he wanted on each one, and only he could choose the sidemen who would help to create those sounds. J.D. owned the master of *Somewhere Between* and in 2000 remastered it and four additional sides Keith Whitley had cut for Rounder before going with RCA. The title song, "Sad Songs and Waltzes," a Willie Nelson lament for the state of country music, was an outtake from *Somewhere Between*. The collection (Rounder 0399) includes some of the best harmony singers in bluegrass and country music: Dale Ann Bradley, Steve Gulley, Wes Hightower, Carl Jackson, Gene Johnson, and Alison Krauss and backup singers the Jordanaires.

Carefully chosen Nashville sidemen (some of whom, Steve Bryant, Glen Duncan, Randy Howard, and Jeff White, also played bluegrass) are joined by J.D. Crowe on banjo on two cuts, to create *real* country music, the kind not heard for more than a generation, as a tribute to and a collaboration with Keith's extraordinary voice.

The result is a rich and varied representation of the man J.D. called "a singer's singer," produced with skill and caring by the man often called "a banjo player's banjo player," proving once again that Crowe's talents are not limited to his picking and that he knows as much about country music as he does about bluegrass.

In the late 1990s, Rickey Wasson bought a music store, and Dwight, who had a day job, was trying to build a house, and had a baby on the way, so they both took off a year or so.[15]

"It was 'cause I was playing too much, and they couldn't make all the shows," J.D. said.[16] "Robert Hale was in the band when I disbanded. When I came back, there was a point when I hired [him] back into the band, also Darrell Webb [mandolin], whom I had used before, and of course, Curt Chapman and myself, and that was the band [with Phil on Dobro] for quite a while. It was a good band, and I enjoyed that time. Robert Hale is a great singer, and Darrell Webb is a great singer and musician."[17]

"I had filled in several times," Robert said, "and when Crowe asked if I'd think about coming back, it was like putting on a pair of well-fitting shoes. Phil and Curt and Darrell Webb were in the band and also playing in Dollywood; I sort of inherited that. It turned out to be the beginning of Wildfire."

"[At one point], we [Crowe's band] weren't playing much," Phil said. "I used to play at Dollywood when it was Silver Dollar City and Goldrush Junction. I knew people who were there, and they asked us to come and play. We weren't planning to start a band or nothing. We wanted a record to sell at the park, and Pinecastle Records picked it up."[18]

"Wildfire," Curt said, "was a sideline at Dollywood during the week for extra money; we did the album to sell to tourists for extra money, too."[19]

"Phil talked to me about [working at Dollywood]," J.D. said, "and I didn't want to do that, and I said, 'You guys go on and do it, and just do it as a foursome, or get somebody else to play the banjo,' 'cause I didn't really want to do it, and they did."[20]

In 2001, Barry Crabtree joined Wildfire as banjo player, and the band was attracting more interest and bookings. Eventually, the guys decided to leave J.D. and go out on their own. "It started really looking good, like things were going to happen," Phil said, "but none of us wanted to leave J.D. We liked him so much, and enjoyed playing, and stuff. We'd mess around a lot, thinking of ideas of how to tell him, but I just couldn't tell him about it."[21]

"I could see this thing developing," J. D. said, "and I could tell that they was wanting to get out and do something other than what they were doing with me."[22]

"Finally," Phil said, "we were at Shepherdsville [Kentucky] and told J.D., and he started laughing. He said, 'I've had more fun with this. I knew that you guys were doing this, and I loved watching you all sweat, waiting to tell me.'"[23]

"We dreaded telling him," Robert said, but he said, 'I was wondering when y'all were going to tell me.' He made it easy for us; he said, 'If I hadn't done what y'all are doing, I'd still be a Sunny Mountain Boy.'"

"So that's how that worked out," J.D. said. "It was all right with me, 'cause I was dissatisfied also. Some things work out for the best, from both sides."[24]

J.D. has said that four or five years is the normal tenure for his musicians. "Then you get tired and want to try something new," he said in *Frets Magazine*. "It's great at the time, but I don't want to continue doing what I did in 1970." His band members have gone into other kinds of music or started their own groups. "That's where progress comes from," he said, "how new groups evolve."[25] He is pleased with what they did together, that they had fun doing it, and that they are all still friends.

"Speaking for Wildfire," Curt said, "we wouldn't be doing this without J.D.'s help. He was all for it and gave us pointers and stuff."[26]

"I played with him for eleven years," Phil said. "They were good years. I think Crowe was ready for a change, because we had got away from what J.D.'s sound was. He rehired Rickey and Dwight and got his sound back that I like to hear Crowe do. I think J.D. was ready to turn the page at that point, and he turned a good one. I think they sound really good; they're a good fit for him."[27]

"The evolution of J.D.'s band sound changes drastically from band to band," Harold Nixon said. He followed Curt on bass but began when Robert Hale was still in the band.

"When Phil and them started Wildfire," Dwight said, "I called J.D. I've been here nine years now." Rickey returned at the same time. "There's a sort of bond between me and Rickey and J.D.," Dwight said. "We all have a big part in the band."

The trio they had fell back into place instantly, with Rickey's rich, resonant lead balanced by Dwight's strong tenor. Instrumentation was different, however, without the Dobro—Aubrey Haynie came in on fiddle for a short time, but he was a busy session musician and could not travel so much.

From nearby Winchester, Kentucky, Harold Nixon had played with local bands John Cosby and the Bluegrass Drifters, Don Stanley and Middle Creek, and Billie Renée and the Cumberlands as well as with Unlimited Tradition, Dave Evans, and frequently with Richard Bennett. He brought to the band classical training—he started to play in the sixth grade and was in the Kentucky All-State Youth Orchestra—and the flawless timing Crowe required.

"I was a little apprehensive," Harold said. "The only recording [of Crowe's] I'd ever heard was *Blackjack,* but I'd heard all of his songs in jam sessions. J.D.'s material is jam material; the songs are standards. I was comfortable from the beginning. I liked the idea of no dress code. It was neat that these guys clustered together and were having a good time. I enjoyed the lack of competition. My favorite part: none of the groups I had played with had J.D.'s high profile."

After Aubrey, a succession of fiddle players, including Bobby Hicks, Mike Cleveland, Steve Thomas, and Ron Stewart, filled in, until Ron became the New South's full-time fiddler in August 2003 at the J.D. Crowe Festival.

The festival began in 2001 and is held annually at Wilmore, Kentucky, near Lexington. With sponsorship by parks and recreation groups, the Jessamine County Fiscal Court, and St. Joseph's Hospital, it is one of the best-managed festivals anywhere. "Dean Osborne does the booking," J.D. said. "I'm involved, but he does the calling; I don't talk to anybody [about booking]." At the festival, J.D. "holds court" backstage, surrounded by fans and old friends, and his band always performs.

Multi-instrumentalist Stewart had a wealth of experience; as "Little Ronnie Stewart," he had played in his family's band for fifteen years before joining the Lynn Morris Band, where he stayed for six years, playing and recording on banjo, fiddle, and occasionally mandolin and guitar. He had also produced a recording on which he played all the instruments. He was IBMA's Fiddle Player of the Year in 2000.

"Crowe had called me before Lynn's illness," he said, "and I told J.D., 'If I could ever help you, I'd like to work with you.' He gave me an open invitation." Ron described his rehearsal for his first "fill-in" at the Birchmere: "It was one song. We played 'No Mother or Dad,' and I tried to play as close to Benny Sims as I could. Crowe said, 'If you know that, my stuff is easy.' I knew all that old [Flatt and Scruggs] stuff, and that's what he cared about. I respect him a lot for that."

Ron was filling in with Crowe when Lynn suffered a stroke. "I wasn't about to jump ship! She had a whole season's worth of shows booked. I felt like I needed to finish out the season and help them do what they needed to do." Ron played out the season with Lynn's husband, bassist Marshall Wilborn, and mandolin player Jesse Brock, filling in with the New South when he had an open date:

> What a great band! And to get to work with a banjo player who backs the fiddle up the way he does. I was nervous when I started, because there'd been no fiddle [in the band] since Bobby [Slone]. I didn't want the whole thing to change—the whole dynamic of the band. I needed to make this work, but Crowe loves the fiddle. That seemed odd to me after hearing all this stuff all these years, but [he] said, "I love the fiddle."
>
> He can play fiddle, too, and he's played with the greatest fiddle players in the world. And, [me] being a banjo player [also], getting to hear some of that at first hand. We'd sit up in the front of the bus with two banjos, sometimes for a couple of hundred miles. We'd watch Flatt and Scruggs videos and stay up all night watching those things.
>
> Hanging out with J.D.'s not like hanging out with a band leader. It's like hanging out with a buddy. I have nothing but good things to say about working with him.

"It's almost like being with your family," Rickey said. "You spend 95 percent of your time offstage, rather than onstage. We all like the same things, the same styles of music, and our idols are all the same. It's not always that way—only one rotten egg in the bunch can spoil the whole thing. J.D. don't have to worry about that; he's probably having as much fun as he ever had."

J.D.'s attitude is probably one reason for the high comfort level in his band. In answer to a question in *Frets'* "Questions" column about how he chooses band members, he said, "There's no room in the band for someone who can't feel and enjoy the music. After he's learned the tunes and gotten used to playing with us, he can add some of his own ideas. I hire the pickers, but I don't want them to say they work *for* me. They work *with* me. All I'm interested in is having a good group."[28]

"[J.D.] don't play the leader role," Dwight said. "You pretty much know what your job is, and as long as you're doing it, you don't hear much from him. He never told me how to play anything, never told me how to dress, never told me how to sing something. That's rare. For the most part, he's let me be me."

"I can't remember J.D. ever saying anything [restrictive] to me," Harold said.

"He never tells anybody what to play," Ron said. "I think he's really smart there. He just wants to see where your mind's coming from."

"A lot of J.D.'s music is based around the fiddle and the Dobro," Rickey said. "The slower, more country stuff. I know he's really enjoying playing with Ronnie, because Ronnie knows the old styles and all the different old fiddle players, and it's amazing to watch J.D. and Ronnie communicate with each other, because it's almost like they're not even talking. Ronnie can play something on the fiddle, and J.D. responds with a look or a face that says, 'I know where you're coming from; I know where you heard that.' It's pretty fun to watch them backstage; they have a ball just being around each other and doing that kind of stuff. I know they both equally enjoy that."

After four years of performing together, the current New South finally went into the studio to record. Fans had been clamoring for a new release, and they had been performing several songs that were right (some said "overdue") for recording.

"Lefty's Old Guitar," brought to the band by Rickey, was a natural for people who revere the work of Lefty Frizzell and is an indication of the country flavor of the album. Other songs were "Mississippi River Raft," Larry Sparks's "Just Loving You," the traditional "Rovin' Gambler," "In My Next Life" (recorded by Merle Haggard), Dwight McCall's "I Only Wish You Knew," "Loneliness," "I'm a Hobo," "Too Often Left Alone," "Blue Bonnet Lane" (recorded by Jim and Jesse), "She Knows When You're on My Mind Again," and a gospel song, "You Can Be a Millionaire with Me." The only performers outside the band were pedal-steel player Doug Jernigan on two cuts and Cia Cherryholmes singing harmony on one cut.

Vocal "stacks" vary throughout the CD, with Dwight's transcending tenor carrying the melody on three songs and high-baritone harmony on two. One track is an old-fashioned "brother-style" duet, and a half-dozen others follow a straight trio form, with J.D.'s baritone and Dwight's tenor bracketing Rickey's honest, luxuriant lead—a lead that gives its own meaning to the "story" songs, whether he speaks for a guitar or a dirt farmer.

Lefty's Old Guitar (Rounder 0512-2) was released in October 2006 and was reviewed immediately in the *Washington Post*: "[This album] showcases one of the best bands [Crowe] has ever had." The review explained the title song and the place of Lefty Frizzell in country music, and said, "[Crowe's] terrific new album is full of honky-tonk . . . melodies filtered through . . . a bluegrass quintet."[29]

J.D.'s hometown paper, the *Lexington Herald-Leader,* gave the lie to the old saw that "no man is a hero in his own backyard," selecting *Lefty's Old Guitar* as the "Critic's Pick" and saying that it "illustrates the sense of taste that . . . pervades Crowe's sublime music." The review praised all the musicians and called Ronnie Stewart "possibly the finest instrumentalist to enter the Crowe ranks in 15 years." The album "is the work of an ensemble that is scholarly in more ways than one."[30]

Reviewed in the *Bluegrass Unlimited* of March 2007, *Lefty's Old Guitar* is the Highlight Album and is called "bluegrass at its best." "The banjo . . . and the man behind it *are* bluegrass. This band [has] all the components required. . . . Great talent coalesces with that archetypal trio. [Crowe] has not forgotten that . . . bluegrass is country music. We get that . . . blend of hard country and bluegrass that has been the Crowe sound for these thirty years. Some of the best music we can listen to."[31]

The CD was nominated for a Grammy. "Cool factor–wise," Harold Nixon said, "it was really neat to be on a Grammy-nominated record. Dwight and I were the only ones that went [to the ceremony], and it was neat being there."

Two of the three Kentucky Mountain Boys recordings, *The Model Church* (Rebel CD-1585) and *Ramblin' Boy,* retitled *Blackjack* (Rebel CD-1583), had been available on CD for some time, but the sound quality of their first album, *Bluegrass Holiday* (Lemco LLP 609), was considered too poor for transfer. As technology changed, however, Rebel Records was able to produce an acceptable, if not perfect, product, and in April 2007 reissued this historic collection, including four tracks from singles recorded at the same time, with an inspired vintage postcard cover. Nearly forty years old, this music of J.D. Crowe, Doyle Lawson, Red Allen, and Bobby Slone is as fresh and exciting as ever and helps to explain the instant popularity that followed its initial release.

The *Bluegrass Holiday* reissue (Reb-CD-1598) was reviewed in the May 2007 *Bluegrass Unlimited*, calling it "long-hoped for" and "fabulous," preceded by an enthusiastic "At last!"[32]

"Crowe played a show at my old high school [in Pinehurst, North Carolina]," Greg Luck said, "and I filled in for Ronnie [Stewart] on fiddle. We ended up in the van, listening to Haggard and George Jones, the CD they did together. We had done that all the time [I was in the band], riding up the road and listening to old country music."

Later that year, both Ron and Harold left the band. "There was no horribleness when I left," Harold said. "Ronnie was leaving, and I didn't know who might be coming in." They were replaced by John Bowman, bass, and Steve Thomas, fiddle; the year 2010 saw the departure of both Bowman and Thomas, with Matt DeSpain joining on resonator guitar and Kyle Perkins on bass. There is always a long list of musicians who are eager to work with Crowe; all he needs to do is make a telephone call.

"There were rumors that there was jealousy between us [J.D. and Ron]," Ron said. "I had written something on the Bluegrass Blog; I told Crowe I wouldn't use it if he didn't want it, but I wanted to do that out of respect for him. Leaving was just something I needed to do; it was the hardest gig I ever quit. So much was just how I felt about Crowe. I've played with him a lot since, and [still] fill in anytime I get a chance." When someone leaves Crowe, Ron said, "there isn't any weirdness. I hold a high regard for him in that. He separates music from the personal as best as anyone could do."

"There's a feeling of satisfaction," Dwight said, "when you know you're where you're supposed to be, and you feel the music is the way you imagined it in your head, like driving a perfect car. The fact that I was a part of it was a sense of completion I'd never had. A lot of it is his banjo, and the timing of his banjo playing. That's a satisfaction you rarely, rarely ever get. That was my drug. I'll be driving down the highway and look over and say, 'I'm playing with J.D. Crowe, my childhood hero!' And he'll be over there snoring."

In his long career, J.D. Crowe has done many "different things": he learned to play Scruggs-style banjo when hardly anyone else was trying; adapted his banjo playing to Jimmy Martin's style and timing, becoming Martin's yardstick for "Jimmy Martin banjo"; developed his own distinctive sound on the banjo and influenced thousands; brought material from many sources into his own music and made it fit; defied opinion to experiment with "electric bluegrass"; played his own eclectic "American music"; made a foray into pure country music when the genre had been taken over by the "Nashville Sound"; and returned to his own brand of bluegrass, to even greater praise and recognition. Most important, he changed the sound of bluegrass music forever. He has set a standard for bandleaders; never dictatorial, he has taught by example. His business methods are exemplary, and his professionalism is beyond question.

J.D.'s description of how to work in a band might also be a good description of how to live: "In a band," he said, "you're part of a puzzle, and whatever part you play has to fit in. If you're a bass player, you're not a lead player, but you're just as important; your part is just as important as anyone's. Everybody has what they've got to do, and if they don't do it, the music won't be right."[33]

CODA
TONE, TOUCH, TIMING, AND TASTE

In a lifetime of public performance, J.D. Crowe has won just about every award available to him, although honors and recognition have never been among his goals. They are, however, the only tangible way for a devoted public to let an artist know he is appreciated, to "give back" for the hours of enjoyment his work has provided.

Among his awards are the Grammy for Best Country Instrumental Performance in 1983 for "Fireball," with the reunited 1975 New South, on *Bluegrass: The World's Greatest Show,* and Grammy nominations for Best Bluegrass Album for *Flashback* in 1994 and for *Lefty's Old Guitar* in 2008 with later versions of the New South.

J.D. Crowe received the Kentucky Governor's Award in the Arts' Folk Heritage Award for 2001, was named a "Kentucky Star" by the Kentucky League of Cities and the Downtown Lexington Corporation in 2003 (his star is in the sidewalk in front of Lexington's historic Kentucky Theatre), and was inducted into the Kentucky Music Hall of Fame and Museum in 2004.

As a participant in the Bluegrass Album Band, he won the (professional) International Bluegrass Music Association's Instrumental Group of the Year award in 1990 and the IBMA Instrumental Album of the Year in 1997.

Other honors include the IBMA's Album of the Year award in 2006 with the New South as part of the compilation album *Celebration of Life: Musicians against Childhood Cancer.* The New South recording *Lefty's Old Guitar* tied for IBMA Album of the Year in 2007, and the title song won the SPBGMA's Song of the Year award in 2008.

A finalist practically every year, Crowe won the IBMA Banjo Player of the Year award in 1994 and 2004 and was inducted into the IBMA Hall of Honor (now Hall of Fame) in 2003.

The (fan-based) Society for the Preservation of Blue Grass Music in America awarded J.D. Crowe "Banjo Performer of the Year" in 1984, 1985, 1986, 1994, and 1995 before giving him the Masters Gold Award in 1996. He was inducted into the SPBGMA's Preservation Hall of Greats in 1991.

In 2006, J.D. Crowe was inducted into the Bill Monroe Bluegrass Hall of Fame at Bean Blossom Park in Indiana.

Crowe has had a long association with GHS Strings, for whom he compiled a very successful set of banjo strings under his name; the Gibson Company has designed two banjos to his specifications, the "J.D. Crowe Model" and the "Blackjack." In 2008, he was asked to design a custom thumb pick for BlueChip Picks.

In Lexington, Kentucky, in 2008, a painting of a youthful J.D. Crowe was included with other musicians in a huge mural at the corner of North Limestone and West Seventh streets, just a stone's throw from the building that housed Martin's Place.

Perhaps more telling than plaques and statues are the words of musicians who have known J.D. Crowe, men who have said sincere and sentimental things in interviews they almost undoubtedly have never said to his face. In describing their relationships with him, the most frequently occurring phrase was, "We never had a cross word," repeated by colleagues, band members, and friends. In a career that spans six decades, that is a remarkable achievement.

> SONNY OSBORNE: "Because we were the same age and played the banjo and both Kentucky guys, we didn't have to *become* friends; we just were. If you've got him as a friend, you've got the best friend you ever had in your life."

PAUL WILLIAMS: "Since November 1957, J.D. Crowe and I have been good friends. It does my heart good to see J.D. get the recognition he deserves—he has lived to get the roses while he's alive, and that makes me glad for him. He's just a super person, and I'm glad I've known him. We all know what the word *friend* means, but he makes all the criteria of what the word means."

DOYLE LAWSON: "I've been a professional musician now for over forty-four years, and forty-one of those years, I've known J.D. Today, J.D. is as close to me as a brother, and even though we haven't worked in a band on a constant basis, we've just never really drifted apart that much. We may not talk to each other sometimes for six months, but when I talk to him, or when I see him, it's just like it was yesterday. That's a pretty long friendship, and true friends are hard to find, and when you get one, you need to treasure it. More than anything, in all the good music I got to play with J.D. over the years, the thing I value most is my friendship with him."[1]

TONY RICE: "If I could count my major influences on one hand—which I could—then J.D. would probably be the one person who had more of a direct influence on what my own general musicianship would evolve into—particularly the rudiments of my own musicianship—the majority of that would come from J.D. Crowe, more so than any other single person. Yes.

"It's hard to explain what you derive from [influences], because sometimes you derive facets of their musicianship and you don't even really know it's happening. But with J.D. Crowe, it was more or less deliberate."

JERRY DOUGLAS: "A lot of people will say 'It says "J.D. Crowe and the New South," but he's just the banjo player and the baritone singer' They don't work for him; they don't know the decisions that are made, and all these things that go on back there. He is in control, and it's just fine with everybody else, 'cause he's making the right moves all the time."

RICKY SKAGGS: "J.D. Crowe has had his influence and left his mark in bluegrass music: legendary banjo [player], legendary band leader, and still playing great. He's an awesome musician. I thank God for our friendship; I love J.D.—we're great friends. Everybody loves J.D."

DWIGHT McCALL: "Even when me and Rickey left [the band, briefly], when I asked if I could play his banjo, he let me take it. If that doesn't tell you what kind of guy he is, nothing will."

CURT CHAPMAN: "[J.D.] quit being my boss after the first two or three shows; he became a friend, and I think that's his relationship with everybody that has played in the New South. To be as good on his instrument [as he is], and a master of his craft, he has got more humility in him than anybody I know."[2]

ROBERT HALE: "Crowe's good about helping people. When my dad passed away, I had a memorial show for him because he'd played music and was well known in the region. It was not a benefit show, just a memorial. Crowe came all the way from Lexington [to West Virginia] to play. That pretty much sums up Crowe, that he would do that. I have nothing but love and respect for him."

FRANK SCHOEPF: "The first night I sat in front of J.D. was, without any exaggeration, a life-changing experience. It took me in a totally different direction. I couldn't have asked for better friends than I've found through playing bluegrass, and it all started there at Martin's."

GENE JOHNSON: "I admire him as a person, as well [as a musician]. It doesn't make any difference whether you're playing music or digging a ditch, it's the people you play with that make the difference."

JERRY DOUGLAS: "I couldn't believe I was actually going to play with this guy; I would have done it for free."

GREG LUCK: "J.D.'s the kind of guy you can work for and be friends with afterward, and know the friendship means something to him."

WENDY MILLER: "In a time in Kentucky when the rest of them went to Nashville, J.D. stayed here. He's been a tremendous asset to the 5-string banjo and to bluegrass music."[3]

DON RIGSBY: "J.D. is one of the single most important figures in bluegrass, both from the modern side and the traditional side. He's not afraid to step out on a limb, but he always comes back to the trunk. He's bent every one of the 'unwritten rules' of bluegrass, but never broken one. The best thing is, if you've got him as a friend, you'll always have him for a friend. Most people are acquaintances, but that's something different."

BARRY CRABTREE: "He's an idol, but he's your buddy, too."

PAUL ADKINS: "J.D.'s just one of the nicest people you'd ever want to meet. He's somebody you can count on—whatever he told you, that was what he did."

RAYMOND W. McLAIN: "J.D.'s always so gracious, not only to let his band members shine, but to make it about the other people. He doesn't make it a star trip for himself; he just wants to play good music."

ALAN MUNDE: "J.D. raised my sensibility of tone and timing. No matter what I played, I wanted the notes to have that clarity. He set a standard of what a good banjo player could be. He was always real nice to me on a personal level; he treated me as if we were equals, like I was part of his community and not just a kid from Oklahoma."

RICHARD BENNETT: "I've never played with anyone else I had as much fun with as Crowe. We had a lot in common besides music. [J.D.] to me was like a father figure or a brother; we enjoyed each other's company."

SONNY OSBORNE: "J.D.'s musical ability is nothing compared to what he is as a person. He's just untouchable—he's as good as it gets."

DOYLE LAWSON: "I believe J.D. right now is having probably as good a time playing music as he has ever had. He's a very happy man; he's got a great band, he's working about what he wants to work, and I'm happy for him, 'cause he's got it where it does what he wants to do, and that's good."[4]

TERRY BAUCOM: "I consider J.D. a close and good friend; he's such a good guy."

RON STEWART: "I value who he is and his friendship above anything musically."

SAM BUSH: "One of my most proud moments on behalf of Courtney Johnson was when J.D. said, 'Do you want to hear my Courtney lick?' That let me know right then he could be as progressive as anybody; he knows what everyone is doing and how to do it, but he has stuck with his own style. Maybe that's why everyone wants to play like J.D."

EDDIE ADCOCK: "J.D.'s just as nice as anyone you ever met; he doesn't make waves. He's always trying to get along with everybody. We hug each other when we meet and have at least a short conversation. He knows I've been through it, and he's been through it, too."

DAN BROCK: "[J.D.] creates an environment; if you're able to get better, you're going to get better. He's got the best training school—he teaches by example—and he has a way of making everybody who plays with him sound good. It's not an accident; for one thing, they *are* good, but when they leave him, they're superior musicians. He knows how to sublimate his ego for the good of the group."

When his long association with Earl Scruggs ended in 1969 Lester Flatt proposed the ultimate testament to J.D.'s musicianship. Through Josh Graves, "He asked me to join his band," J.D. said. "It killed me to turn him down, but I'm glad now . . . you don't replace *The Man!*" Besides, he added modestly, "We had this new thing going and it looked pretty promising."[5]

NOTES

Chapter 1. I Never Heard a Sound Like That

1. B. Crowe interview, February 3, 1998.
2. J.D. interview, January 9, 2008.
3. Orval Crowe obituary, *Lexington Herald-Leader*, February 17, 1989.
4. J.D. interview, October 29, 2008.
5. B. Crowe interview, June 27, 2007.
6. J.D. interview, January 9, 2008.
7. B. Crowe interview, February 3, 1998.
8. J.D. interview, January 9, 2008.
9. B. Crowe interview, June 27, 2007.
10. J.D. interview, January 29, 2008.
11. Ibid.
12. Collett interview, February 3, 1998.
13. J.D. interview, January 29, 2008.
14. B. Crowe interview, February 3, 1998.
15. J.D. interview, January 9, 2008.
16. B. Crowe interview, June 27, 2007.
17. J.D. interview, January 9, 2008.
18. J.D. interview, March 10, 1981.
19. J.D. interview, January 14, 1981.
20. J.D. interview, January 29, 2008.

21. Collett interview, February 3, 1998.

22. Collett interview, June 27, 2008.

23. Collett interview, February 3, 1998.

24. J.D. interview, January 9, 2008.

25. Collett interview, June 27, 2007.

26. J.D. interview, January 29, 2008.

27. J.D. interview, September 7, 1994.

28. J.D. interview, January 15, 2002.

29. Ibid.

30. J.D. interview, January 29, 2008.

31. *Kentucky Mountain Barn Dance Song Book*. No copyright date but probably 1950, as photographs in the booklet clearly show the WKLX banner, and the *Barn Dance* moved from WVLK to WKLX in April 1950 but did not leave Clay Gentry until December.

32. Ibid.

33. *Lexington Leader,* September 10, 1949.

34. John D. Wright Jr., *Lexington: Heart of the Bluegrass* (Lexington: Lexington-Fayette County Historic Commission, 1982), 177.

35. *Lexington Leader,* September 10, 1949.

36. *Lexington Leader,* September 16, 1949.

37. J.D. interview, January 29, 2008.

38. J.D. interview, January 9, 2008.

39. J.D. interview, May 17, 1976.

40. J.D. interview, September 7, 1994.

41. J.D. interview, May 17, 1976.

42. J.D. interview, September 7, 1994.

43. J.D. interview, January 9, 2008.

44. J.D. interview, September 7, 1994.

45. Ibid.

46. J.D. interview, January 9, 2008.

47. J.D. interview, January 15, 2002.

48. *Lexington Leader,* September 23, 1949.

49. Scruggs interview, February 24, 1996.

50. Jake Lambert and Curly Sechler, *The Good Things Out Weigh the Bad: A Biography of Lester Flatt* (Hendersonville, Tenn.: Jay-Lyn Publication, 1982), 13.

51. J.D. interview, May 17, 1976.

52. J.D. interview, January 9, 2008.

53. B. Crowe interview, June 27, 2007.

54. J.D. interview, January 9, 2008.

55. *Kentucky Mountain Barn Dance Song Book.*

56. Collett interview, February 3, 1998.

57. Collett interview, June 27, 2007.

58. J.D. interview, May 17, 1976.

59. J.D. interview, January 9, 2008.

60. J.D. interview, May 17, 1976.

61. Collett interview, June 27, 2007.

62. B. Crowe interview, June 27, 2007.

63. Ibid.

64. Collett interview, June 27, 2007.

65. J.D. interview, January 9, 2008.

66. Collett interview, February 3, 1998.

67. B. Crowe interview, June 27, 2007.

68. Collett interview, June 27, 2007.

69. Collett interview, June 7, 2008.

70. B. Crowe interview, June 27, 2007.

71. J.D. interview, May 20, 2008.

72. Collett interview, June 27, 2007.

73. *Lexington Leader,* November 16, 1951.

74. J.D. interview, January 9, 2008.

75. Ibid.

76. Scruggs interview, September 5, 2007.

77. J.D. interview, May 17, 1976.

78. J.D. interview, January 9, 2008.

79. J.D. interview, May 17, 1976.

80. J.D. interview, January 9, 2008.

81. J.D. interview, July 19, 2008.

82. J.D. interview, September 13, 2006.

83. J.D. interview, January 26, 1996.

84. J.D. interview, January 9, 2008.

85. J.D. interview, May 17, 1976.

86. J.D. interview, September 7, 1994.

87. Ibid.

88. J.D. interview, January 9, 2008.

Chapter 2. I Just Wanted to Pick

1. J.D. interview, January 9, 2008.

2. J.D. interview, September 7, 1994.

3. Ivan Tribe, "Esco Hankins, Traditional Country and Gospel Singer," *Bluegrass Unlimited,* February 1985, 17–18.

4. *Kentucky Mountain Barn Dance Song Book.*

5. *Crazy* indicated sponsorship by the Crazy Water Crystals company; Hankins likely lost his sponsor when he moved out of their area.

6. *Lexington Herald-Leader,* November 19, 1990.

7. J.D. interview, January 15, 2002.

8. J.D. interview, January 9, 2008.

9. Collett interview, June 27, 2007.

10. B. Crowe interview, June 27, 2007.

11. J.D. interview, January 9, 2008.

12. J.D. interview, May 20, 2008.

13. J.D. interview, January 25, 2002.

14. J.D. interview, January 9, 2008.

15. *Lexington Leader,* April 1, 1950.

16. *Lexington Leader,* April 12, 1950.

17. *Lexington Leader,* December 15, 1950.

18. J.D. interview, January 9, 2008.

19. J.D. interview, May 20, 2008.

20. J.D. interview, January 9, 2008.

21. B. Crowe interview, June 27, 2007.

22. J.D. interview, January 9, 2008.

23. J.D. interview, January 29, 2008.

24. J.D. interview, May 20, 2008.

25. Ibid.

26. Ibid.

27. Ed McClanahan, "Little Enis Pursues His Muse," *Playboy,* March 1974, 117–204.

28. J.D. interview, May 20, 2008.

29. J.D. interview, September 7, 1994. There were actually three LPs recorded at Lemco Studio: *Bluegrass Holiday,* with Red Allen, and *Ramblin' Boy* and *The Model Church,* with Larry Rice. The two 45-rpm singles recorded there during the same time period also included Red Allen and were issued on the King Bluegrass label. Doyle Lawson and Bobby Slone appeared on all the above recordings with J.D.

30. J.D. interview, March 12, 1996.

31. Dan Foy, "Gibson Banjo Shipments by Year, 1948–1979," Banjophiles.com. Used by permission.

32. J.D. interview, July 19, 2008.

33. Foy, "Gibson Banjo Shipments."

34. J.D. interview, March 12, 1996.

35. Doug Hutchens, "Rudy Lyle, Classic Bluegrass Banjo Man," *Bluegrass Unlimited,* April 1985, 44–49.

36. Scruggs interview, February 24, 1996. "Graphophone" was Columbia's counterpart to Victor's "Victrola" record player.

37. B. Crowe interview, February 3, 1998.

38. J.D. interview, January 29, 2008.

39. J.D. interview, May 20, 2008.

40. Ibid.

41. J.D. interview, March 12, 1996.

42. J.D. interview, May 20, 2008.

43. Ibid.

44. Ibid.

45. Ibid.

46. J.D. interview, January 9, 2008.

47. Frank Godbey, "Pee Wee Lambert," *Bluegrass Unlimited,* January 1979, 12–20.

48. J.D. interview, May 20, 2008.

49. J.D. interview, September 7, 1994.

50. Ibid.

51. J.D. interview, May 20, 2008.

52. Godbey, "Pee Wee Lambert."

53. J.D. interview, January 9, 2008.

54. J.D. interview, September 7, 1994.

55. J.D. interview, September 13, 2006.

56. Collett interview, February 3, 1998.

57. J.D. interview, January 9, 2008.

58. Glenna Fisher and Bernie Fisher, "WPFB, Where the Bluegrass Tradition Lives On," *Bluegrass Unlimited,* February 1985.

59. J.D. interview, May 20, 2008.

60. J.D. interview, September 7, 1994.

61. Ibid.

62. J.D. interview, January 9, 2008.

Chapter 3. *The Road to Detroit*

1. J.D. interview, May 20, 2008.

2. J.D. interview, July 19, 2008.

3. Foy, "Gibson Banjo Shipments" (see chap. 2, n. 31).

4. Ibid.

5. J.D. interview, September 7, 1994.

6. J.D. interview, May 20, 2008.

7. J.D. interview, January 29, 2008.

8. J.D. interview, May 20, 2008.

9. J.D. interview, January 29, 2008.

10. Ibid.

11. J.D. interview, May 20, 2008.

12. J.D. interview, July 19, 2008.

13. J.D. interview, January 29, 2008.

14. J.D. interview, September 7, 1994.

15. J.D. interview, May 20, 2008.

16. J.D. interview, July 19, 2008.

17. J.D. interview, May 20, 2008.

18. Medline Plus, a service of the U.S. National Library of Medicine and the National Institutes of Health, http://www.nlm.nih.gov. See also the Canadian Lung Association.

19. Collett interview, February 3, 1998.

20. Canadian Lung Association.

21. J.D. interview, May 20, 2008.

22. Collett interview, February 3, 1998.

23. J.D. interview, September 7, 1994.

24. Collett interview, February 3, 1998.

25. Collett interview, June 27, 2007.

26. J.D. interview, May 20, 2008.

27. J.D. interview, January 9, 2008.

28. B. Crowe interview, July 27, 2007.

29. J.D. interview, September 7, 1994.

30. J.D. interview, January 9, 2008.

31. J.D. interview, September 7, 1994.

32. J.D. interview, May 20, 2008.

33. J.D. interview, January 15, 2002.

34. J.D. interview, July 19, 2008.

35. J.D. interview, May 17, 1976.

36. J.D. interview, July 19, 2008.

37. J.D. interview, January 9, 2008.

38. J.D. interview, May 20, 2008.

39. J.D. interview, January 15, 2002.

40. J.D. interview, May 20, 2008.

41. J.D. interview, January 15, 2002.

42. J.D. interview, May 20, 2008.

43. J.D. interview, January 15, 2002.

44. J.D. interview, July 19, 2008.

45. J.D. interview, May 20, 2008.

46. J.D. interview, January 9, 2008.

47. J.D. interview, July 19, 2008.

48. Tom Ewing, "Earl Taylor: One of the Bluegrass Greats," *Bluegrass Unlimited,* September 1976, 10–14.

49. J.D. interview, January 15, 2002.

50. J.D. interview, July 19, 2008.

51. J.D. interview, January 15, 2002.

52. J.D. interview, January 9, 2008.

53. Ibid.

54. Ibid.

55. Ibid.

56. Ibid.

57. Schoepf interview.

58. J.D. interview, September 7, 1994.

59. Ibid.

60. J.D. interview, May 20, 2008.

61. J.D. interview, September 7, 1994.

62. J.D. interview, January 9, 2008.

63. J.D. interview, October 29, 2008.

64. J.D. interview, July 19, 2008.

65. Ibid.

Chapter 4. Louisiana to Wheeling and Home Again

1. J.D. interview, May 17, 1976.

2. Lawson interview, May 19, 2007.

3. J.D. interview, January 9, 2008.

4. Ibid.

5. J.D. interview, September 7, 1994.

6. J.D. interview, October 29, 2008.

7. J.D. interview, January 29, 2008.

8. J.D. interview, July 19, 2008.

9. J.D. interview, February 26, 1996.

10. J.D. interview, October 29, 2008.

11. Collett interview, June 27, 2007.

12. J.D. interview, October 29, 2008.

13. J.D. interview, July 19, 2008.

14. J.D. interview, October 29, 2008.

15. Ibid.

16. J.D. interview, September 7, 1994.

17. J.D. interview, July 19, 2008.

18. J.D. interview, January 9, 2008.

19. J.D. interview, January 15, 2002.

20. J.D. interview, September 7, 1994.

21. J.D. interview, January 29, 2008.

22. J.D. interview, July 19, 2008.

23. Collett interview, June 27, 2007.

24. J.D. interview, January 29, 2008.

25. Leon Smith, "Talking with the Stars: Two Interviews from *A Bluegrass Hornbook*," *Bluegrass Unlimited*, September 1976, 24.

26. Lawson interview, May 19, 2007.

27. J.D. interview, January 9, 2008.

28. Joslin interview, March 30, 2004.

29. Ibid.

30. Audiotapes from 1964 and 1966 in the possession of Ed Stacy.

31. Whitaker interview.

32. J.D. interview, January 9, 2008.

33. J.D. interview, January 15, 2002.

34. Joslin interview, March 30, 2004.

35. J.D. interview, January 9, 2008.

36. Joslin interview, March 31, 2004.

37. J.D. interview, July 19, 2008.

38. Joslin interview, March 31, 2004.

39. Joslin interview, March 30, 2004.

40. Joslin interview, March 31, 2004.

41. J.D. interview, September 7, 1994.

42. J.D. interview, July 19, 2008.

43. Richard K. Spotswood, "The Commercial Recordings of Charlie Monroe," *Bluegrass Unlimited,* May 1969, 3–6.

44. J.D. interview, March 3, 1996.

45. J.D. interview, September 7, 1994.

46. Joslin interview, March 31, 2004.

47. Audiotape in the possession of Ed Stacy.

48. Ibid.

49. J.D. interview, September 7, 1994.

50. Scott interview, December 1, 2003.

51. Scott interview, December 16, 2003.

Chapter 5. *Why Don't You Come Down to Martin's?*

1. Slone interview, February 15, 1978.

2. Ibid.

3. J.D. interview, September 7, 1994.

4. Slone interview, February 15, 1978.

5. Joslin interview, March 31, 2004.

6. Scott interview, December 1, 2003.

7. J.D. interview, May 20, 2008.

8. Scott interview, December 5, 2003, and July 7, 2008.

9. Marty Godbey, "The Lost Fiddler, Art Stamper," *Bluegrass Unlimited,* November 1982, 24–27.

10. J.D. interview, January 15, 2002.

11. Scott interview, July 7, 2008.

12. J.D. interview, July 19, 2008.

13. J.D. interview, January 29, 2008.

14. Scott interview, December 9, 2003.

15. J.D. interview, January 9, 2008.

16. Slone interview, February 15, 1978.

17. J.D. interview, January 15, 2002.

18. J.D. interview, March 10, 1981.

19. Scott interview, December 9, 2003.

20. J.D. interview, September 7, 1994.

21. J.D. interview, January 9, 2008.

22. J.D. interview, September 7, 1994.

23. Lawson interview, May 19, 2006.

24. Lawson interview, November 18, 2006.

25. Lawson interview, May 19, 2007.

26. Lawson interview, November 18, 2006.

27. J.D. interview, January 9, 2008.

28. Scott interview, December 5, 2003.

29. Lawson interview, November 18, 2006.

30. J.D. interview, September 7, 1994.

31. Lawson interview, May 19, 2007.

32. John E. Kleber, ed., *Kentucky Encyclopedia* (Lexington: University Press of Kentucky, 1992), 243.

33. J.D. interview, January 29, 2008.

34. Lawson interview, November 18, 2006.

35. J.D. interview, July 19, 2008.

36. Lawson interview, November 18, 2006.

37. J.D. interview, July 19, 2008.

38. Scott interview, December 5, 2003.

39. Ibid.

40. Lawson interview, May 19, 2007.

41. Lawson interview, November 18, 2006.

42. Scott interview, December 1, 2003.

43. Scott interview, December 16, 2003.

44. Scott interview, December 5, 2003.

45. Lawson interview, November 18, 2006.

46. Slone interview, February 15, 1978.

47. Ibid.

48. J.D. interview, July 19, 2008.

49. J.D. interview, September 7, 1994.

50. J.D. interview, July 19, 2008.

51. Lawson interview, November 18, 2006.

52. Ibid.

53. J.D. interview, January 9, 2008.

54. J.D. interview, July 19, 2008.

55. J.D. interview, January 9, 2008.

56. Audiotape made by Frank Godbey, July 6, 1968.

57. Travis DuPriest, e-mail, June 23, 2008.

58. Mabel DuPriest, e-mail, June 23, 2008.

59. Ibid.

60. J.D. interview, January 29, 2008.

61. Lawson interview, November 18, 2006.

62. Slone interview, February 15, 1996.

63. J.D. interview, January 29, 2008.

64. J.D. interview, January 9, 2008.

65. Ibid.

66. Lawson interview, November 18, 2006.

67. J.D. interview, September 7, 1994.

Chapter 6. The Red Slipper Lounge

1. Lawson interview, May 19, 2008.

2. J.D. interview, January 9, 2008.

3. J.D. interview, January 29, 2008.

4. Lawson interview, November 18, 2006.

5. Lawson interview, May 19, 2007.

6. J.D. interview, January 29, 2008.

7. Lawson interview, May 19, 2007.

8. Frank Godbey, "Bluegrass in the Cocktail Lounge," *Bluegrass Unlimited,* February 1969, 9.

9. J.D. interview, January 9, 2008.

10. J.D. interview, January 29, 2008.

11. J.D. interview, September 7, 1994.

12. "Record Reviews," *Bluegrass Unlimited,* July 1969, 35.

13. "Record Reviews," *Bluegrass Unlimited,* December 1969, 23.

14. J.D. interview, July 19, 2008.

15. Lawson interview, May 19, 2007.

16. Lawson interview, November 18, 2006.

17. Ibid.

18. Slone interview, February 15, 1978.

19. Lawson interview, November 18, 2006.

20. Ibid.

21. J.D. interview, September 12, 2006.

22. Lawson interview, May 19, 2007.

23. Lawson interview, November 18, 2006.

24. Lawson interview, May 19, 2007.

25. J.D. interview, September 7, 1994.

26. Lawson interview, November 18, 2006.

27. J.D. interview, January 15, 2002.

28. Slone interview, February 22, 1996.

29. J.D. interview, September 7, 1994.

30. J.D. interview, November 4, 2008.

31. J.D. interview, October 29, 2008.

32. Ibid.

33. Ibid.

34. Lawson interview, May 19, 2007.

35. *Bluegrass Unlimited,* July 1971.

36. Doug Benson, "Breakthrough in Bluegrass Repertoire," *Bluegrass Unlimited,* October 1969, 3 (emphasis in the original).

37. Lawson interview, November 18, 2006.

38. J.D. interview, October 29, 2008.

39. *Bluegrass Unlimited,* March 1971, 16.

40. *Bluegrass Unlimited,* December 1971.

41. Lawson interview, May 19, 2007.

42. Lawson interview, November 18, 2008.

43. Doug Hutchens, "Banjo's 'n Bluegrass," Yahoo.com lists, posted July 20, 2008. Used by permission.

44. J.D. interview, January 29, 2008.

45. Ibid.

46. Slone interview, February 15, 1978.

47. J.D. interview, January 29, 2008.

48. Slone interview, February 15, 1978.

Chapter 7. Rounder 0044 *and the Convergence of 1975*

1. J.D. interview, September 7, 1994.

2. J.D. interview, November 29, 2008.

3. J.D. interview, May 17, 1976.

4. J.D. interview, January 15, 2002.

5. J.D. interview, October 29, 2008.

6. J.D. interview, January 29, 2008.

7. Ibid.

8. Ibid.

9. Slone interview, February 15, 1978.

10. J.D. interview, September 7, 1994.

11. Ibid.

12. Lawson interview, May 19, 2007.

13. J.D. interview, September 7, 1994.

14. Ibid.

15. Ibid.

16. Ibid.

17. J.D. interview, January 29, 2008.

18. J.D. interview, February 23, 1982.

19. J.D. interview, January 29, 2008.

20. J.D. interview, January 26, 1996.

21. J.D. interview, September 7, 1994.

22. J.D. interview, January 29, 2008.

Chapter 8. The New South

1. J.D. interview, January 29, 2008.

2. David Haney, "Rounder, 15 Years on the Edge," *Bluegrass Unlimited,* September 1986, 23–31.

3. Ibid.

4. "Record Reviews," *Bluegrass Unlimited,* November 1975, 22.

5. "New South (band)," Wikipedia.com.

6. J.D. interview, January 26, 1996.

7. J.D. interview, January 29, 2008.

8. Talbot interview, May 20, 2002.

9. Slone interview, February 15, 1979.

10. Marty Godbey, *"Bluegrass, Bluegrass,* a Television Series," *Bluegrass Unlimited,* November 1977, 9–11.

11. J.D. interview, January 29, 2008.

12. "Record Reviews," *Bluegrass Unlimited,* July 1979, 30.

13. J.D. interview, October 29, 2008.

14. J.D. interview, January 29, 2008.

15. Johnson interview.

16. J.D. interview, January 29, 2008.

17. Talbot interview, May 20, 2002.

18. J.D. interview, March 10, 1981.

19. J.D. interview, March 2, 1996.

20. Talbot interview, September 4, 2007.

21. Slone interview, February 15, 1979.

22. J.D. interview, March 10, 1981.

23. Marty Godbey, "Bobby Slone for President," *Bluegrass Unlimited,* April 1979, 71–79.

24. J.D. interview, January 29, 2008.

25. Charles Wolfe, *Kentucky Country,* 108.

26. *Bluegrass Unlimited,* May 1980, 39.

27. *Frets Magazine,* September 1980, 47.

28. *Banjo Newsletter,* October 2002, 6.

29. J.D. interview, January 29, 2008.

30. *Bluegrass Unlimited,* January 1988, 39.

31. J.D. interview, January 29, 2008.

32. Lawson interview, May 19, 2007.

33. J.D. interview, January 29, 2008.

34. *Frets Magazine,* March 1982, 49.

35. Lawson interview, May 19, 2007.

36. J.D. interview, January 29, 2008.

37. Lawson interview, May 19, 2007.

38. Miller interview, February 22, 1996.

39. Miller interview, November 28, 2007.

40. Miller interview, February 22, 1996.

41. Miller interview, November 28, 2007.

42. J.D. interview, March 10, 1981.

43. J.D. interview, January 29, 2008.

44. Miller interview, November 28, 2007.

45. J.D. interview, January 29, 2008.

46. Miller interview, November 28, 2007.

Chapter 9. Burn Out, Time Out, and Second Wind

1. Miller interview, February 22, 1996.

2. Hayes interview, December 2, 2008.

3. Hayes interview, February 26, 1996.

4. Hayes interview, December 2, 2008.

5. J.D. interview, February 24, 1982.

6. *Frets Magazine,* April 1983, 62.

7. "The Crowe Doesn't Always Fly Straight to Bluegrass," *Columbus Dispatch,* November 6, 1983, F2.

8. Hayes interview, December 2, 2008.

9. Ibid.

10. Miller interview, November 28, 2007.

11. Hayes interview, December 2, 2008.

12. Miller interview, November 28, 2007.

13. Hayes interview, February 26, 1996.

14. Miller interview, November 28, 2007.

15. Hayes interview, December 2, 2008.

16. Miller interview, November 28, 2007.

17. Ibid.

18. Ibid.

19. J.D. interview, January 15, 2002.

20. *Frets Magazine,* May 1983, 55.

21. There was no Bluegrass Grammy Award until 1988.

22. J.D. interview, January 29, 2008.

23. Ibid.

24. J.D. interview, October 29, 2008.

25. J.D. interview, January 29, 2008.

26. "Record Reviews," *Bluegrass Unlimited,* April 1987, 38.

27. Chapman interview, October 14, 2003.

28. Hayes interview, February 26, 1996.

29. Chapman interview, December 19, 2007.

30. Chapman interview, October 14, 2003.

31. Chapman interview, December 19, 2007.

32. Chapman interview, October 14, 2003.
33. Chapman interview, December 19, 2007.
34. J.D. interview, September 7, 1994.
35. J.D. interview, August 12, 2002.
36. Miller interview, November 28, 2007.
37. J.D. interview, January 29, 2008.
38. Chapman interview, December 19, 2007.
39. Lawson interview, May 19, 2007.
40. J.D. interview, January 29, 2008.
41. *Lexington Herald Leader,* February 17, 1989.
42. Slone interview, February 22, 1996.
43. Slone interview, February 15, 1979.
44. Miller interview, November 28, 2007.
45. *Lexington Herald Leader,* May 10, 1989, B1.
46. Slone interview, February 22, 1996.
47. J.D. interview, January 29, 2008.
48. J.D. interview, September 7, 1994.
49. Chapman interview, February 20, 1996.
50. J.D. interview, January 29, 2008.
51. Ibid.
52. Chapman interview, December 19, 2007.
53. Leadbetter interview, January 17, 1996.
54. Leadbetter interview, November 18, 2006.
55. J.D. interview, January 29, 2008.
56. Chapman interview, December 19, 2007.
57. J.D. interview, July 20, 2010.
58. J.D. interview, September 7, 1994.
59. Ibid.

Chapter 10. The New *New South*

1. Chapman interview, December 19, 2007.
2. Leadbetter interview, December 14, 2007.
3. J.D. interview, September 7, 1994.
4. "Reviews," *Bluegrass Unlimited,* April 1995, 57.
5. *Bluegrass Now,* January–February 1995, 46.
6. Chapman interview, December 19, 2007.
7. Chapman interview, October 14, 2003.
8. Leadbetter interview, December 14, 2007.
9. Chapman interview, October 14, 2003.
10. *AcuTab Transcriptions.*
11. J.D. interview, January 29, 2008.

12. Jim Spriggs, "Band Can Match Crowe's Picking," *Columbus Dispatch,* April 20, 1998, B6.

13. "Reviews," *Bluegrass Unlimited,* May 1999, 75.

14. "Picks and Pans," *People Online,* January 18, 1999.

15. McCall interview.

16. J.D. interview, October 29, 2008.

17. J.D. interview, January 29, 2008.

18. Leadbetter interview, December 14, 2007.

19. Chapman interview, December 19, 2007.

20. J.D. interview, January 29, 2008.

21. Leadbetter interview, December 14, 2007.

22. J.D. interview, January 29, 2008.

23. Leadbetter interview, December 14, 2007.

24. J.D. interview, January 29, 2008.

25. Herschel Freeman, "J.D. Crowe, a Bluegrass Giant in Transition," *Frets Magazine,* December 1981, 38.

26. Chapman interview, October 14, 2003.

27. Leadbetter interview, December 14, 2007.

28. "Questions," *Frets Magazine,* May 1982, 50.

29. "J.D. Crowe and the New South: *Lefty's Old Guitar,*" *Washington Post,* November 3, 2006, WE9.

30. "J.D. Crowe and the New South: *Lefty's Old Guitar,*" *Lexington Herald-Leader,* October 13, 2006, 6.

31. "J.D. Crowe and the New South: *Lefty's Old Guitar,*" Review Highlight, *Bluegrass Unlimited,* March 2007, 71.

32. "Compilations and Reissues," *Bluegrass Unlimited,* May 2007, 83.

33. J.D. interview, March 1, 1996.

Coda

1. Lawson interview, May 19, 2007.

2. Chapman interview, December 19, 2007.

3. Miller interview, February 22, 1996.

4. Lawson interview, May 19, 2007.

5. J.D. interview, May 25, 2011.

SELECTED LISTENING

Ideally, a discography should list all recordings participated in by the subject, but as the session material on many of J.D. Crowe's Rounder recordings has been lost, this is not possible here. Such information as is available, gathered from individual reports, reviews, and other sources, is given in the text of the book but is by no means complete.

Information about recordings made when Crowe recorded with Jimmy Martin (1956–60 plus 1963) is included in the excellent discography that accompanies Bear Family's five-CD box set, BCD-15705-EI, *Jimmy Martin and the Sunny Mountain Boys,* which is the only source for those recordings at this time.

The following recordings are representative of Crowe's work at various times, and all of them are currently available on CD.

With Jimmy Martin

1950S–1960S

Don't Cry to Me
Compilation Thrill Jockey 145c
> Contains nine performances recorded live at the *Louisiana Hayride* with Jimmy Martin and Paul Williams.

CA. 1960

Big Jam Session
Live / private party
Old Homestead 159
    A private picking party with Jimmy Martin and Paul Williams.

The Kentucky Mountain Boys

1969

Bluegrass Holiday
Originally on Lemco
Rebel CD 1598
    With Red Allen, Doyle Lawson, and Bobby Slone.

1970

Blackjack
Originally *Ramblin' Boy* on Lemco
Rebel CD 1583
    With Doyle Lawson, Larry Rice, and Bobby Slone.

1971

The Model Church
Originally on Lemco
Rebel CD 1585
    With Doyle Lawson, Larry Rice, and Bobby Slone.

The New South

1973

J.D. Crowe and the New South "Bluegrass Evolution"
Originally *J.D. Crowe and the New South,* Starday SLP 489, released June 1977
Starday-0489-CD
    With Tony Rice, Larry Rice, and Nashville studio musicians.

1975

The New South
Rounder CD 0044
    With Tony Rice, Ricky Skaggs, Jerry Douglas, and Bobby Slone.
Holiday in Japan
Originally issued in Japan as two LPs on the Towa and Trio labels
New South Music (remastered)
    Two-CD set, recorded live. Same personnel as above.

1979

My Home Ain't in the Hall of Fame
Rounder CD 0103
   With Keith Whitley, Jimmy Gaudreau, Bobby Slone (f), and Steve Bryant.
Live in Japan
Issued in 1987
Rounder CD 0159
   With Keith Whitley, Jimmy Gaudreau, Bobby Slone (f), and Steve Bryant.

1981

Somewhere Between
Issued in 1982 as Rounder LP 0153; no longer available
Remastered 2000. Reissued as *Sad Songs and Waltzes* (Rounder CD 0399), under
   Keith Whitley's name.
   With Keith Whitley, Wendy Miller, Bobby Slone (f), and Steve Bryant plus
   Nashville studio musicians.
Sad Songs and Waltzes
Issued in 2000
Rounder CD 0399. Crowe appears on only two cuts, but produced the recording.
   Keith Whitley, Steve Bryant, Glen Duncan, Randy Howard, Jeff White; harmony
   vocals by Dale Ann Bradley, Steve Gulley, Wes Hightower, Carl Jackson, Gene
   Johnson, and Alison Krauss.

1986

Straight Ahead
Rounder CD 0202
   With Tony King, Bobby Slone (f), Wendy Miller, Sam Bush, Steve Bryant, Randy
   Hayes, and Jerry Douglas.

1994

Flashback
Rounder CD 0322
   With Richard Bennett, Don Rigsby, Phil Leadbetter, Curt Chapman, and Randy
   Howard.

1999

Come on Down to My World
Rounder CD 0422
   With Greg Luck, Dwight McCall, Phil Leadbetter, Curt Chapman, Rickey Was-
   son, Glen Duncan, and Buddy Spicher.

2007

Lefty's Old Guitar
Rounder CD 0512
    With Rickey Wasson, Dwight McCall, Ron Stewart, and Harold Nixon.

The Bluegrass Album Band

1981

The Bluegrass Album, Vol. 1
Rounder CD 0140

1982

The Bluegrass Album, Vol. 2
Rounder CD 0164
    These two volumes feature Tony Rice, J.D. Crowe, Doyle Lawson, Bobby Hicks, and Todd Phillips.

1983

The Bluegrass Album, Vol. 3, *California Autumn*
Rounder CD 0180
    Jerry Douglas is added and appears on all remaining Bluegrass Album Band volumes.

1985

The Bluegrass Album, Vol. 4
Rounder CD 0210

1990

The Bluegrass Album, Vol. 5, *Sweet Sunny South*
Rounder CD 0240
    Mark Schatz replaces Todd Phillips and Vassar Clements replaces Bobby Hicks on this volume.

1996

The Bluegrass Album, Vol. 6, *Bluegrass Instrumentals*
Rounder CD 0330
    Todd Phillips returns; Clements and Hicks play twin fiddles.

Selected Special Projects

2004

Tribute to Jimmy Martin
Koch International CD 9819
    Includes Paul Williams, Audie Blaylock, Michael Cleveland, Kenny Ingram, Ben
    Isaacs, and others.

2008

Longview: Deep in the Mountains
Rounder CD 0578
    Includes Lou Reid, Don Rigsby, James King, Ron Stewart, and Marshall Wilborn.

2010

Old Friends Get Together
Mountain Home
    Includes Paul Williams, Doyle Lawson, Ron Stewart, Ben Isaacs, and others.

ADDITIONAL READING

To gain insight into J.D. Crowe and his music, it is necessary to understand the musical environment in which he has lived and worked. There is no better reference than Neil V. Rosenberg's *Bluegrass: A History* (Urbana: University of Illinois Press, 1985), which covers bluegrass music from its prehistory until the publication date.

Bluegrass Unlimited (P.O. Box 771, Warrenton, VA 20188-0771; http://www .bluegrassmusic.com) began as a newsletter in 1966 and became a national magazine in 1970. It provides a great deal of information in its "General Store" and "Notes & Queries" sections, performance listings, venue references, advertisements, letters, and feature articles, among which are serious studies of historical and current musicians. The *Banjo Newsletter* (P.O. Box 3418, Annapolis, MD 21403-0418; http://www.banjonews.com), established in 1973, concentrates on everything to do with banjos and those who play them, not limited to bluegrass. Both magazines have featured J.D. Crowe several times.

In the twenty-first century the Internet plays a crucial role in the music business, and the value of an online presence was recognized early by J.D. Crowe and the New South. To keep up with the latest news about the band, visit their Web site, http://www.jdcrowe.net/. Several online discussion groups exist; http://www.banjohangout.org is one of the more popular, and Crowe is a frequent topic.

Short-lived magazines with an interest in bluegrass music have appeared from time to time, and many fan-based groups have newsletters that may be of use when there is a dearth of original source material and little public documentation. A caveat here: articles written by fans and nonprofessionals, however well intentioned, often tend to perpetuate inaccurate information from earlier sources and should be carefully checked.

There are several related books in the works: a biography of longtime Flatt and Scruggs sideman Curly Sechler is being written by Penny Parsons, and a biography of Eddie Adcock is being written by Martha Herron Adcock.

General References

AcuTab Transcriptions. Vol. 1, *J.D. Crowe*. Roanoke: AcuTab Publications, 1976. Tablature transcriptions from *Flashback* (Rounder 0322) and *The New South* (Rounder 0044).

Artis, Bob. *Bluegrass*. New York: Hawthorne Books, 1975. Out of print but a wonderful window on bluegrass music in the 1970s.

Fleischhauer, Carl, and Neil Rosenberg. *Bluegrass Odyssey*. Urbana: University of Illinois Press, 2001. Masterful photographs and text document some aspects of bluegrass music from 1966 to 1986.

Mills, Jim. *Gibson Mastertone Flathead 5-String Banjos of the 1930's and 1940's*. Anaheim Hills, Calif.: Centerstream Publishing, 2009. Histories and descriptions of some of the premier Gibson banjos of the period, with anecdotes about their owners, past and present.

Skinker, Chris. *Jimmy Martin and the Sunny Mountain Boys*. Notes accompanying Bear Family "box set" BCD 15705, Bremen, Germany, 1994. A history of Martin's career, with information about J.D. Crowe's early years with Martin and a full discography.

Spann, Joseph E. *Spann's Guide to Gibson, 1902–1941*. Anaheim Hills, Calif.: Centerstream Publishing, 2011. An analysis of Gibson's instrument production in the years before WWII.

Stafford, Tim, and Caroline Wright. *Still Inside: The Tony Rice Story*. Kingsport, Tenn.: Word of Mouth Press, 2010. An unusual nonlinear biography, including a narrative by Tony, interviews, and comments by Tony's friends and fellow musicians.

Wolfe, Charles K. *Kentucky Country*. Lexington: University Press of Kentucky, 1982. A brief overview of the history of country music in Kentucky and Kentucky performers.

INTERVIEWS

When little original source material is available to document the life of an individual, it becomes necessary to rely upon the memories of those who have been involved with the subject. Realizing all too well the fallibility of human recollection, I have tried to collect information from several people in each instance, when possible, to present a balanced picture of J.D. Crowe, his music, and the time and circumstances in which he has lived.

With my husband, Frank, I first interviewed J.D. Crowe in 1976 for the *Banjo Newsletter*, at the request of its founder and first editor, Hub Nitchie. Other interviews with Crowe, for many different publications, followed. I have kept the notes from these and from interviews with many other musicians, compiled over more than thirty years, to form the bulk of the information I have gleaned for this book. Large portions of these interviews have necessarily been published, but some are seen here for the first time. Additional interviews have been conducted especially for this project, cuts from some of which were used for the Kentucky Educational Television documentary *A Kentucky Treasure: The J.D. Crowe Story* © 2008, produced by H. Russell Farmer. Interviews were conducted in person unless otherwise stated.

Adcock, Eddie. Telephone interview, February 14, 2008.

Adkins, Paul. Telephone interview, December 4, 2008.

Allen, Harley "Red." Dayton, Ohio, April 14, 1979.

Bartlett, J.G. "Lightning." Telephone interview, October 8, 2008.

Baucom, Terry. Telephone interview, December 4, 2008.

Becker, Frank. Lexington, Ky., April 21, 2008.

Bennett, Richard. Richmond, Ky., April 12, 2008.

Bickel, Harry. Louisville, Ky., April 15, 2004.

Brock, Dan. Lexington, Ky., April 9, 2008.

Bush, Sam. Telephone interview, November 14, 2008.

Chapman, Curt. Lexington, Ky., December 19, 2007. Telephone interviews, February 20, 1996; October 14, 2003.

Clyburn, Wayne. Via email, October 17, 2008.

Collett, Rosa Marie Crowe. Lexington, Ky., February 3, 1998; June 27, 2007.

Combs, Don. Nicholasville, Ky., November 2, 2008.

Cooley, Steve. Louisville, Ky., April 15, 2004.

Crabtree, Barry. Telephone interview, October 27, 2008.

Crabtree, Billy Ray. Telephone interview, October 27, 2008.

Crase, Noah. Telephone interview, October 28, 2008.

Crowe, Bessie Lee Nichols. Lexington, Ky., February 3, 1998; June 27, 2007.

Crowe, J.D. Lexington, Ky., May 17, 1976 (with Frank Godbey); January 29, 2008. Nicholasville, Ky., January 14, March 10, 1981; February 23, 1982; September 7, 1994; January 26, 1996; January 15, August 12, 2002; September 13, 2006; January 9, May 20, July 19, October 29, 2008; October 28, 2009. Telephone interviews, April 7, 1982; February 26, March 1, 12, December 18, 2006; November 4, 2008; July 20, 2010; May 25, 2011 (Frank Godbey).

Douglas, Jerry. Lexington, Ky., July 24, 2007.

DuPriest, Mabel Benson, and Travis DuPriest. Via email, June 23, 2008.

Fields, Wayne. Richmond, Ky., December 9, 2007.

Foy, Dan. Via email, May 13, 2008.

Gaudreau, Jimmy. Telephone interview, October 22, 2008.

Hale, Robert. Telephone interview, December 5, 2008.

Haney, David. Telephone interview, April 4, 2008.

Hayes, Randy. Telephone interviews, February 26, 1996; November 14, December 2, 2008.

Hutchens, Doug. Telephone interview, April 29, 2008. Also posting on *Banjo's 'n Bluegrass,* July 20, 2008. Used by permission.

Irwin, Ken. Telephone interview, April 21, 2008.

Johnson, Gene. Telephone interview, November 24, 2008.

Joslin, Charles. Lexington, Ky., March 30, 31, 2004.

King, Tony. Telephone interview, April 21, 2009.

Knight, Gene. Telephone interview, November 19, 2008.

Landreth, Ken. Maryville, Tenn., January 11, 2008.

Lawson, Doyle. Wilmington, Ohio, November 18, 2006; McKee, Ky., May 19, 2007.

Lawson, Glen. Telephone interview, November 18, 2008.

Leadbetter, Phil. Wilmington, Ohio, November 18, 2006; Knoxville, Tenn., December 14, 2007. Telephone interview, January 17, 1997.

Luck, Greg. Telephone interview, April 1, 2009.

Martin, Jimmy. Hermitage, Tenn., September 9, 2003.

McCall, Dwight. Clay City, Ky., April 4, 2009.

McGinnis, Bill. Lexington, Ky., April 13, 2008.

McLain, Raymond W. Telephone interview, November 10, 2008.

Miller, Wendy. Stanton, Ky., November 28, 2007. Telephone interview, February 22, 1996.

Morris, Joyce. Telephone interview, July 29, 2008.

Munde, Alan. Louisville, Ky., October 1, 2003.

Neat, Frank. Telephone interview, July 30, 2008.

Osborne, Sonny. Nashville, Tenn., September 4, 2007.

Powell, Brian. Telephone interview, August 16, 2003.

Rice, Tony. Pigeon Forge, Tenn., August 11, 2007.

Riddle, Bill. Lexington, Ky., May 15, 2007.

Rigsby, Don. Telephone interview, October 22, 2008.

Ritchie, Wayne. Telephone interview, October 19, 2008.

Rodgers, Bob. Via email, February 11, 2009.

Schoepf, Frank. Telephone interview, January 27, 2009.

Scott, Gordon. Telephone interviews, December 1, 5, 16, 2003; July 7, 2008.

Scruggs, Earl. Madison, Tenn., February 24, 1996; Nashville, Tenn., September 5, 2007.

Skaggs, Ricky. Hendersonville, Tenn., September 3, 2007.

Slone, Bobby. Lexington, Ky., February 15, 1978. Telephone interview, February 22, 1996.

Stacy, Ed. Lexington, Ky., December 9, 2003.

Stewart, Ron. Telephone interview, November 11, 2009.

Sturgill, Hugh. Telephone interview, March 31, 2008.

Talbot, Dave. Lexington, Ky., April 19, 2002; Bowling Green, Ky., March 29, 2002; Winchester, Ky., May 20, 2002; Nashville, Tenn., September 4, 2007.

Warner, Chris. McKee, Ky., May 19, 2007.

Wasson, Ricky. Stanton, Ky., November 28, 2007.

Whitaker, Ruby Gilkerson. Lexington, Ky., June 4, 2008.

Williams, Paul. Wilmore, Ky., September 22, 2006.

Wiseman, Mac. Telephone interview, September 19, 2006.

Wood, J. Telephone interview, February 3, 2005.

Zack, George. Telephone interview, December 9, 2008.

INDEX

A prolific writer and photographer, the late **MARTY GODBEY** published extensively on history, architecture, food, travel, and bluegrass music. She lived in Lexington, Kentucky, where she watched J.D. Crowe play locally for more than 40 years.

MUSIC IN AMERICAN LIFE

Henry Cowell, Bohemian   *Michael Hicks*
Rap Music and Street Consciousness   *Cheryl L. Keyes*
Louis Prima   *Garry Boulard*
Marian McPartland's Jazz World: All in Good Time   *Marian McPartland*
Robert Johnson: Lost and Found   *Barry Lee Pearson and Bill McCulloch*
Bound for America: Three British Composers   *Nicholas Temperley*
Lost Sounds: Blacks and the Birth of the Recording Industry, 1890–1919   *Tim Brooks*
Burn, Baby! BURN! The Autobiography of Magnificent Montague
    Magnificent Montague with Bob Baker
Way Up North in Dixie: A Black Family's Claim to the Confederate Anthem
    Howard L. Sacks and Judith Rose Sacks
The Bluegrass Reader   *Edited by Thomas Goldsmith*
Colin McPhee: Composer in Two Worlds   *Carol J. Oja*
Robert Johnson, Mythmaking, and Contemporary American Culture
    Patricia R. Schroeder
Composing a World: Lou Harrison, Musical Wayfarer   *Leta E. Miller and
    Fredric Lieberman*
Fritz Reiner, Maestro and Martinet   *Kenneth Morgan*
That Toddlin' Town: Chicago's White Dance Bands and Orchestras, 1900–1950
    Charles A. Sengstock Jr.
Dewey and Elvis: The Life and Times of a Rock 'n' Roll Deejay   *Louis Cantor*
Come Hither to Go Yonder: Playing Bluegrass with Bill Monroe   *Bob Black*
Chicago Blues: Portraits and Stories   *David Whiteis*
The Incredible Band of John Philip Sousa   *Paul E. Bierley*
"Maximum Clarity" and Other Writings on Music   *Ben Johnston, edited by
    Bob Gilmore*
Staging Tradition: John Lair and Sarah Gertrude Knott   *Michael Ann Williams*
Homegrown Music: Discovering Bluegrass   *Stephanie P. Ledgin*
Tales of a Theatrical Guru   *Danny Newman*
The Music of Bill Monroe   *Neil V. Rosenberg and Charles K. Wolfe*
Pressing On: The Roni Stoneman Story   *Roni Stoneman, as told to Ellen Wright*
Together Let Us Sweetly Live   *Jonathan C. David, with photographs by
    Richard Holloway*
Live Fast, Love Hard: The Faron Young Story   *Diane Diekman*
Air Castle of the South: WSM Radio and the Making of Music City
    Craig P. Havighurst
Traveling Home: Sacred Harp Singing and American Pluralism   *Kiri Miller*
Where Did Our Love Go? The Rise and Fall of the Motown Sound   *Nelson George*
Lonesome Cowgirls and Honky-Tonk Angels: The Women of Barn
    Dance Radio   *Kristine M. McCusker*
California Polyphony: Ethnic Voices, Musical Crossroads   *Mina Yang*
The Never-Ending Revival: Rounder Records and the Folk Alliance   *Michael F. Scully*
Sing It Pretty: A Memoir   *Bess Lomax Hawes*

The University of Illinois Press
is a founding member of the
Association of American University Presses.

———————————————————

Designed by Jim Proefock
Composed in 10.75/15 Dante
with Goshen display
at the University of Illinois Press
Manufactured by Thomson-Shore, Inc.

University of Illinois Press
1325 South Oak Street
Champaign, IL 61820-6903
www.press.uillinois.edu